THE MEL BAY MODERN GUITAR METHOD COMPLETE EDITION

Part 1/Grades 1-4

Audio

Online Audio

Video

Online Video

YouTube

To access the online audio and video, scan the QR codes above or go to:

Audio

www.melbay.com/30504

Video

dv.melbay.com/30504

YouTube

www.melbay.com/30504V

I0792715

ONLINE AUDIO TRACKS FOR PART 1/GRADE 1

Disc 1

Tk	Pg	Title
1		TuneUp [1:38]
2	6	E-Whole Notes, Half, Quarter [0:54]
3	8	Playing the Notes [0:54]
4		Working the Fingers [0:52]
5	9	1st-String Etude [0:31]
6		Etude No. 2 [0:31]
7		The Mixmaster [0:32]
8	10	B-Whole Notes, Half, Quarter [1:11]
9		B-E, B-F, B-G, C-E [1:19]
10		C-F, C-G, D-E, D-F, D-G [1:31]
11	12	March [0:49]
12		Steps [0:30]
13		Study #1 [0:18]
14		Study #2 [0:19]
15	13	Inch Worm [0:31]
16		Frolic [0:50]
17		E-B [0:30]
18		Indian Drum [0:30]
19	14	3/4 Song [0:22]
20		3/4 Study [0:22]
21		Waltz [0:22]
22		The Merry Men [0:37]
23	15	A Study on the Third String [0:27]
24		Sparkling Stella [0:40]
25	16	Prelude [0:50]
26		Descending [0:28]
27		Acending [0:36]
28		Sunset [0:51]
29		Aura Lee [0:50]
30	18	When the Saints Go Marchin' In [0:38]
31		Two Note Pick-up [0:23]
32		One Note Pick-up [0:22]
33		Psalm 100 [0:41]
34		Red River Valley [0:41]
35	20	D-Whole, Half and Quarter [1:12]
36	21	Native Flute [0:27]
37		Bear Dance [0:27]
38		Prairie Song [0:35]
39		Native Drum [0:28]
40	22	Cockles and Mussels [0:36]
41		Hymn [0:32]
42		German Waltz [0:22]
43	23	1/8 Note Studies 1-10 [2:27]
44	24	Tudor Dance [0:26]
45		Mohican Lament [0:27]
46		Dance of the Royal Court [0:36]
47		Village Waltz [0:23]
48	25	Amazing Grace [0:39]
49		Tenting Tonight [1:00]
50		Melancholy [0:42]
51	26	A-Notes Whole, Half, Quarter [1:08]
52	27	Wilderness Trail [0:27]
53		Westward Ho! [0:27]
54		Chord Waltz [0:24]
55		Elsie's Waltz [0:19]
56		Buffalo Gals [0:39]
57		Chester [0:38]
58		Kum-Ba-Ya [0:37]
59		Michael, Row the Boat Ashore [0:25]
60	30	Mountain Flower [0:31]
61		Quest [0:28]
62		Homeward Bound [0:24]
63	31	Note Review - Daydreams, Ozark Stream, Waterfall, Mountain Trail [1:41]
64	31	E-Notes Whole, Half, Quarter [1:09]
65	33	Driving Bass [0:24]
66		Low Gear [0:26]
67		Running the Notes [0:41]
68	34	Minor Melody [0:33]
69		Hitting on All Six [0:43]
70	35	Smoky Ridge [0:33]
71		Voyage [0:41]
72	36	Our First Duet [0:40]
73		The Repeater [0:31]
74	37	Two Guitars [0:39
75		Sunset [0:40]
76	38	The Chord Waltz [0:33]
77		The Builder [0:35]
78		Small Chord Etude [0:28]
79	39	Chord March [0:25]
80		Autumn [0:27]
81		Chording Along [0:22]
82		Echoes [0:37]
83	40	Building the F Chord / Two, Three and Four Notes [0:54]
84		Four-String Chord Study 1 [0:25]
85		Four-String Chord Study 2 [0:27]
86		Chimes [0:28]
87	41	Bottom Floor [0:38]
88		Chord Walk [0:26]
89		May Song [0:41]
90		Running in the Chord [0:25]
91	42	My Country Tis of Thee [0:37]
92		Green Grow the Lilacs [0:43]
93		Chord Bouquet [0:32]
94	43	Follow the Leader [0:49]
95		Tallis Canon
96	44	Bass Solos with Chord Accompaniment [0:33]
97		Gliding Along [0:32]
98	45	Hymn [0:34]
99		Country Waltz [0:29]

Disc 2

Tk	Pg	Title
1	45	Western Song [0:35]
2	46	Oh Bury Me Not on the Lone Prairie [0:43]
3		Red River Valley [0:43]
4		Sawdust Trail [0:28]
5	47	Scale Studies 1 [0:14]
6		Scale Studies 2 [0:25]
7		Scale Studies 3 [0:24]
8	48	Scale Studies 4-8 [1:45]
9	49	Shenandoah & Advanced Version [2:28]
10	50	Blues Bells of Scotland & Advanced Version [2:11]
11	51	Chords C Accompaniment - Alt. & in 3-4 Time [0:54]
12	52	Chord Studies in C 1-7 [1:25]
13	53	A Daily Scale Study [0:44]
14		Running Around [0:38]
15	54	Home, Home, Can I Forget Thee [0:54]
16		Long, Long Ago [1:10]
17	56	Sharps 1st String, Sharps & Naturals, 2nd String [0:42]
18		Sharps 3rd-4th String [0:31]
19		Sharps 5th-6th String [0:32]
20	57	Walking Guitar [0:34]
21		Flats 1st and 2nd Strings [0:30]
22		Flats 3rd and 4th Strings [0:32]
23	58	Flats 5th and 6th Strings [0:32]
24		Benny's Flat [0:35]
25	59	Playtime [0:56]
26	60	A Minor Scales Natural, Harmonic Melodic [0:57]
27	61	Accompaniment Styles in Am All of P61 [2:17]
28	62	A Daily Scale Study in Am [0:25]
29		Picking Studies in Am 1,2 & 3 [1:23]
30	63	All of P63 [1:31]
31	64	Sailing [0:33]
32		Minor Song [0:26]
33		Journey [0:27]
34	65	Wayfaring Stranger [0:40]
35		Another Daily Scale Study in A minor [0:27]
36		A Visit to the Relatives [1:03]
37	66	Shady Glenn [0:46]
38		Careless Love [1:17]
39	67	Foggy Mountain Run [0:52]
40		The Shire [0:24]
41		Bluegrass Sunrise [0:21]
42	68	Craddle Rock [1:09]
43		Blue Ridge Trail [1:00]
44	69	Billy's Duet [1:25]
45		Lafayette Square [1:03]
46	70	Song Without Words [0:56]
47		Terry's Tune [1:36]
48	71	A Dairy Drill [0:39]
49		Picking Studies in G 1-3 [1:05]
50	72	Picking Studies in G 4 & 5 [1:01]
51	73	Acc. Styles in the Key of G [1:08]
52		All Styles 3-6 [0:53]
53	74	G Boogie [0:32]
54		In the Evening Moon [0:50]
55		Etude [0:55]
56	75	The Old Mill [0:40]
57		Two-Four Picking [0:25]
58	76	A Scale Study [1:17]
59		Opening Day [1:14]
60		A Serenade [1:09]
61	77	Australian Hymn [1:11]
62		Home on the Range [1:06]
63	78	The Little Prince [0:49]
64		Carry Me Back to Old Virginity [1:39]
65	79	Two E Minor Scales [0:45]
66		Picking Studies 1-3 [1:12]
67	80	Picking Studies 4-6 [1:15]
68		Picking Studies 7-8 [0:51]
69	81	All Styles Em 4/4, 3/4 & 2/4 [1:25]
70		Chord Studies 1-4 [0:56]
71	82	Morning Song [0:31]
72		Cindy [0:34]
73		Night Song [1:12]
74	83	East River [1:08]
75		Goblins [0:53]
76	84	Lament [1:59]
77	85	Maytime [1:01]
78	86	Rondo [1:13]
79	87	Sor's Waltz [1:24]
80		Bluegrass Waltz [0:31]
81	88	Running the Thirds in G [0:24]
82		A Little Bit of Hannon [0:46]
83		Southern Fried [0:29]

www.melbay.com

How to Hold the Guitar & Pick

The correct way to hold the guitar.

#1

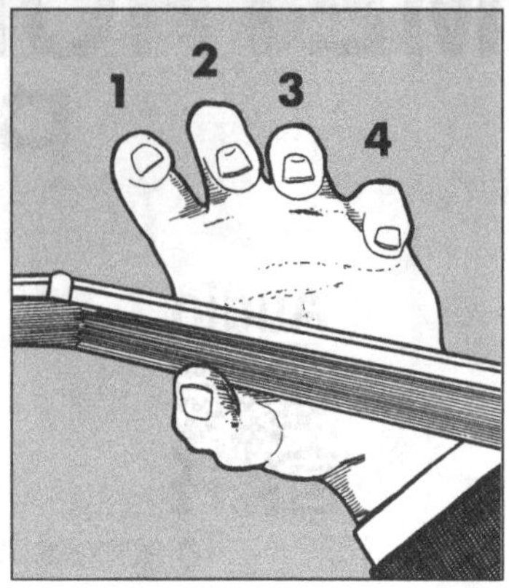

#2

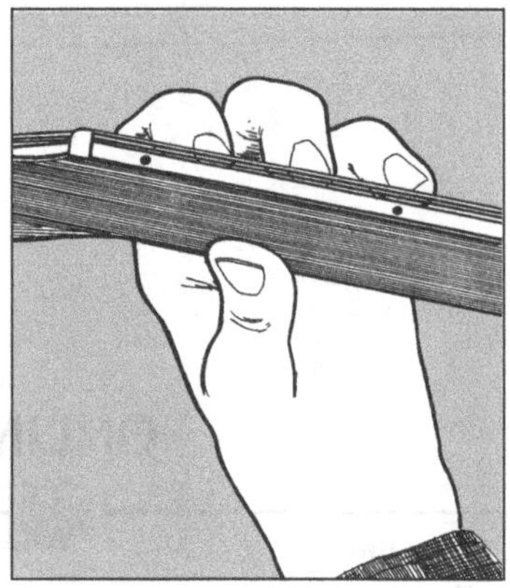

Place your fingers FIRMLY on the strings DIRECTLY BEHIND THE FRETS.

#1

This is the pick.

#2

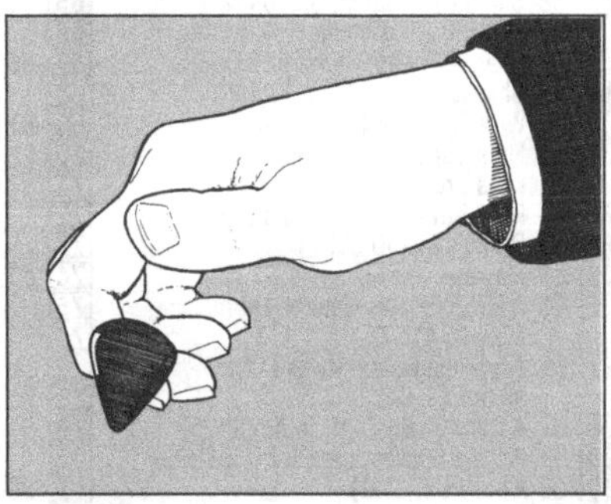

Hold it in this manner firmly between the thumb and first finger.

#3

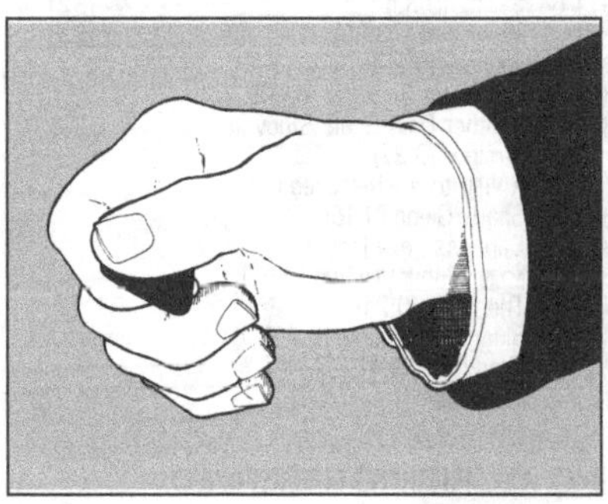

⊓ = Down Stroke of the Pick.

#4

Tuning the Guitar

The six open strings of the guitar will be of the same pitch as the six notes shown in the illustration of the piano keyboard. Note that five of the strings are below the middle C of the piano keyboard.

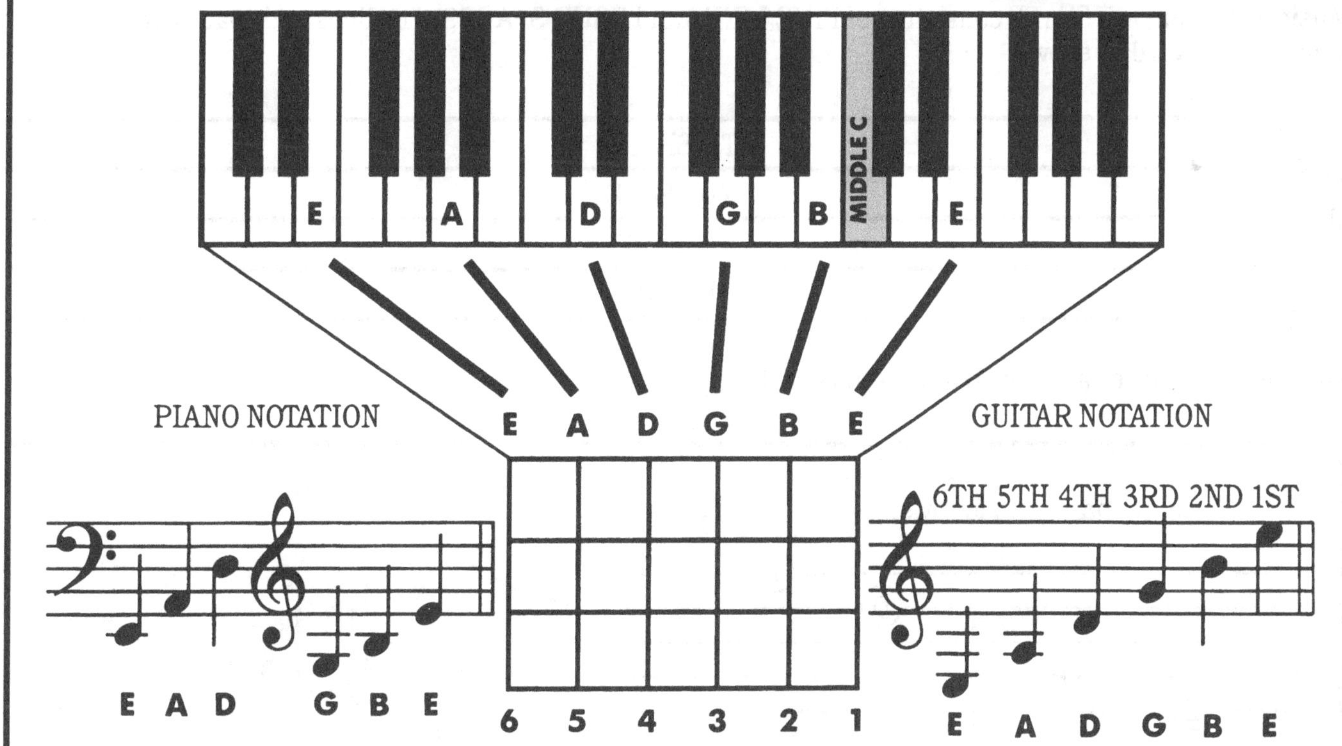

Another Method of Tuning

1. Tune the 6th string in unison with the **E** or 12th white key to the LEFT of MIDDLE C on the piano.
2. Place the finger behind the fifth fret of the 6th string. This will give you the tone or pitch of the 5th string **(A)**.
3. Place finger behind the fifth fret of the 5th string to get the pitch of the 4th string **(D)**.
4. Repeat same procedure to obtain the pitch of the 3rd string **(G)**.
5. Place finger behind the fourth fret of the 3rd string to get the pitch of the 2nd string **(B)**.
6. Place finger behind the fifth fret of the 2nd string to get the pitch of the 1st string **(E)**.

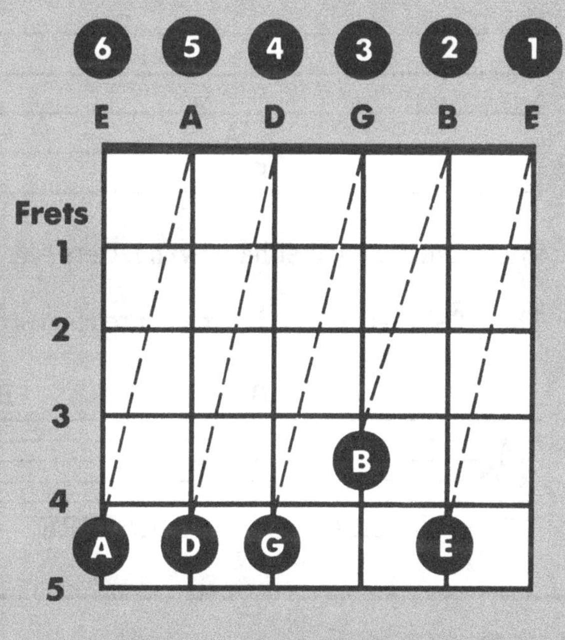

Electronic Guitar Tuner

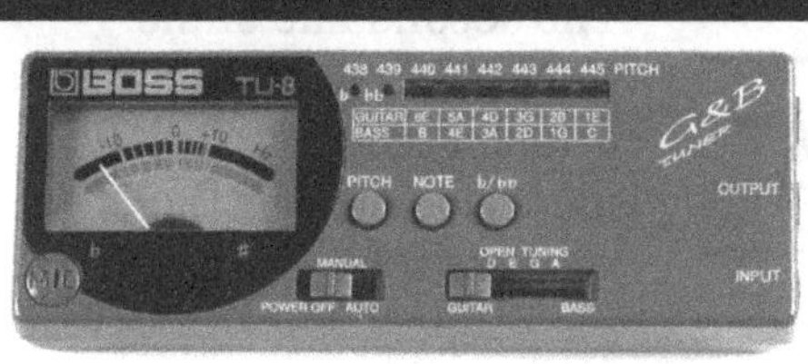

Electronic Guitar Tuners are available at your music store. They are a handy device and highly recommended.

THE RUDIMENTS OF MUSIC

THE STAFF:

Music is written on a STAFF consisting of FIVE LINES and FOUR SPACES. The lines and spaces are numbered upward as shown:

5TH LINE
4TH SPACE
4TH LINE
3RD SPACE
3RD LINE
2ND SPACE
2ND LINE
1ST SPACE
1ST LINE

The lines and spaces are named after letters of the alphabet.

The **LINES** are named as follows:

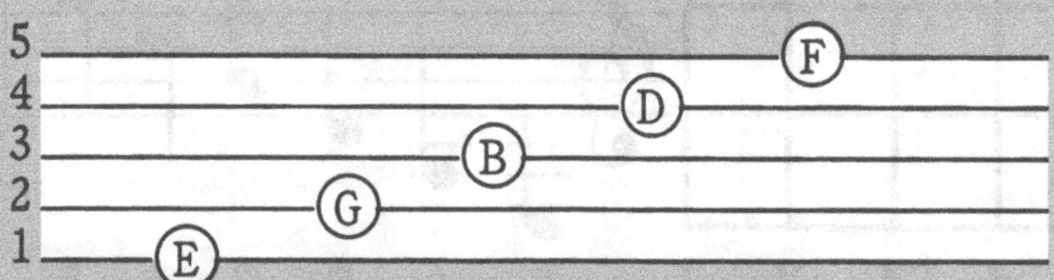

The letters can easily be remembered by the sentence—**E**very **Good** **Boy** **Does** **Fine**

The letter-names of the **SPACES** are:

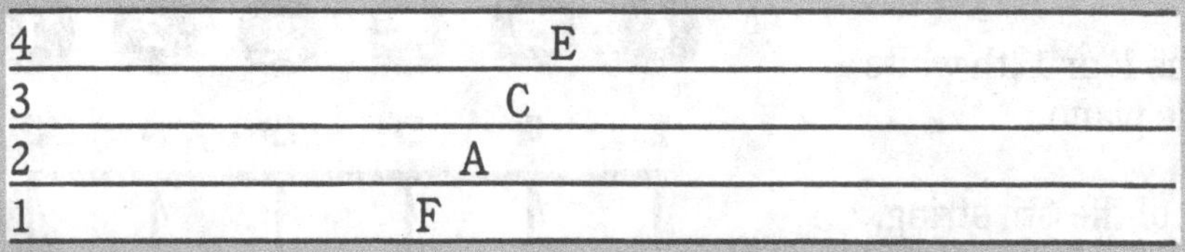

They spell the word **F-A-C-E.**

The musical alphabet has seven letters—**A B C D E F G.**

The **STAFF** is divided into measures by vertical lines called **BARS.**

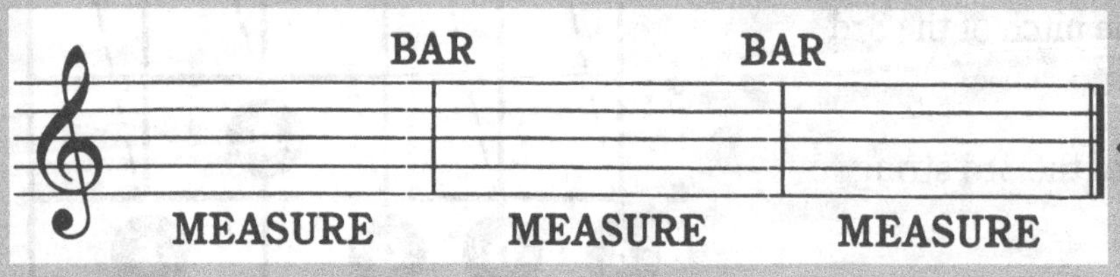

DOUBLE BARS MARK THE END OF A SECTION OR STRAIN OF MUSIC.

THE CLEF:

This sign is the treble or G clef.

All guitar music will be written in this clef.

The second line of the treble clef is known as the G line. Many people call the treble clef the G clef because it circles around the G line.

Notes

THIS IS A NOTE:

A NOTE HAS THREE PARTS. THEY ARE

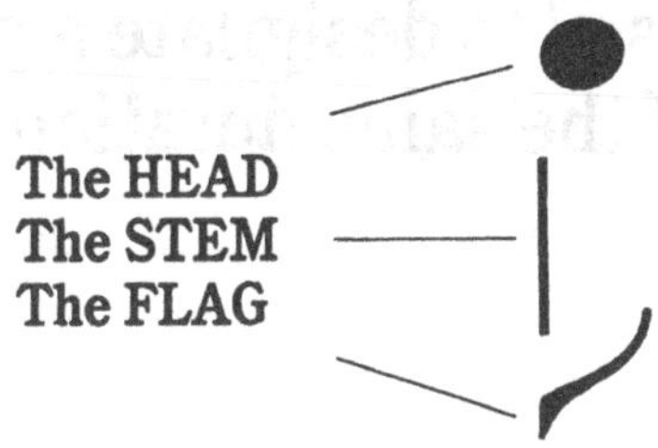

NOTES MAY BE PLACED IN THE STAFF, ABOVE THE STAFF,

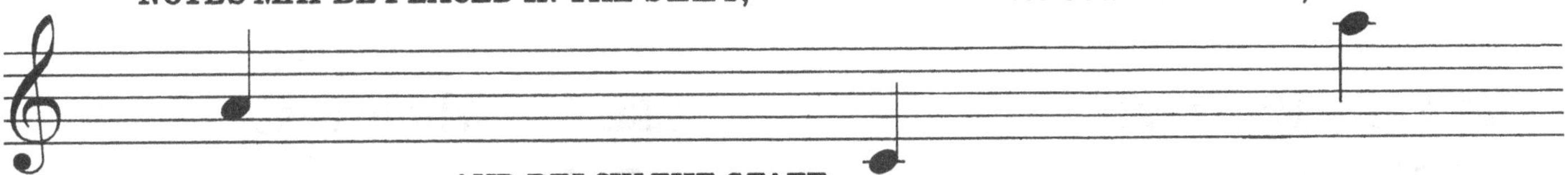

AND BELOW THE STAFF.

A note will bear the name of the line or space it occupies on the staff.
The location of a note in, above, or below the staff will indicate the pitch.

PITCH: the height or depth of a tone.
TONE: a musical sound.

Types of Notes

THE TYPE OF NOTE WILL INDICATE THE LENGTH OF ITS SOUND.

This is a whole note.
The head is hollow.
It does not have a stem.

= 4 Beats
A whole note will receive four beats or counts.

This is a half note.
The head is hollow.
It has a stem.

= 2 Beats
A half note will receive two beats or counts.

This is a quarter note.
The head is solid.
It has a stem.

= 1 Beat
A quarter note will receive one beat or count.

This is an eighth note.
The head is solid.
It has a stem and a flag.

= ½ Beat
An eighth note will receive one-half beat or count.
(2 for 1 beat)

Rest

A REST is a sign used to designate a period of silence. This period of silence will be of the same duration of time as the note to which it corresponds.

 This is an eighth rest.

 This is a quarter rest.

 Half rest

Half rests lie on the line.

 Whole rest

Whole rests hang down from the line.

Notes

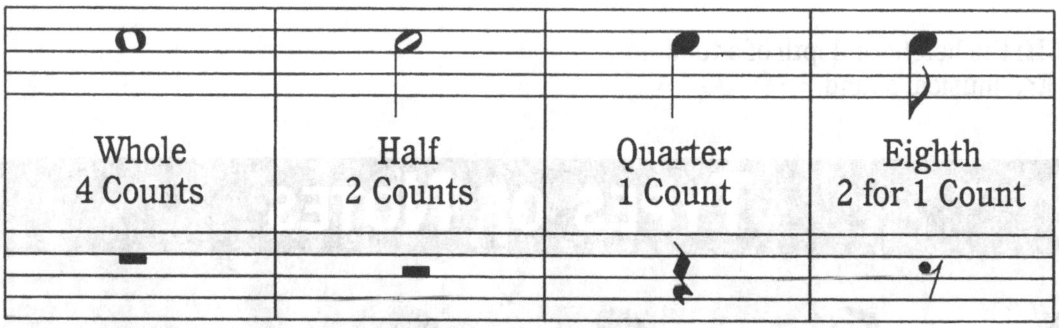

Rests

The Time Signature

The above examples are the common types of time signatures to be used in this book.

The number of beats per measure.	4	Beats per measure
The type of note receiving one beat.	4	A quarter note receives one beat.

Signifies so-called "common time" and is simply another way of designating 4/4 time.

Notes on the E String

First String

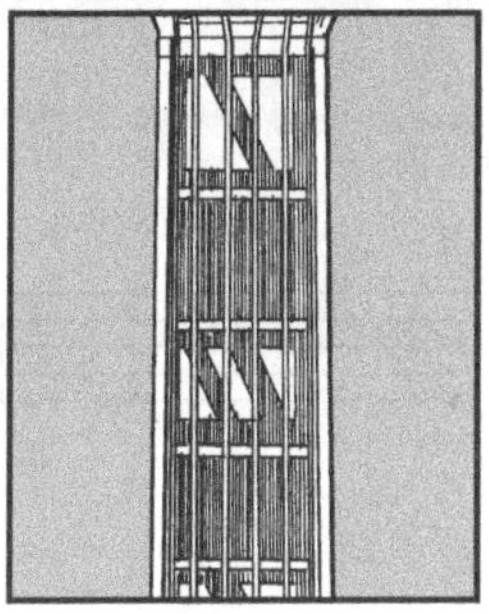

E

Open

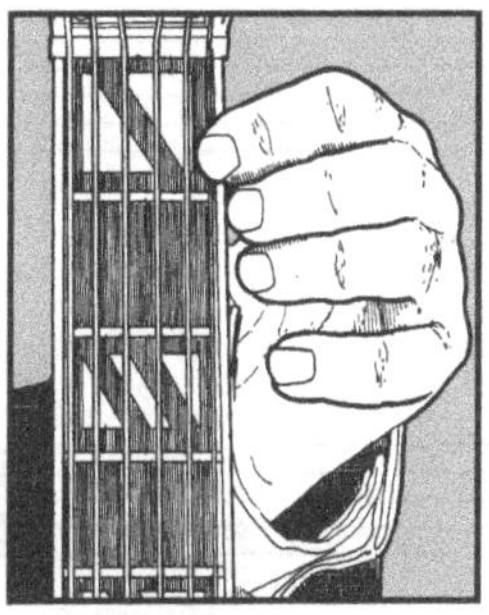

F

1st Fret
1st Finger

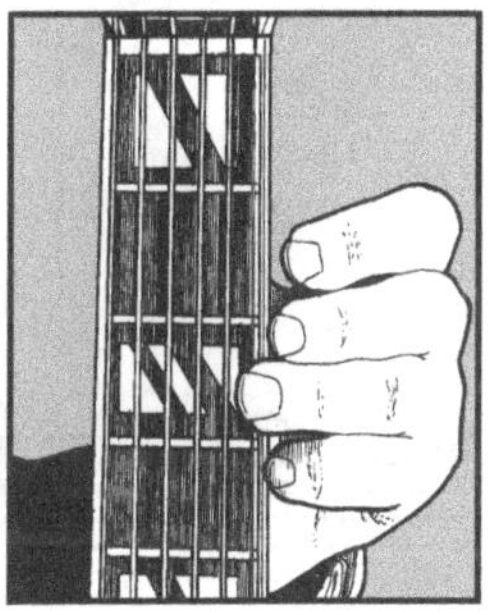

G

3rd Fret
3rd Finger

Note that the numbers of the fret and finger are identical.

Press the fingers firmly behind the frets.

Never place the finger on the frets.

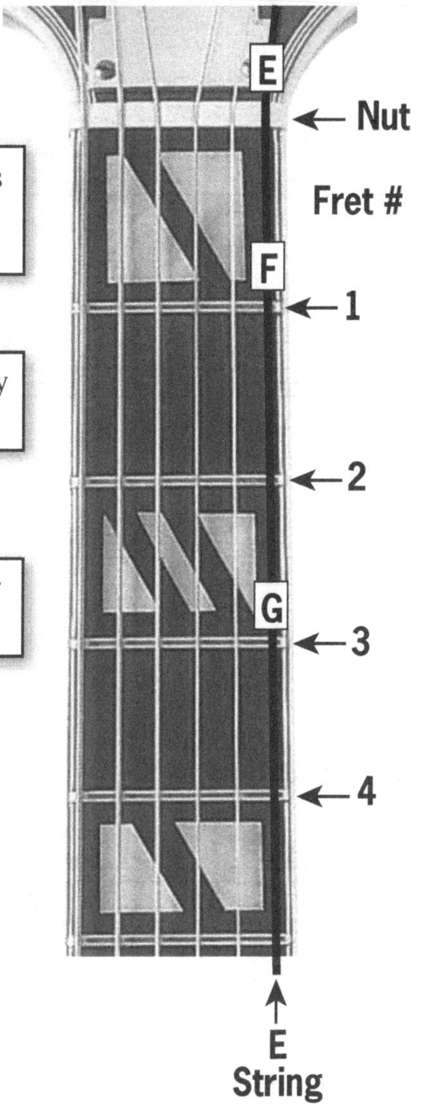

WHOLE Notes (𝅝) receive four beats.

Slow

Count: 1 - 2 - 3 - 4

HALF Notes (𝅗𝅥) receive two beats.

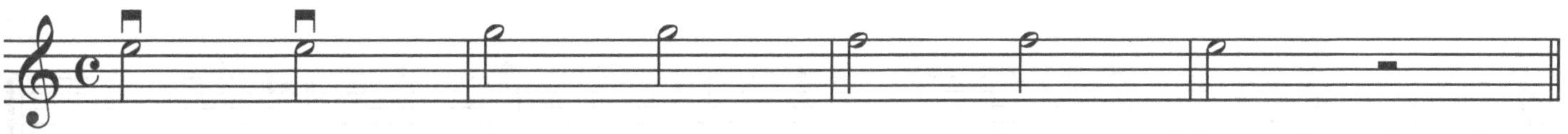

Count: 1 - 2 3 - 4 1 - 2 (3 - 4)
(Rest)

QUARTER Notes (♩) receive one beat.

Count: 1 2 3 4 1 2 3 4

Playing the Notes

Working the Fingers

1st-String Etude

Etude No. 2

The Mixmaster

Notes on the First String
(Fill in the blocks)

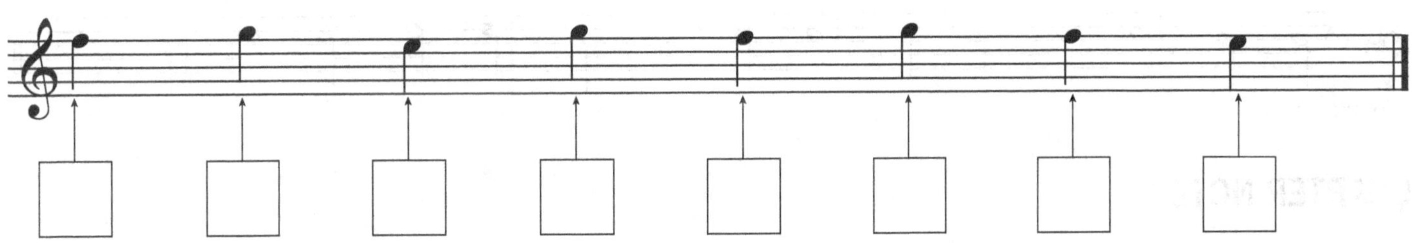

(Complete)

Notes on the B String

Second String

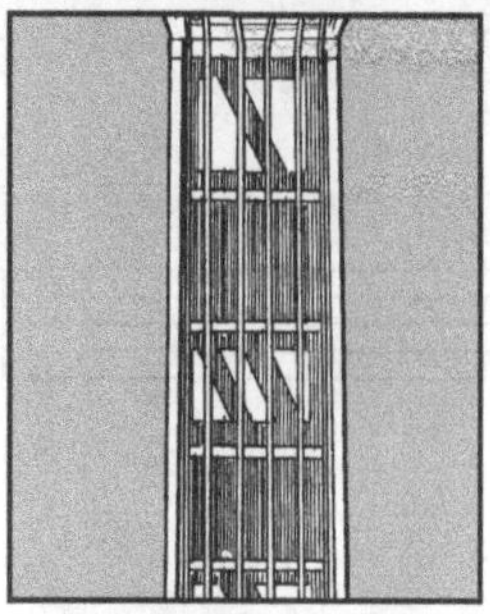

B

Open

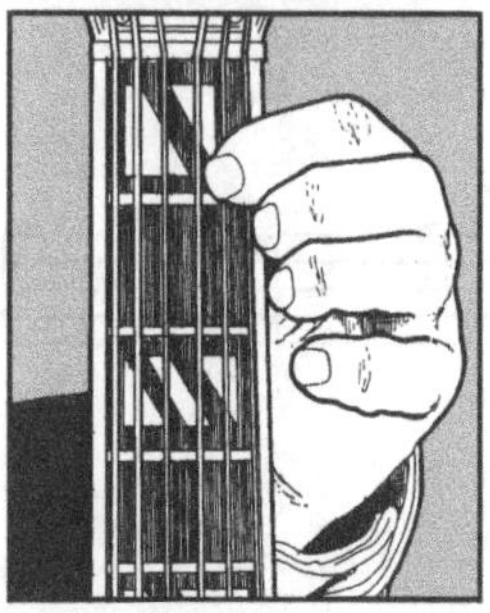

C

1st Fret
1st Finger

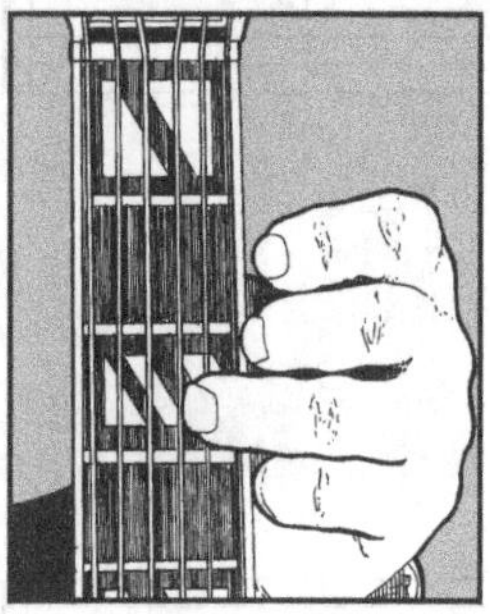

D

3rd Fret
3rd Finger

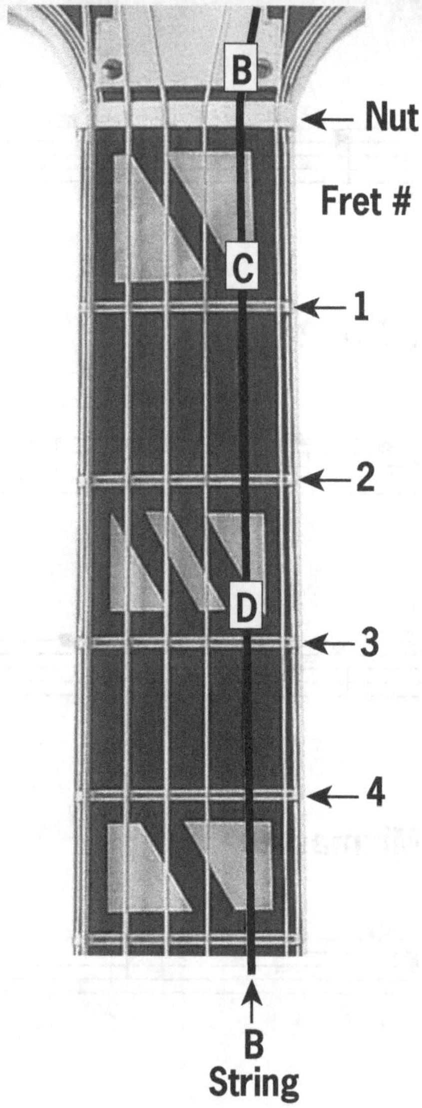

WHOLE NOTES

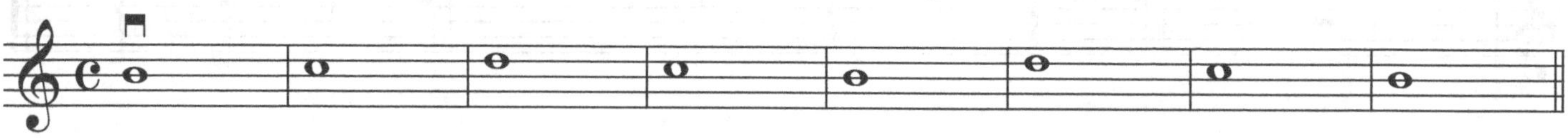

Count: 1 - 2 - 3 - 4

HALF NOTES

Count: 1 - 2 3 - 4

QUARTER NOTES

Count: 1 2 3 4

B - E

B - F

B - G

C - E

C - F

C - G

D - E

D - F

D - G

March

Steps

Study #1

Study #2

Inch Worm

Frolic

E - B

Indian Drum

Three-Four Time

This sign  indicates **three-four** time.

3 – beats per measure.
4 – type of note receiving one beat (quarter note).

In three-four time, we will have three beats per measure.

Dotted Half Notes

A dot (•) placed behind a note increases its value by one-half.

A dotted half note (•) will receive three beats.

Examples: **= 2 counts** **. = 3 counts**

3/4 Song

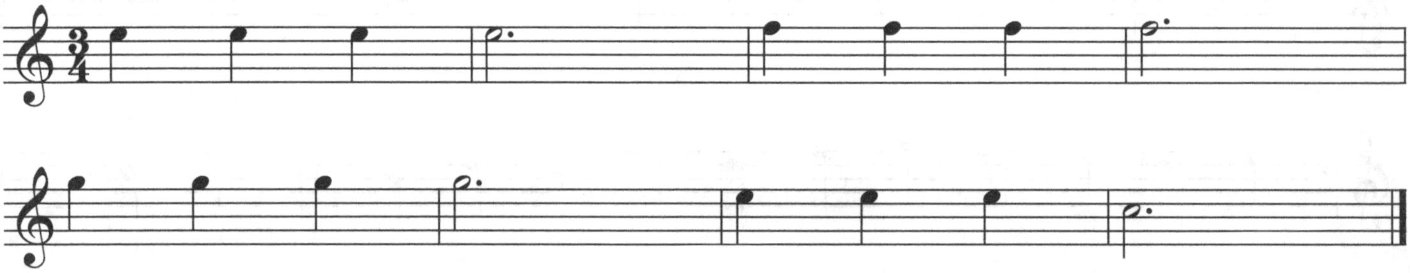

3/4 Study

Waltz

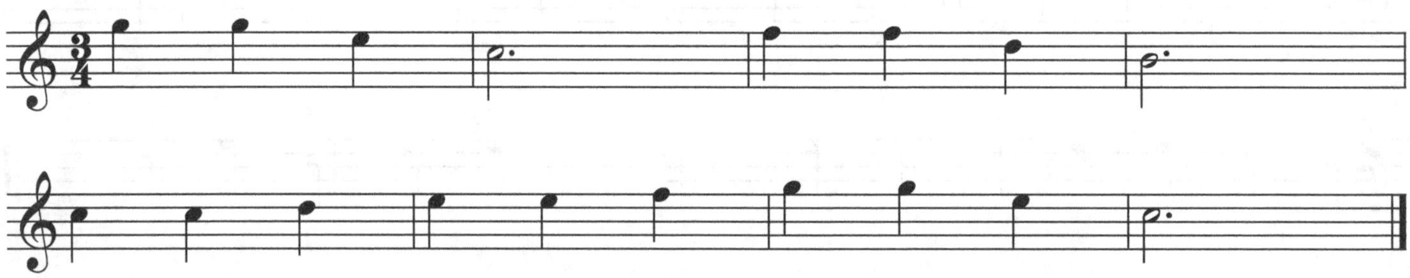

The Merry Men

Notes on the G String

Third String

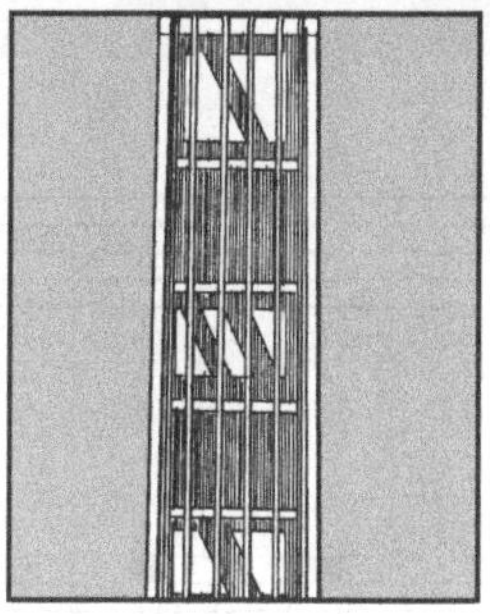

G

Open

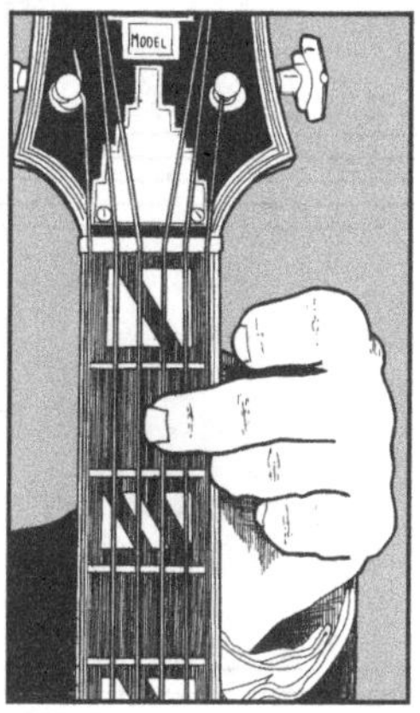

A

2nd Fret
2nd Finger

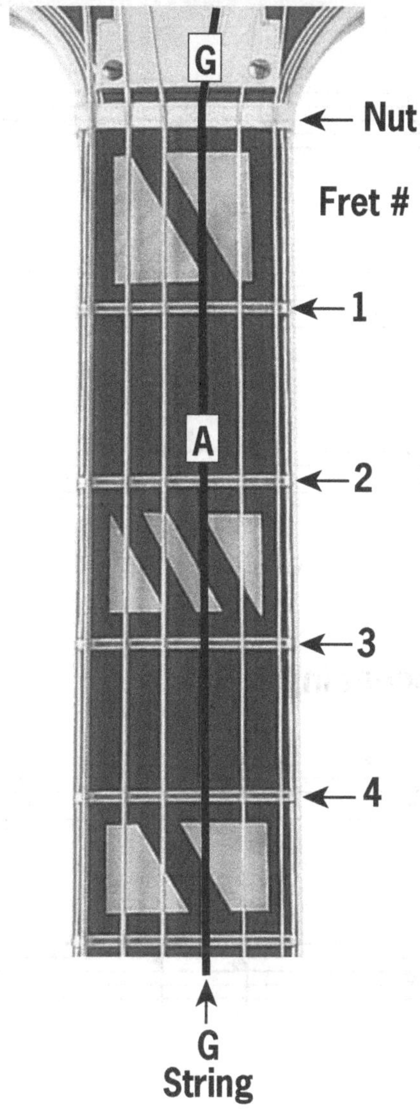

A Study on the Third String

Sparkling Stella

Prelude

Descending

Ascending

Sunset

Teacher Acc.

Aura Lee

Teacher Acc. Folk Song

Pick-Up Notes

One or more notes at the beginning of a strain before the first measure are referred to as **pick-up notes**.

The rhythm for pick-up notes is taken from the last measure of the selection and the beats are counted as such.

When the Saints Go Marchin' In

Teacher Acc. Spiritual

Two Note Pick-up

Teacher Acc.

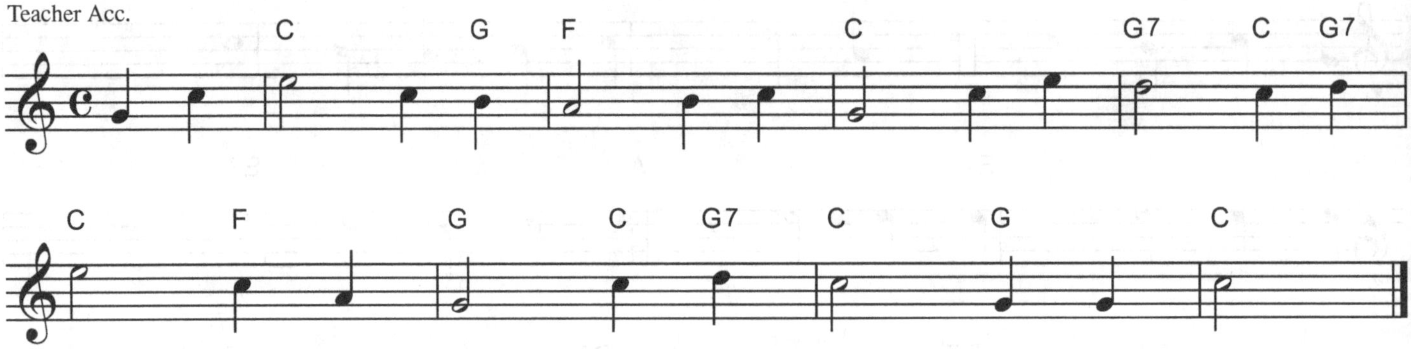

One Note Pick-up

Teacher Acc.

The Tie

The **tie** is a curved line between two notes of the same pitch. The first note is played and held for the time duration of both. The second note is not played, but held.

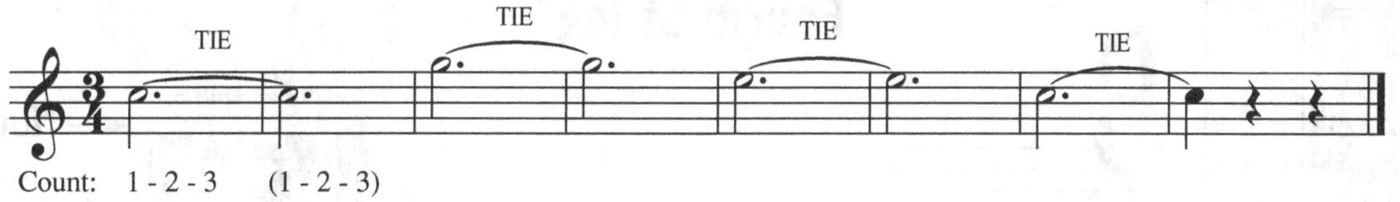

Psalm 100

Teacher Acc.

Louis Bourgeois
1510–1561

Red River Valley

Teacher Acc.

Western Song

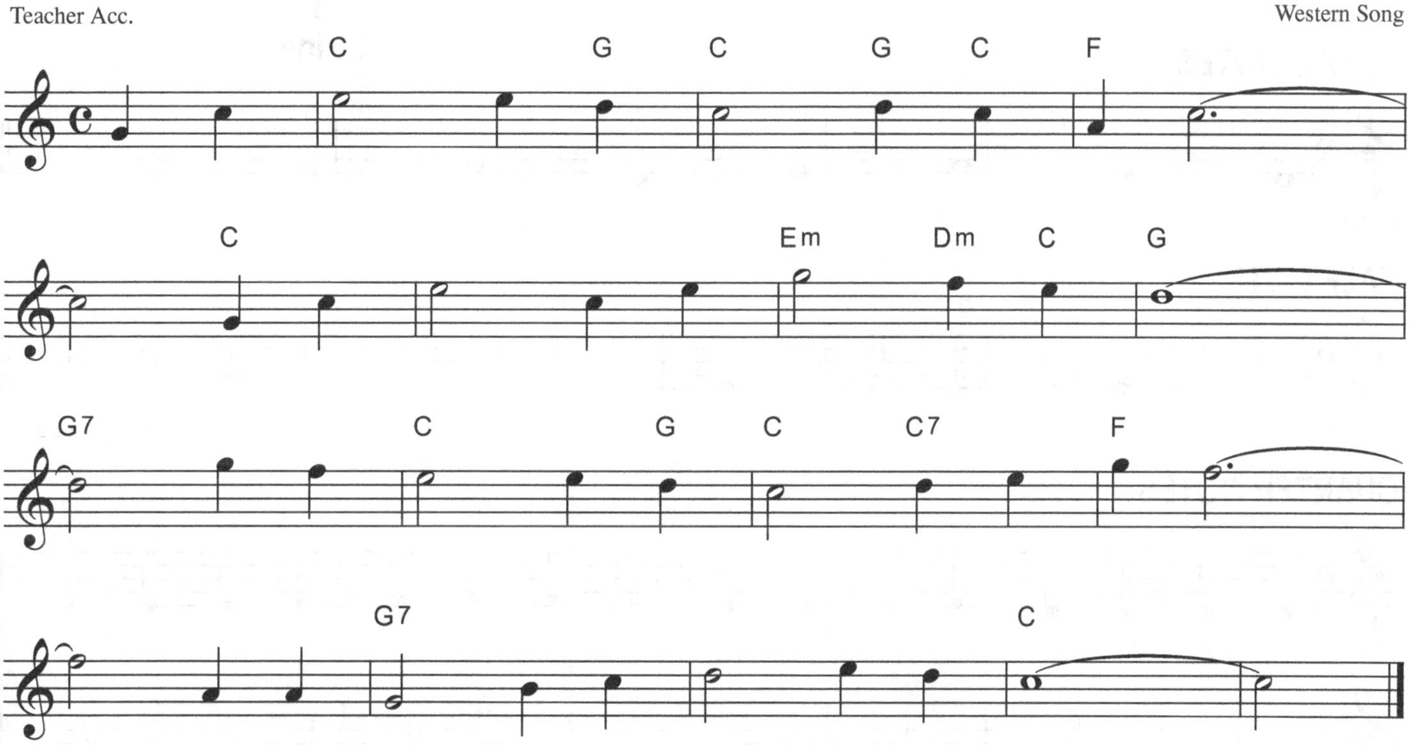

Notes on the D String

Fourth String

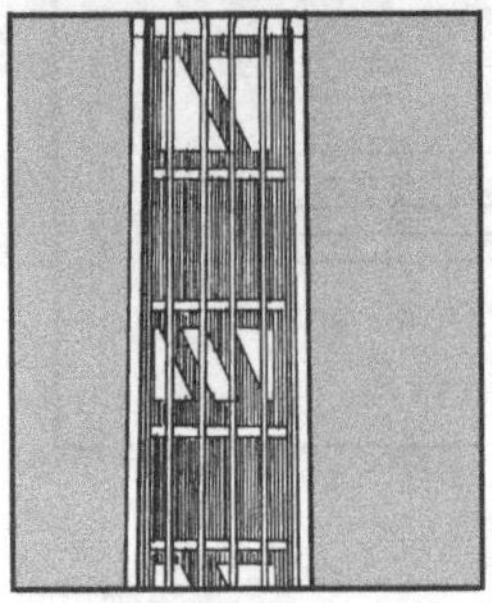

D

Open

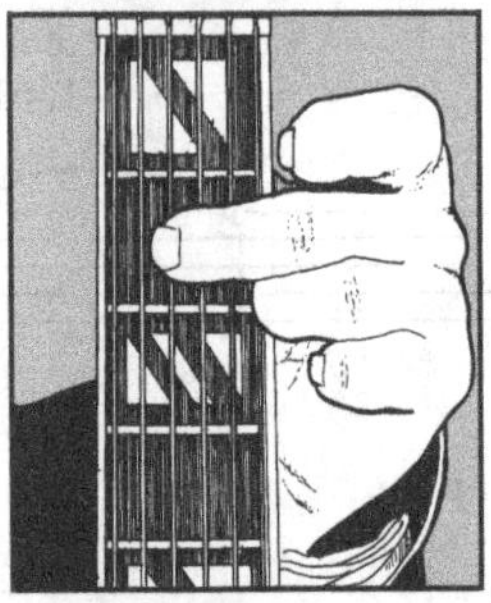

E

2nd Fret
2nd Finger

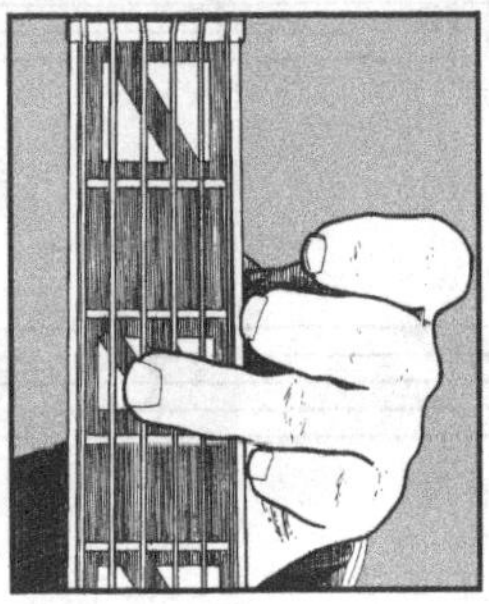

F

3rd Fret
3rd Finger

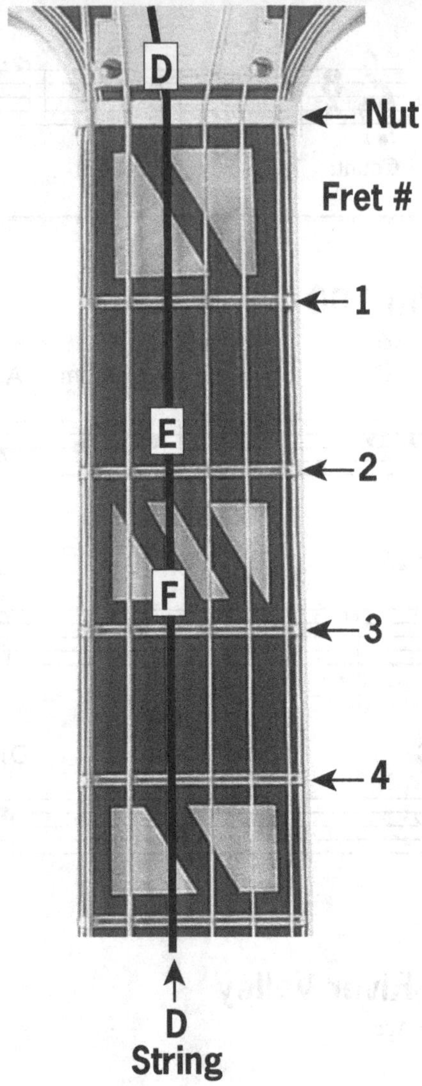

WHOLE NOTES

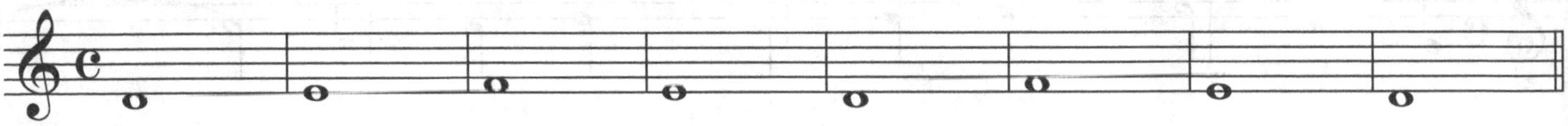

Count: 1 - 2 - 3 - 4

HALF NOTES

(Rest)

Count: 1 - 2 3 - 4 … 1 - 2 (3 - 4)

QUARTER NOTES

Count: 1 2 3 4

(Rest)

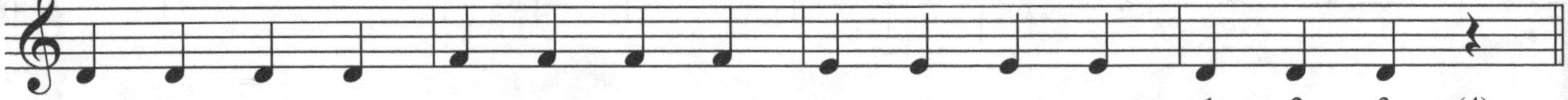

1 2 3 (4)

4 String Note Review

Native Flute

Bear Dance

Prairie Song

Native Drum

Cockles and Mussels

Teacher Acc. Ballad

Hymn

Teacher Acc.

German Waltz

Teacher Acc.

The Eighth Note

An **eighth note** receives one-half beat. (One quarter note equals two eighth notes.)

An eighth note will have a head, stem, and flag. If two or more are in successive order, they may be connected by a beam. (See example.)

EIGHTH NOTES **EIGHTH RESTS**

Eighth-Note Studies

⊓ = Downstroke of Pick V = Upstroke of Pick

①

②
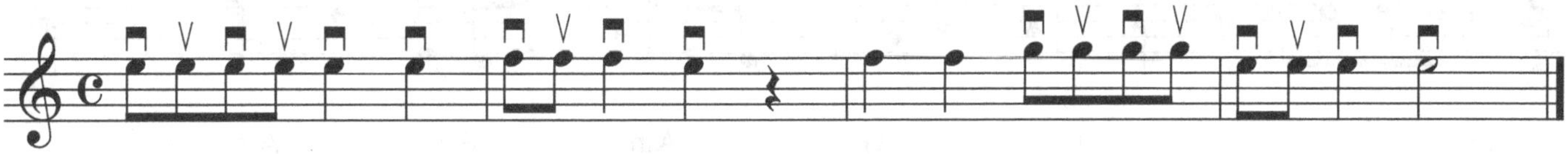

③

④

⑤

⑥

⑦

⑧

⑨

⑩

Tudor Dance

Teacher Acc.

Mohican Lament

Teacher Acc.

Dance of the Royal Court

Teacher Acc.

Village Waltz

Teacher Acc.

Amazing Grace

Teacher Acc. Hymn

Tenting Tonight

Teacher Acc. Song of the Civil War

Melancholy

Teacher Acc. W. Bay

Ledger Lines

When the pitch of a musical sound is below or above the staff, the notes are then placed on or between extra lines called **ledger lines.**

They will be like this:

Notes on the A String

Fifth String

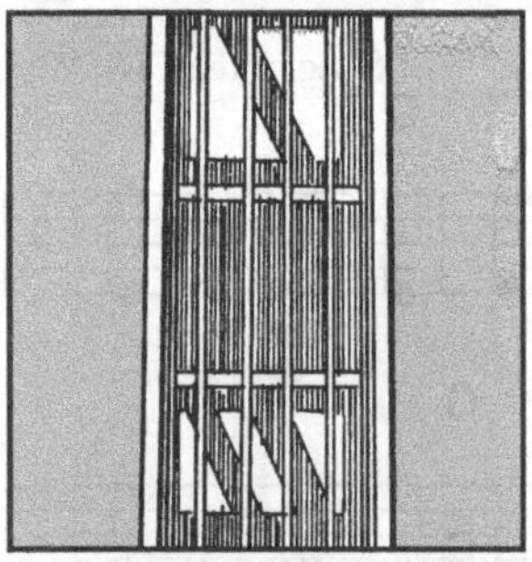

A

Open

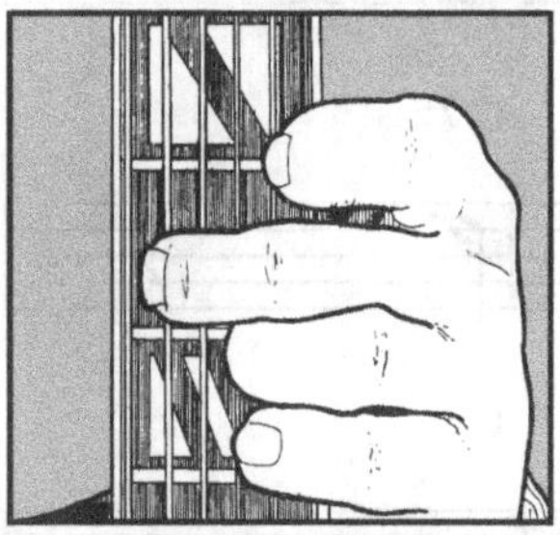

B

2nd Fret
2nd Finger

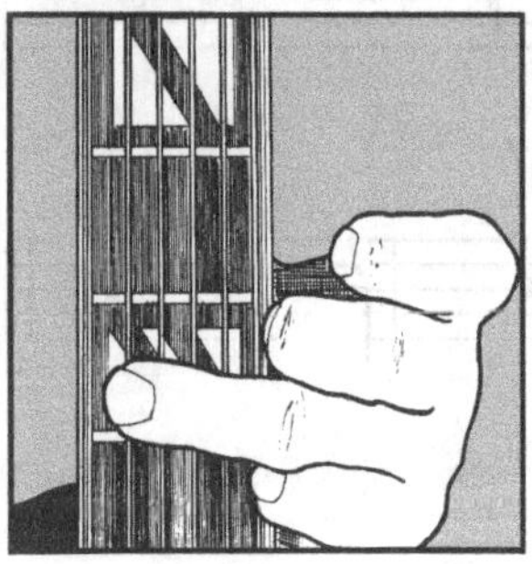

C

3rd Fret
3rd Finger

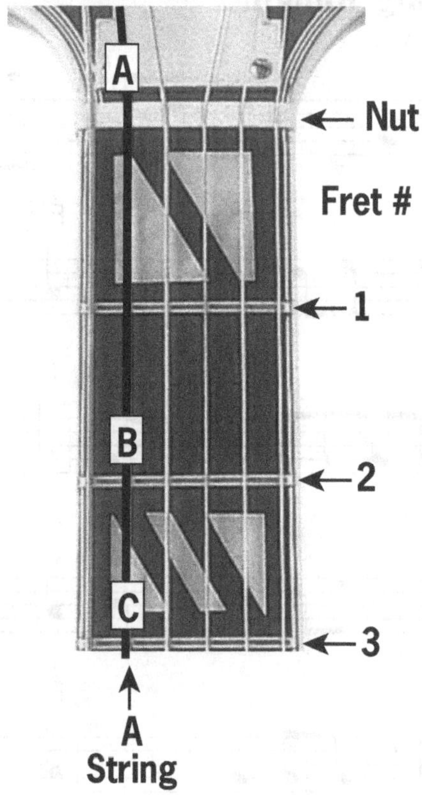

WHOLE NOTES

Count: 1 - 2 - 3 - 4

HALF NOTES

Count: 1 - 2 3 - 4

QUARTER NOTES

Wilderness Trail

Teacher Acc.

Westward Ho!

Teacher Acc.

Chord Waltz

Teacher Acc.

Elsie's Waltz

Teacher Acc.

Buffalo Gals

Teacher Acc.

Western Song

Chester

Teacher Acc.

Song of the Revolutionary War

Dotted Quarter Notes

A **dot** after a note increases its value by one-half.

Dotted Quarter Note (1/4 + 1/8) Equal to (1/4 + 1/8) (Tie) Three Eighths

The count for the dotted quarter note is as follows.

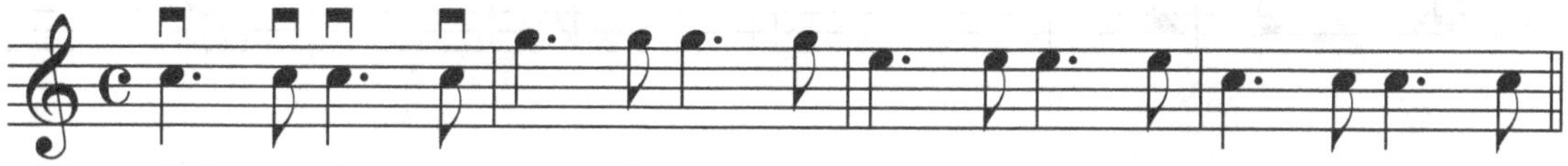

Count: 1 2 & 3 4 & 1 2 & 3 4 & 1 2 & 3 4 & 1 2 & 3 4 &

Kum-Ba-Ya

Teacher Acc.

African Hymn

Michael, Row the Boat Ashore

Teacher Acc.

Spiritual

Mountain Flower

Teacher Acc.

Quest

Teacher Acc.

Homeward Bound

Teacher Acc.

Note Review

Daydreams

Teacher Acc.

Ozark Stream

Teacher Acc.

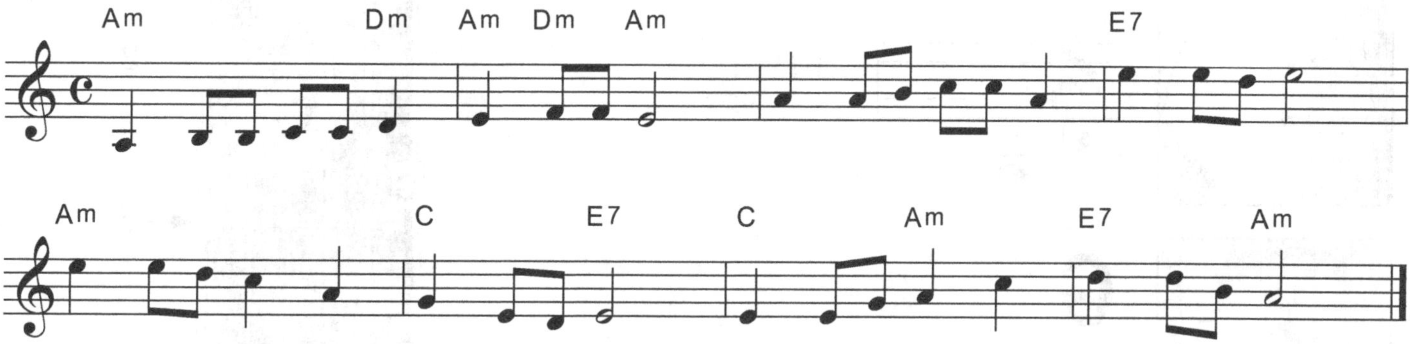

Waterfall

Teacher Acc.

Mountain Trail

Teacher Acc.

Notes on the E String

Sixth String

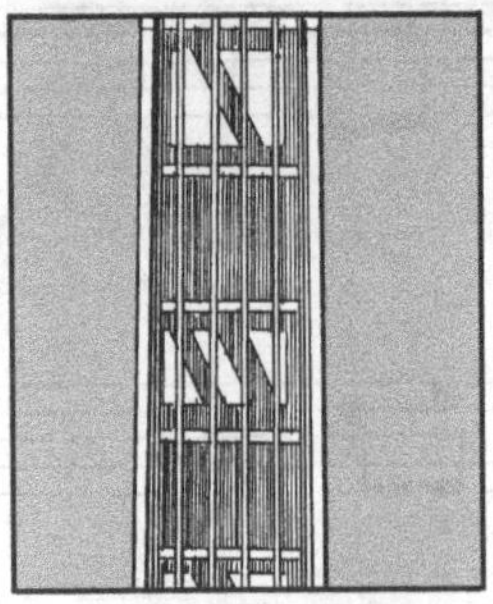

E

Open

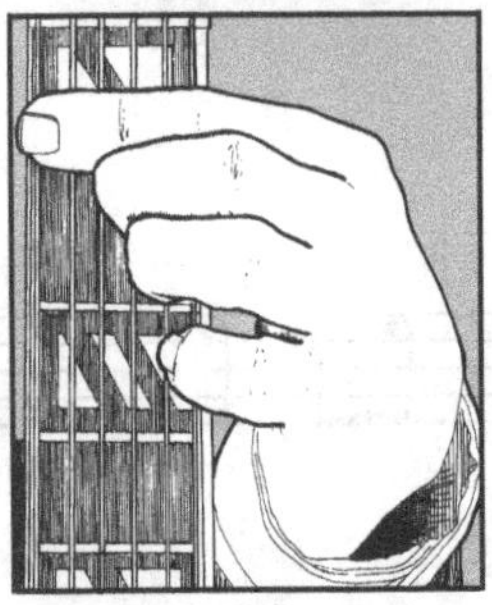

F

1st Fret
1st Finger

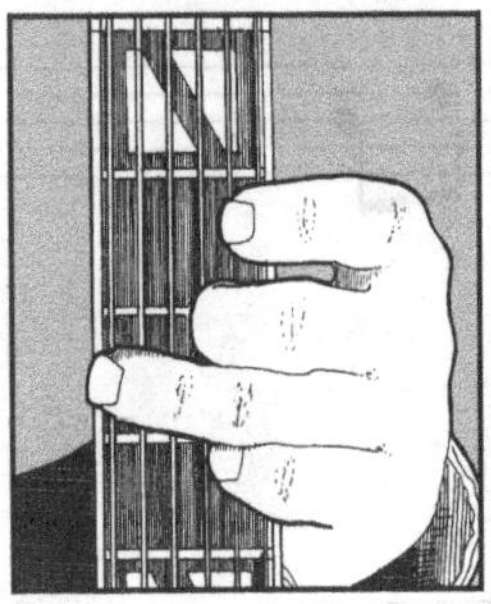

G

3rd Fret
3rd Finger

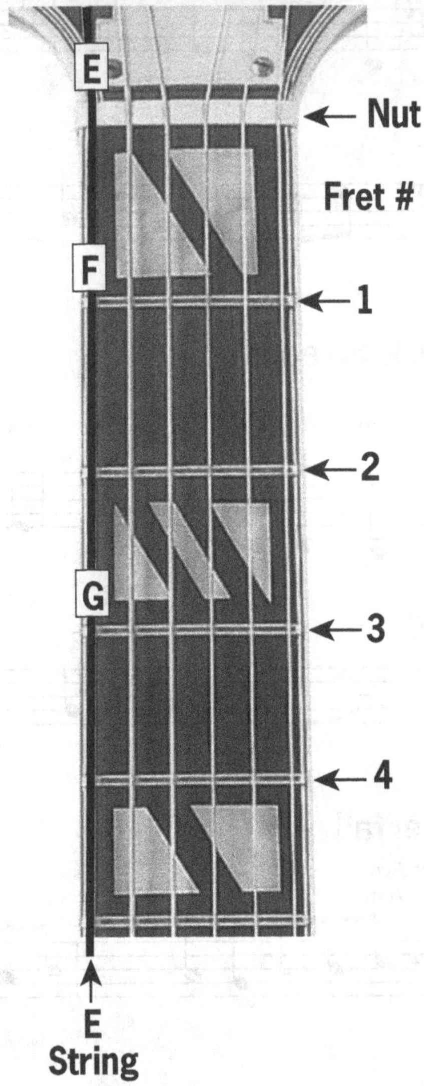

WHOLE NOTES

HALF NOTES

QUARTER NOTES

Driving Bass

Teacher Acc.

Low Gear

Teacher Acc.

Running the Notes

Teacher Acc.

Introducing the A Note

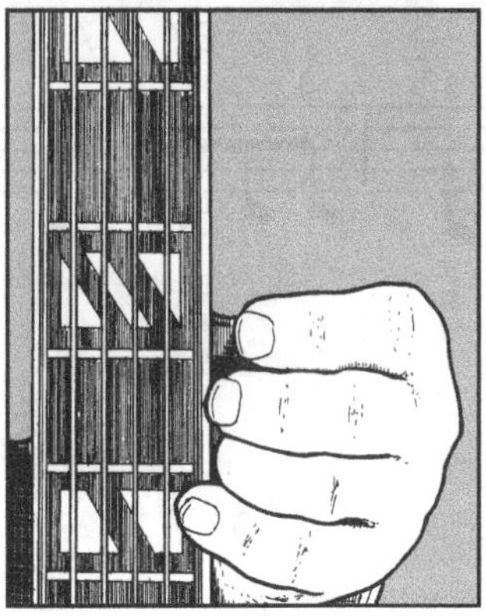

A

5th Fret
4th Finger

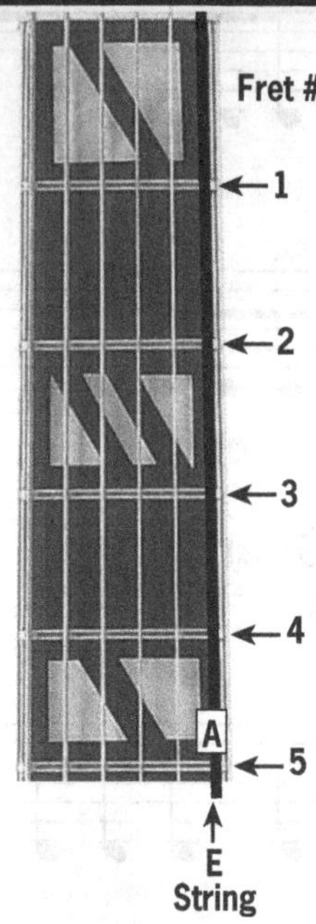

Minor Melody

Teacher Acc. W. Bay

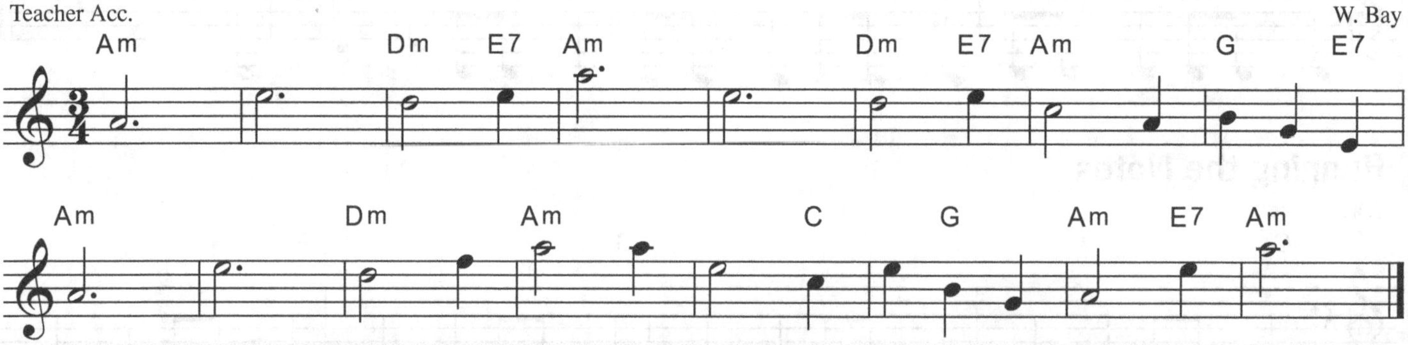

Notes on the Guitar in the First Position

	6th String			5th String			4th String			3rd String		2nd String			1st String			
Frets	0	1	3	0	2	3	0	2	3	0	2	0	1	3	0	1	3	5
	E	F	G	A	B	C	D	E	F	G	A	B	C	D	E	F	G	A

Hitting on All Six

Teacher Acc. Mel Bay

Playing High A

Smoky Ridge

Teacher Acc.

Voyage

Teacher Acc.

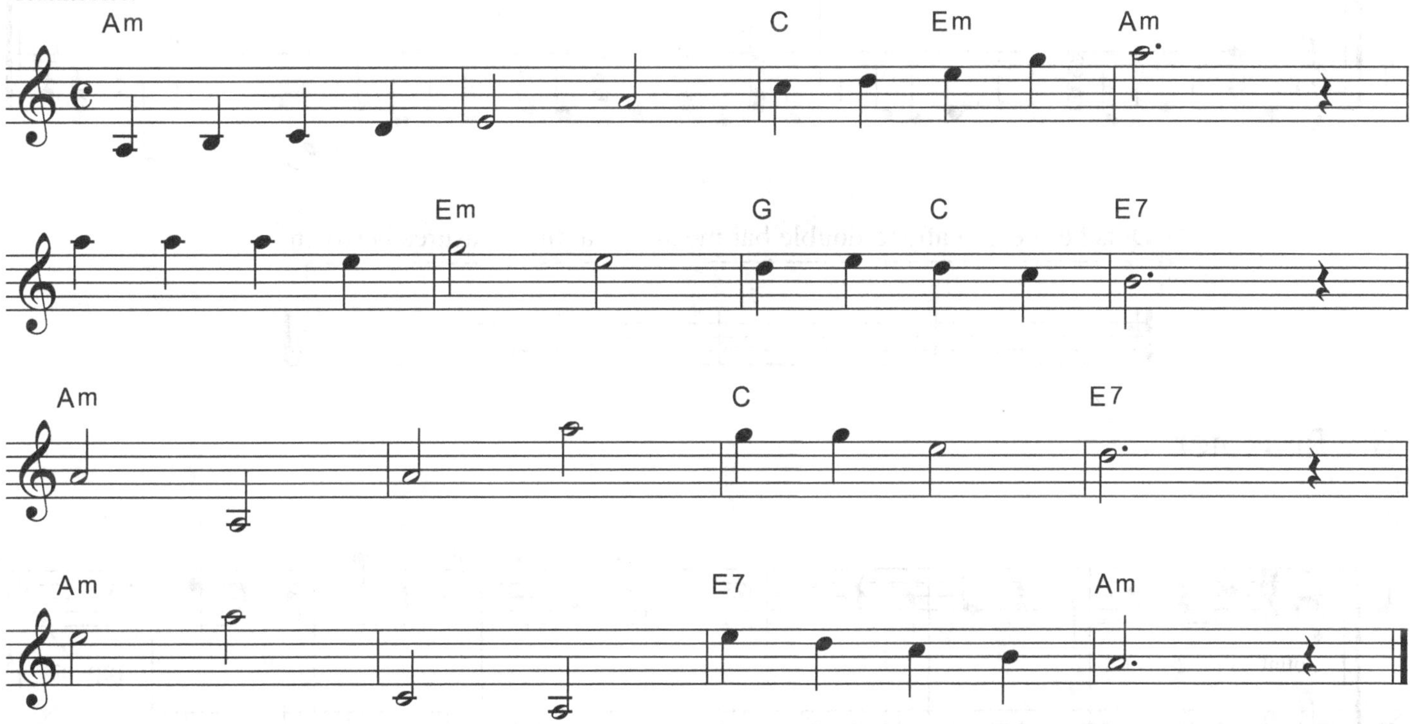

A Word About Duets

One of the first requisites of a good guitarist is the ability to play well with others. It is with this point in mind that I am stressing the value of duet training.

The modern guitarist has to have the ability to play **solo, harmony,** and **rhythm.**

Duet training will teach the student to perform his or her own part independently without the bewilderment or confusion caused by the rhythm or counterpoint appearing in the second part.

This is one of the most important phases of the student training.

The second part in the following duets will be played by the teacher. The student will be required to play both parts later

Our First Duet

Guitar Duet

S = Student T = Teacher

Arr. by Mel Bay

Dots before and after a double bar mean repeat the measures between.

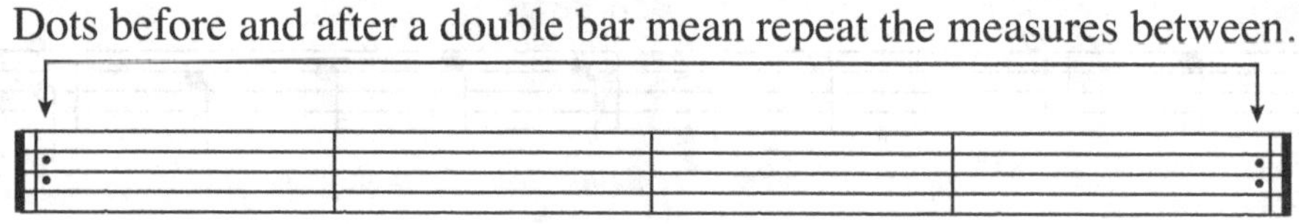

The Repeater

I = 1st Part

II = 2nd Part

The dots placed above and below the third line of the staff at the double bar indicate that the piece is to be repeated.

Two Guitars

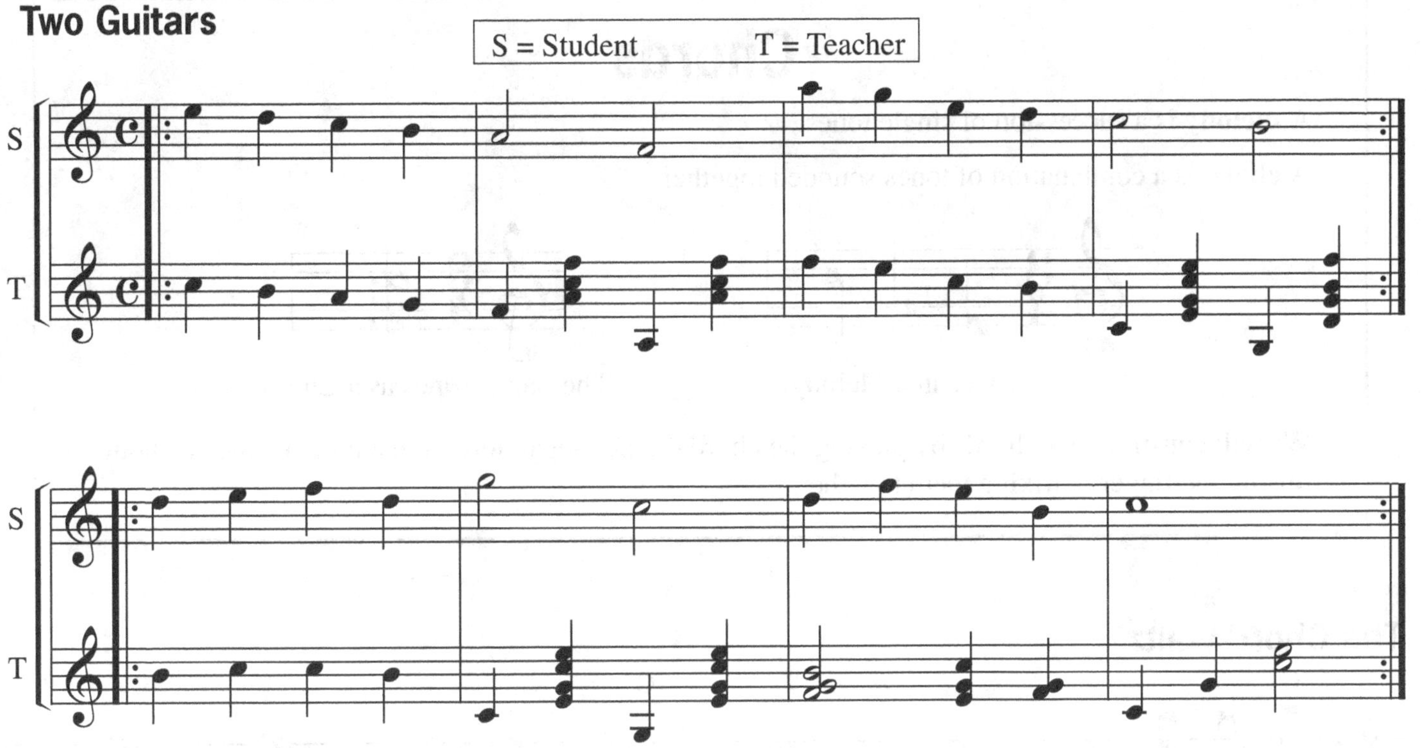

Sunset

Chords

A **melody** is a succession of single tones.

A **chord** is a combination of tones sounded together

Tones in a Melody

The Same Tones as a Chord

We will construct our chords by playing the chordal tones separately as in a melody and, without raising the fingers, striking them together.

The Chord Waltz

Mel Bay

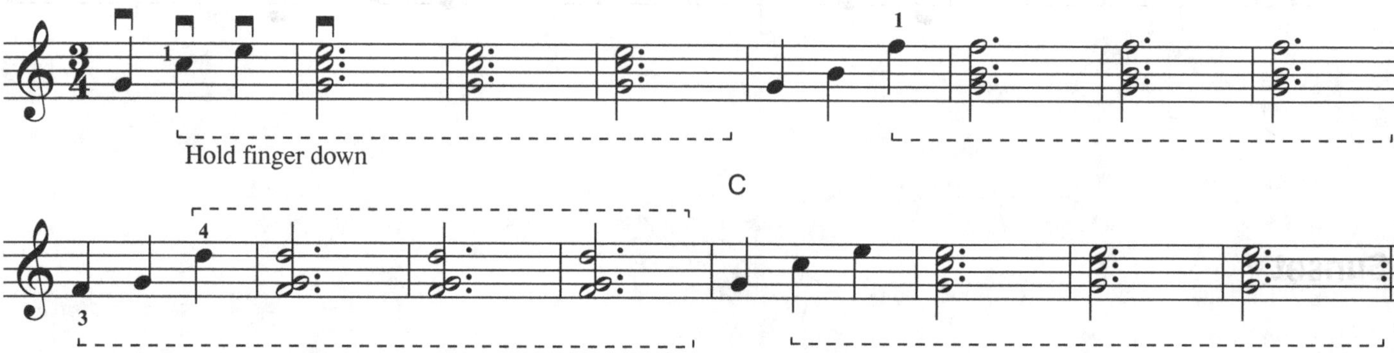

The Builder

Mel Bay

Small Chord Etude

Mel Bay

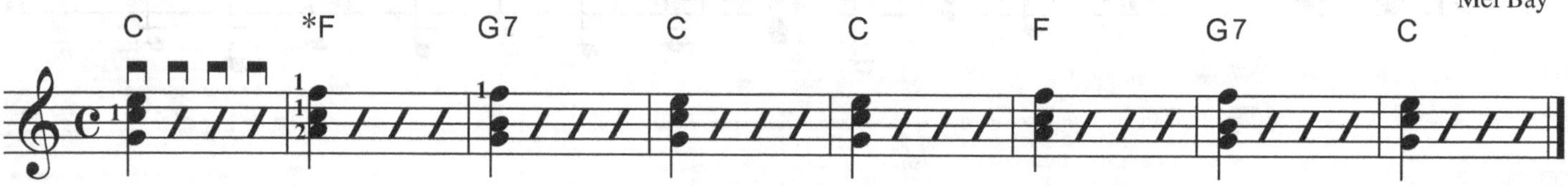

Practice the above etude until it can be played without missing a beat.

*Note that the first finger holds down two notes (C-F) in the second chord.

Chord Songs

Chord March

Autumn

Chording Along

Echoes

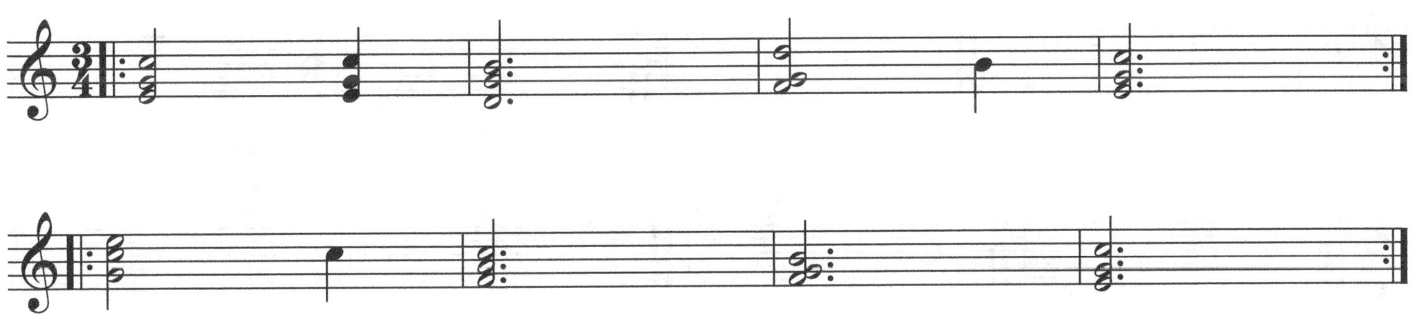

Building the F Chord

Two Notes

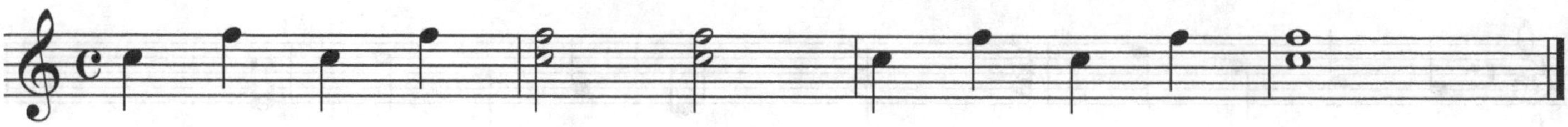

Three Notes

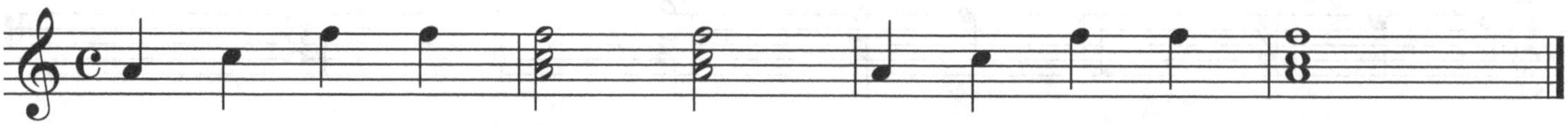

Four Notes

Four-String Chord Study

We use the same method for building four-string chords as we did in building the three-string chords. Play the chordal tones melodically, holding the fingers down until chord is reached, then strike them together producing the desired chord.

Exercise

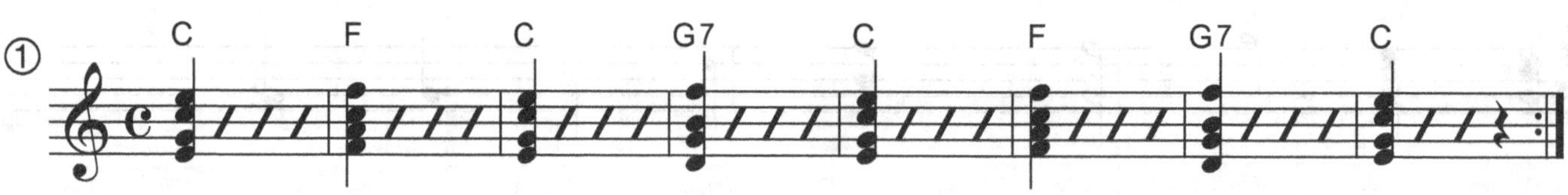

Chimes

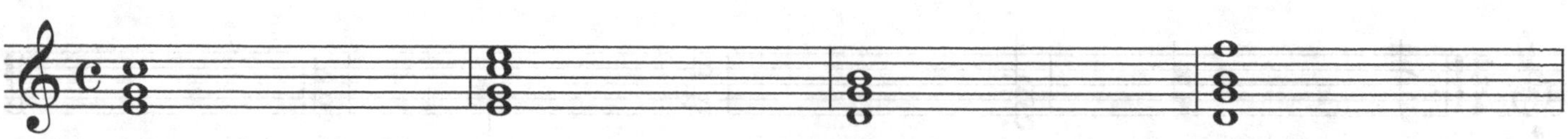

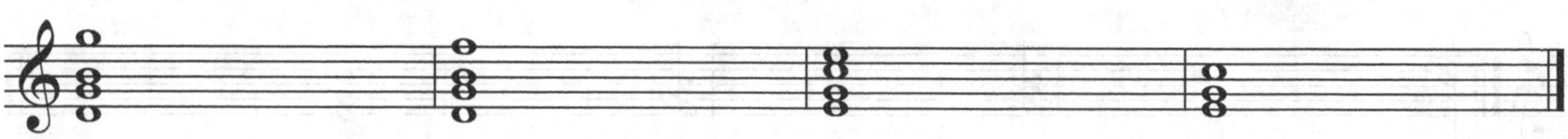

Chord Studies

Bottom Floor

Teacher Acc.

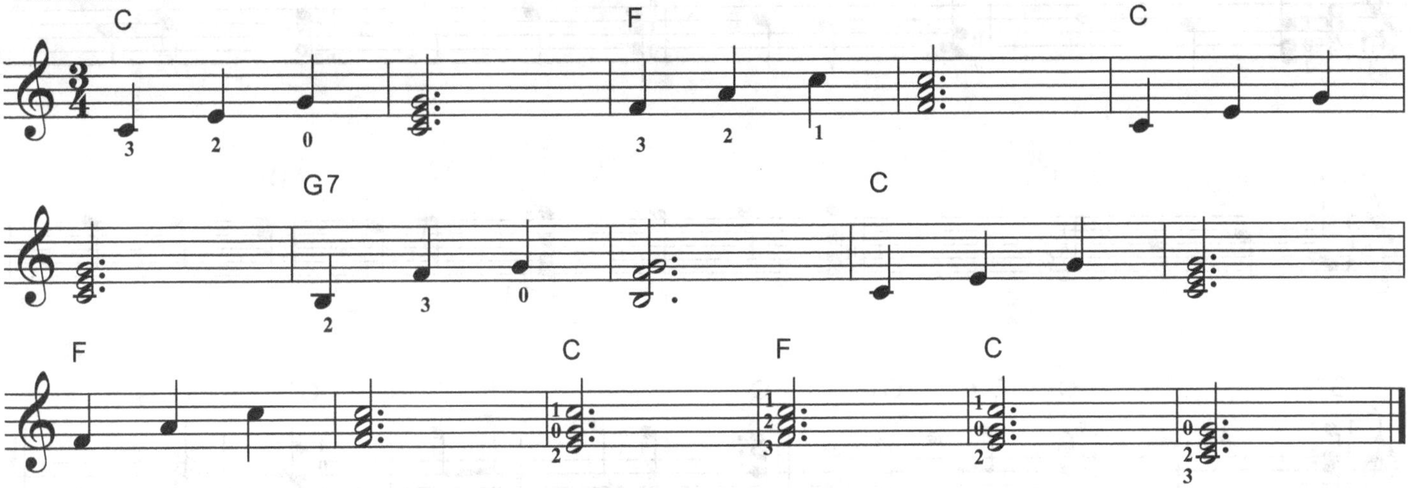

Chord Walk

Teacher Acc.

May Song

Teacher Acc.

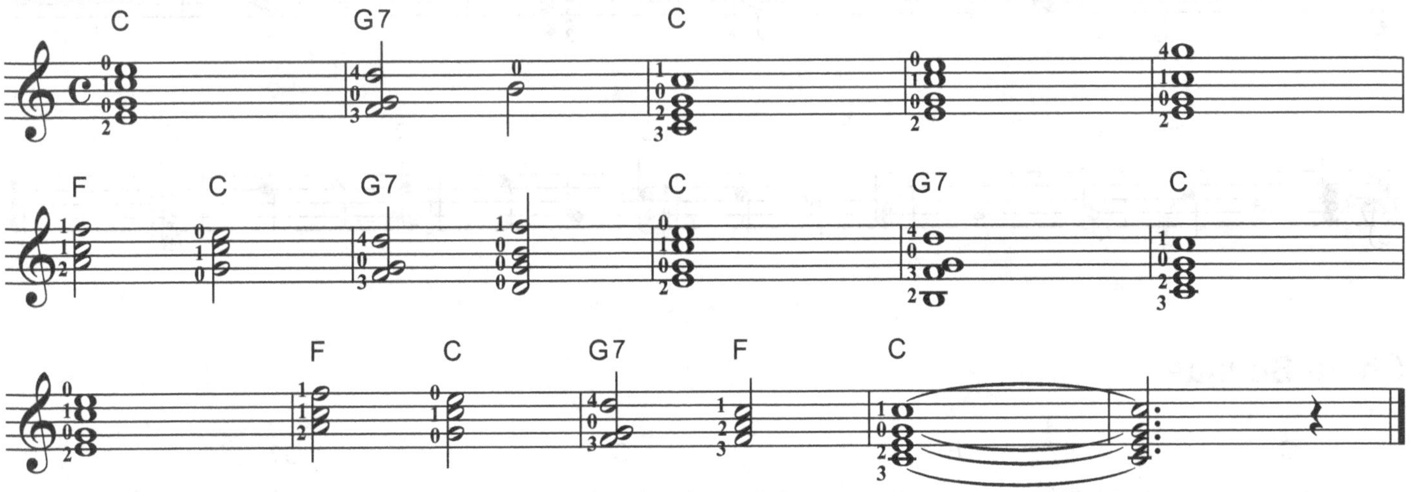

Running in the Chord

Teacher Acc.

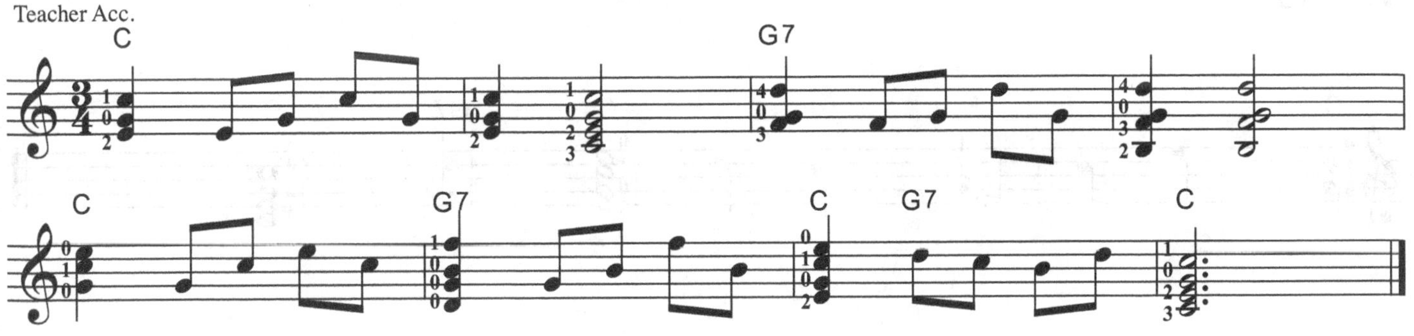

My Country Tis of Thee

Teacher Acc.

Green Grow the Lilacs

Teacher Acc.

Chord Bouquet

Teacher Acc.

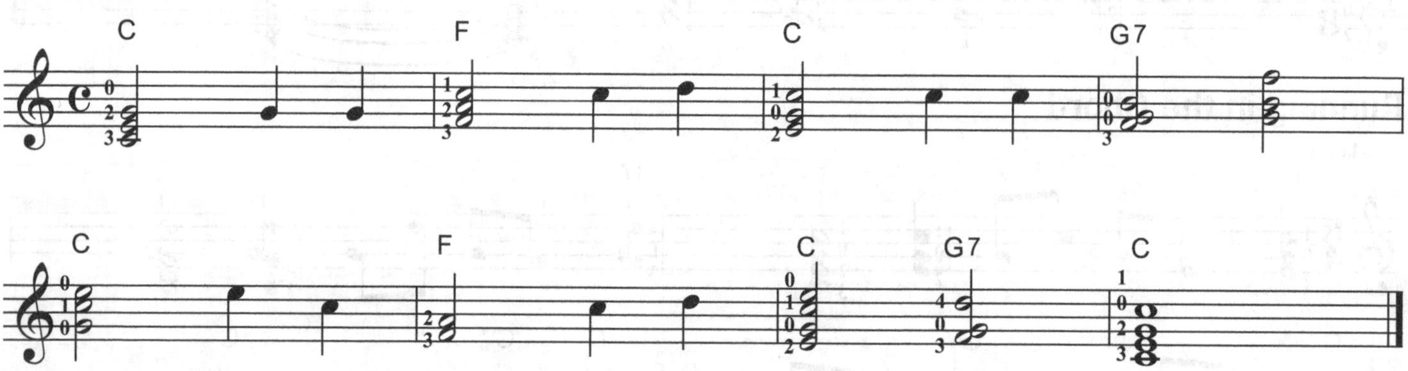

Follow the Leader

Guitar Duet

Arr. by Mel Bay

Tallis Canon

Bass Solos with Chord Accompaniment

When playing bass solos with chord accompaniment, you will find the solo with the stems turned downward and the accompaniment with the stems turned upward.

Count: 1 2 3

In the example shown above, you see the dotted half note (E) with the stem downward. It is played on the count of one and held for counts two and three.

The quarter rest over the dotted half note indicates that there is no chord accompanimet at the count of one. The chords with the stems upward are played on counts two and three.

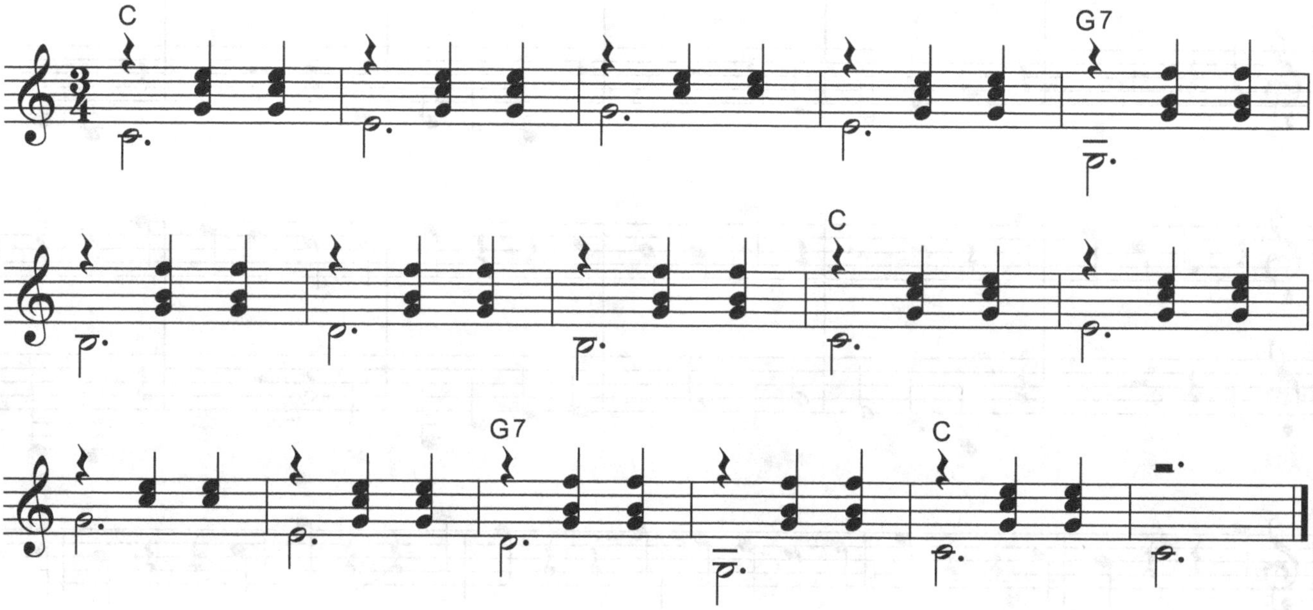

Gliding Along

Mel Bay

Hymn

Teacher Acc.

Country Waltz

Teacher Acc.

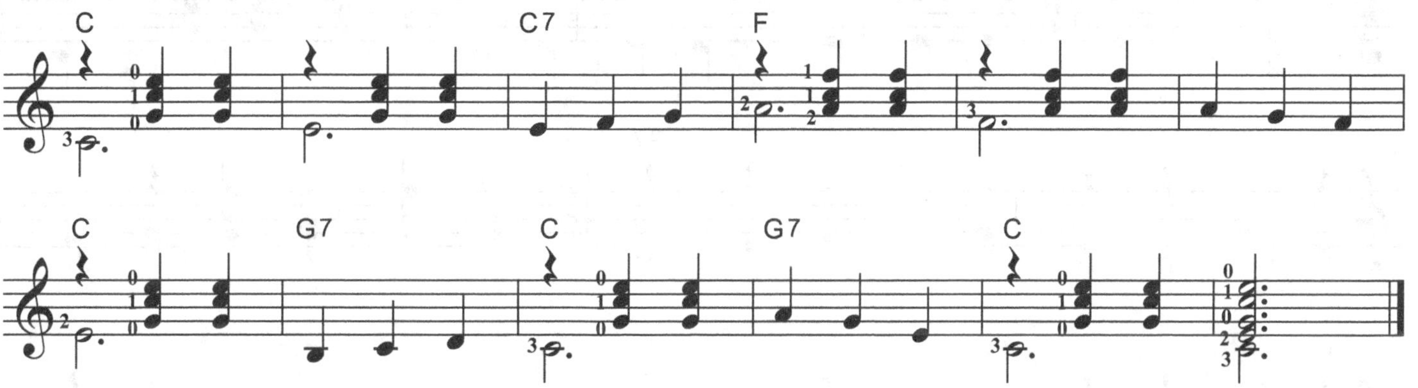

Western Song

Teacher Acc.

Oh Bury Me Not on the Lone Prairie

Teacher Acc.

Red River Valley

Teacher Acc.

Sawdust Trail

Teacher Acc.

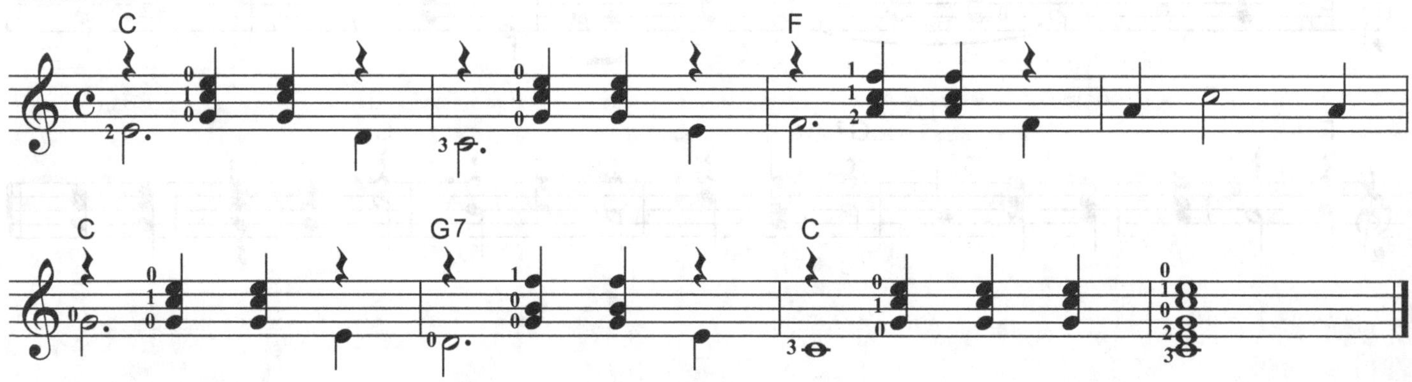

The Key of C

All music studied so far in this book has been in the key of C. That means that the notes have been taken from the C scale (shown at right) and made into melodies.

It is called the C scale because the first note is a C and we proceed through the musical alphabet until C reappears: C-D-E-F-G-A-B-C.

We will cover the subject of keys and scales more thoroughly in the theory and harmony chapters appearing later in this course.

At present we will deal only with basic fundamentals.

The C Scale

Ascending

Descending

Scale Studies

①

②

Teacher Acc.

③

Teacher Acc.

④
Teacher Acc.

⑤
Teacher Acc.

⑥
Teacher Acc.

⑦
Teacher Acc.

⑧
Teacher Acc.

Shenandoah

Teacher Acc.

Shenandoah – Advanced Version

Teacher Acc.

Blue Bells of Scotland

Teacher Acc.

Blue Bells of Scotland – Advanced Version

Teacher Acc.

Chords in the Key of C Major

The key of C has three principal chords. They are C, F, and G7.

C

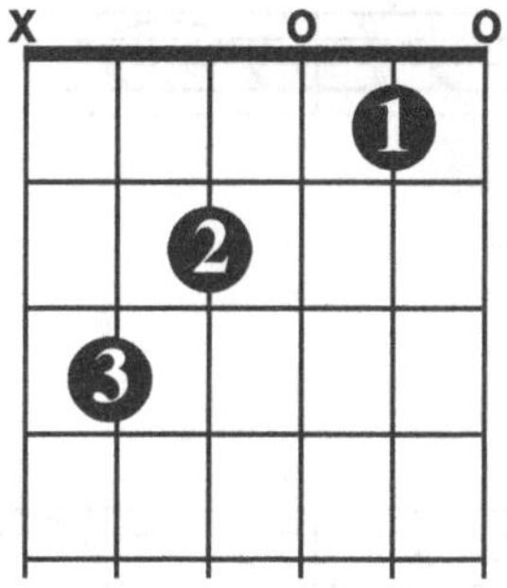

F

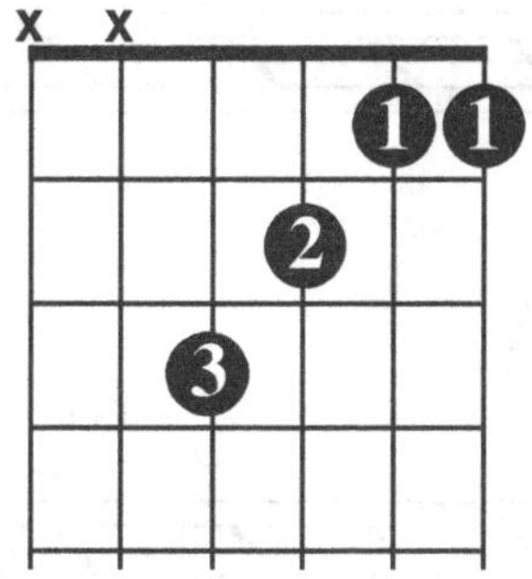

G7

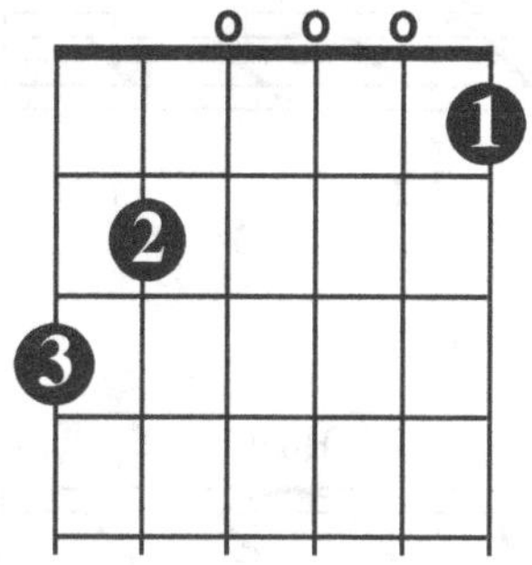

- The circles indicate the position where your fingers should be placed.
- Numerals inside circles indicate the fingers.
- "X" over the strings means that the strings are not to be played.
- "O" over the strings indicates the strings be played open.
- Place fingers in positions indicated by the circles and strike them all together.

Musical Notation of the Chords

C

F

G7

Accompaniment Styles

Alternate Basses

In Three-Four Time

Chord Studies in C

/ = Strum chord down across strings   Down Up = Down – up strum

①

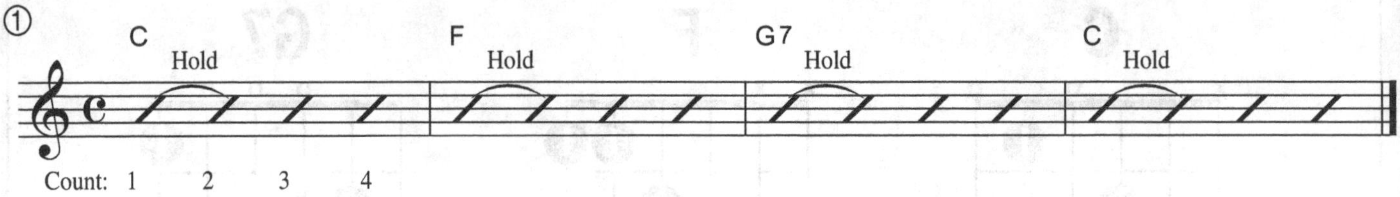

②

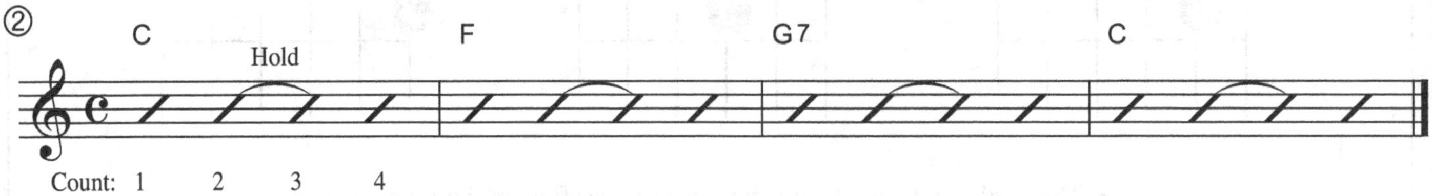

③

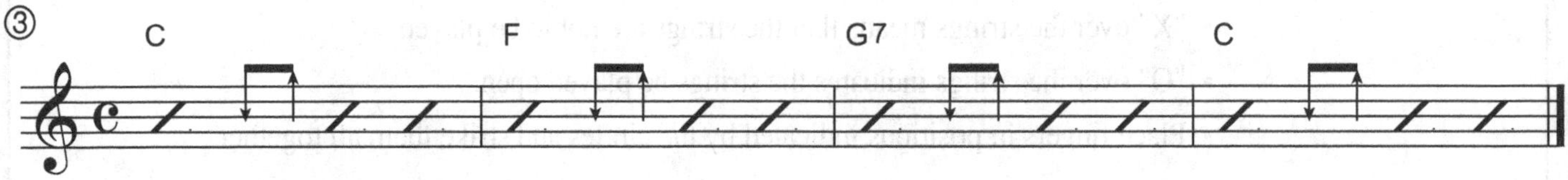

④

⑤

⑥

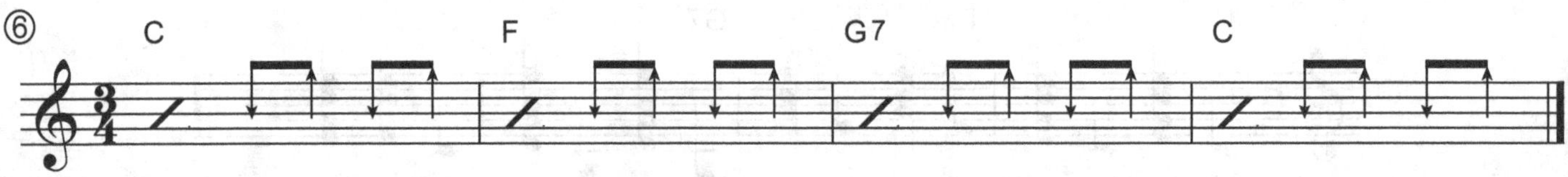

⑦

A Daily Scale Study

> The above study should be played slowly with a gradual increase of speed until a moderate tempo has been reached. It is an excellent daily exercise.

Running Around

Teacher Acc.

Home, Home, Can I Forget Thee

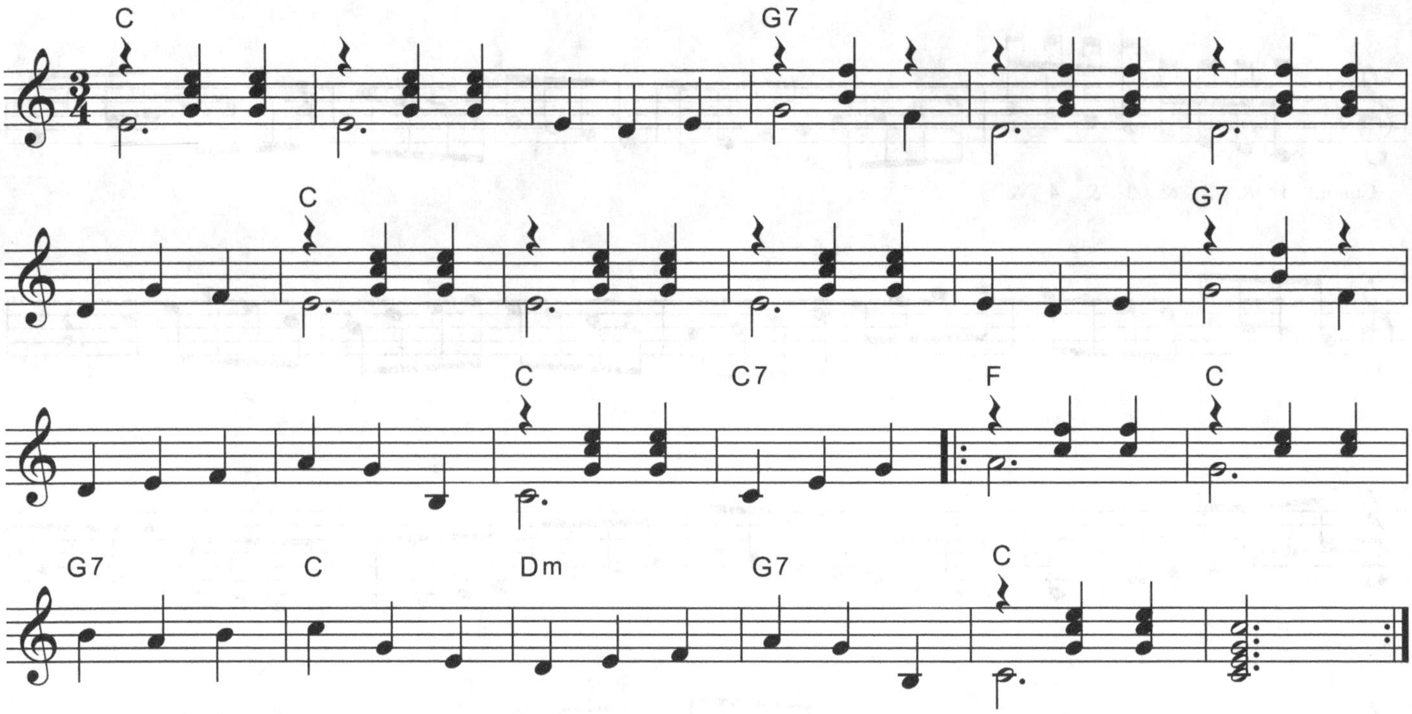

Long, Long Ago

Steps

A half-step is the distance from a given tone to the next higher or lower tone. On the guitar, the distance of a half step is one fret.

A whole step consists of two half steps, The distance of a whole step on the guitar is two frets.

The C scale has two half steps. They are between E-F and B-C. Note the distance of one fret between those notes. The distances between C-D, D-E, F-G, G-A, and A-B are whole steps.

Whole steps and half steps are also referred to as whole tones and half tones, We will refer to them as whole steps and half steps.

Chromatics

The alteration of the pitches of tones is brought about by the use of symbols called **chromatics** (also referred to as **accidentals**).

The Sharp ♯

The sharp placed before a note raises its pitch 1/2 step or one fret.

Fret: 1 2 1 2 0 1 3 4 0 1 3 4 3 4 1 2

The Flat ♭

The flat placed before a note lowers its pitch 1/2step or one fret.

Fret: 2 4 2 3 1 4 1 4 1 4 2

The Natural ♮

The natural restores a note to its normal position. It cancels all accidentas previously used.

Fret: 1 2 2 1 2 3 2 1

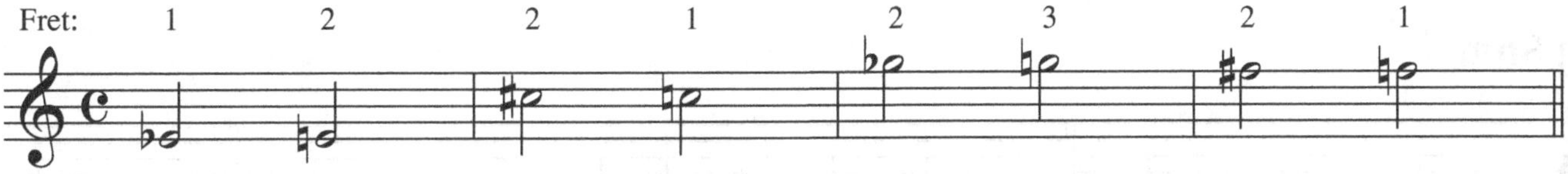

Sharps

A **sharp** placed in front of a note *raises* the pitch 1/2 step or one fret. Study the notes below

1st String

Remember: when a note is sharped, all notes of that pitch remain sharped throughout the measure unless a **natural sign** (♮) appears. A natural sign cancels a sharp.

1st String Sharps & Naturals

2nd String

3rd String

4th String

5th String

6th String

Walking Guitar

Flats

A **flat** (♭) placed in front of a note lowers the pitch 1/2 step or one fret. Study the notes below. A **natural sign** (♮) cancels out the flat.

1st String

2nd String

3rd String

4th String

5th String

6th String

Benny's Flat

Tempo

Tempo is the rate of speed of a musical composition. Three types of tempos used in this book will be: **Andante:** A slow, easy pace. **Moderato:** Moderate. **Allegro:** Lively.

Playtime

Guitar Duet **Moderato**

Pleyel
Arr. by Mel Bay

The Key of A Minor

(Relative to C Major)

- Each major key will have a relative minor key.
- The relative minor scale is built upon the sixth tone of the major scale.
- The key signature of both will be the same.
- The minor scale will have the same number of tones (7) as the major.
- The difference between the two scales is the arrangement of the whole steps and half steps.
- There are three forms of the minor scale: 1) pure or natural, 2) harmonic, 3) melodic.

The A Minor Scale

Natural (Pure)

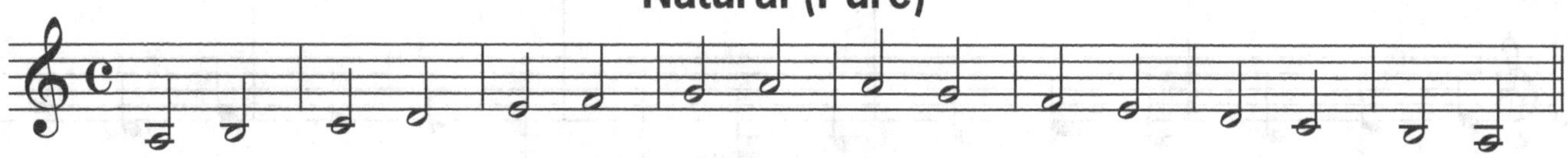

Harmonic

The 7th tone is raised one half step ascending and descending.

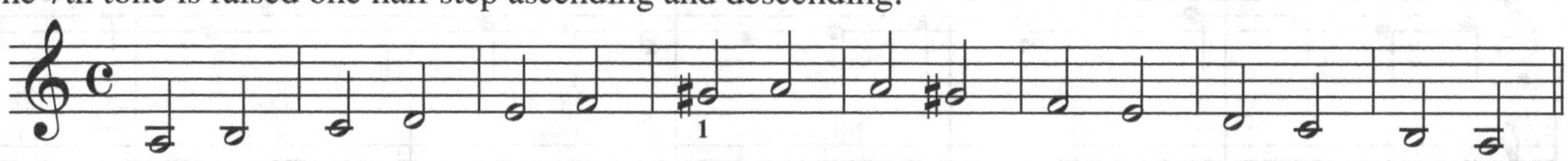

Melodic

The 6th and 7th tones are raised one half step ascending and lowered back to their normal pitch descending.

The Chords in the Key of A Minor

m = minor

Am

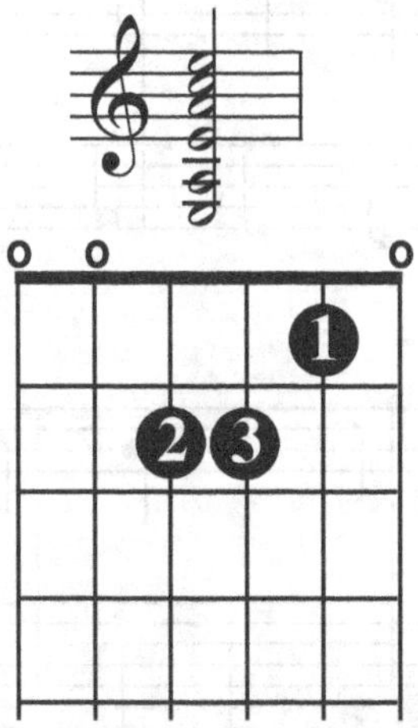

Dm

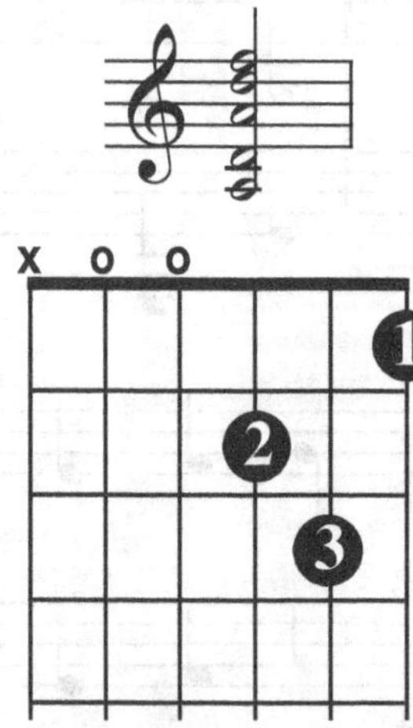

E7

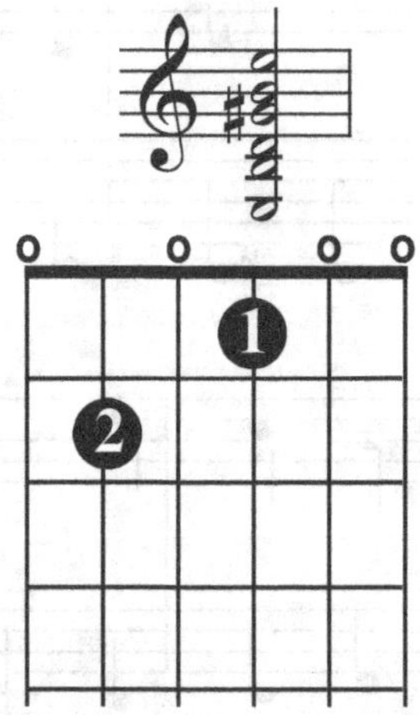

Accompaniment Styles in A Minor

Orchestration Style

The Diagonal line (/) indicates a chord stroke. They will fall only on each beat of the measure.

Repeat the accompaniment exercises until they can be played without missing a beat.

Chord Studies in the Key of Am

/ = Strum chord down across strings   Down Up = Down – up strum

A Daily Scale Study in A Minor

Harmonic

(Repeat ⊓ V ⊓ V)

Picking Studies in A Minor

①

②

③

④

⑤

⑥

⑦

Sailing

Teacher Acc.

Minor Song

Teacher Acc.

Journey

Teacher Acc.

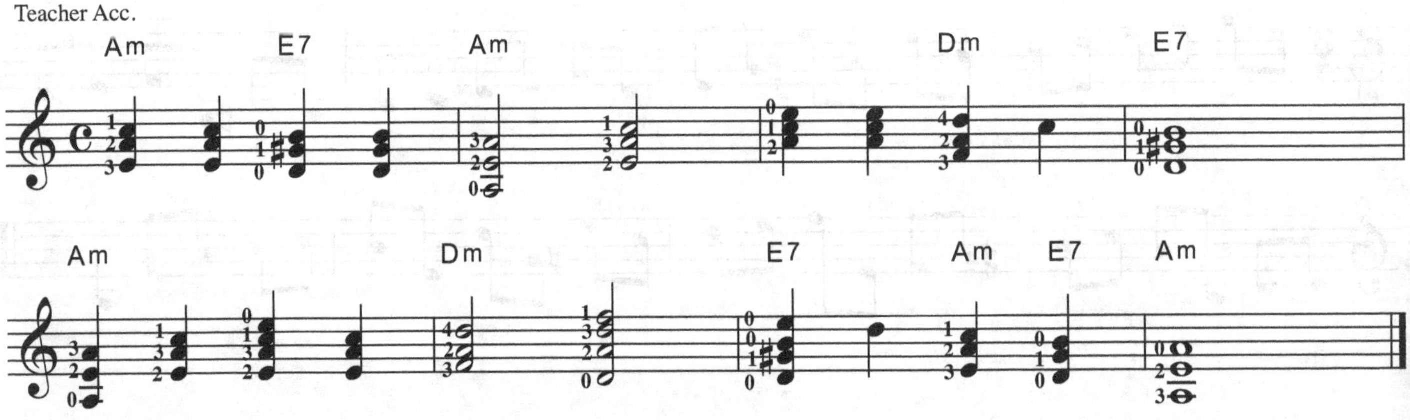

Hold Sign: 𝄐 This sign placed over or under a note or rest indicates the prolonging of its time value.

Wayfaring Stranger

Another Daily Scale Study in A Minor

The Up Stroke: V This stroke will be used on repeated eighth notes of the same pitch.

A Visit to the Relatives

First and Second Endings

Sometimes two endings are required in certain selections... one to lead back into a repeated chorus and one to close it. They will be shown like this:

The first time, play the bracketed ending No. 1. Repeat the chorus. The second time, skip the first ending and play ending No. 2.

Shady Glen

Teacher Acc.

Careless Love

Teacher Acc.

Picking Solos

Foggy Mountain Run

Teacher Acc.

The Shire

Teacher Acc.

Bluegrass Sunrise

Teacher Acc.

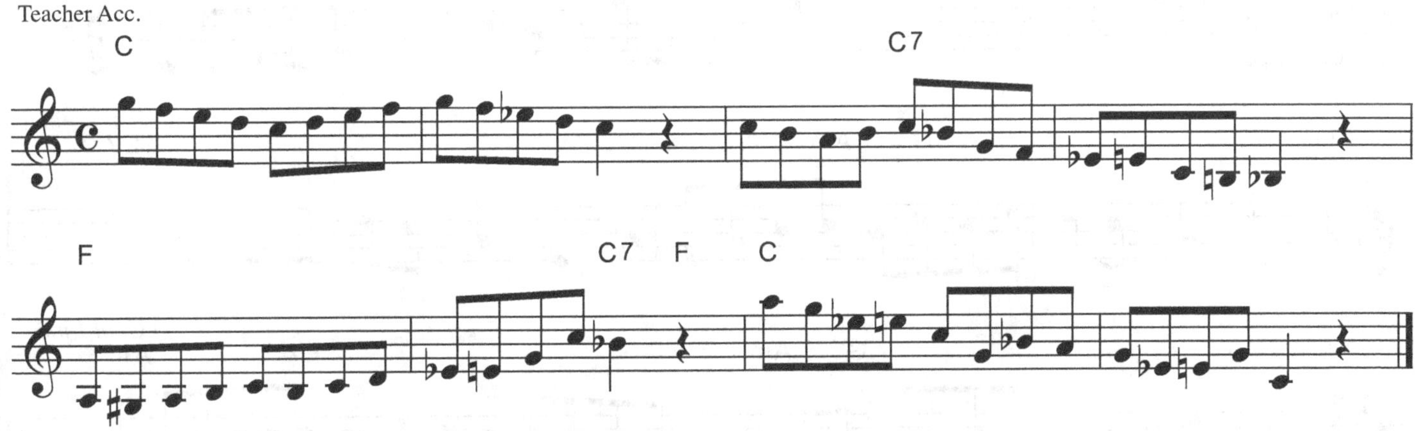

Cradle Song

Teacher Acc.

D.C. al Fine means to go back to the beginning of a piece of music and play until you see the word *Fine* which means "**The End**."

Blue Ridge Trail

Teacher Acc.

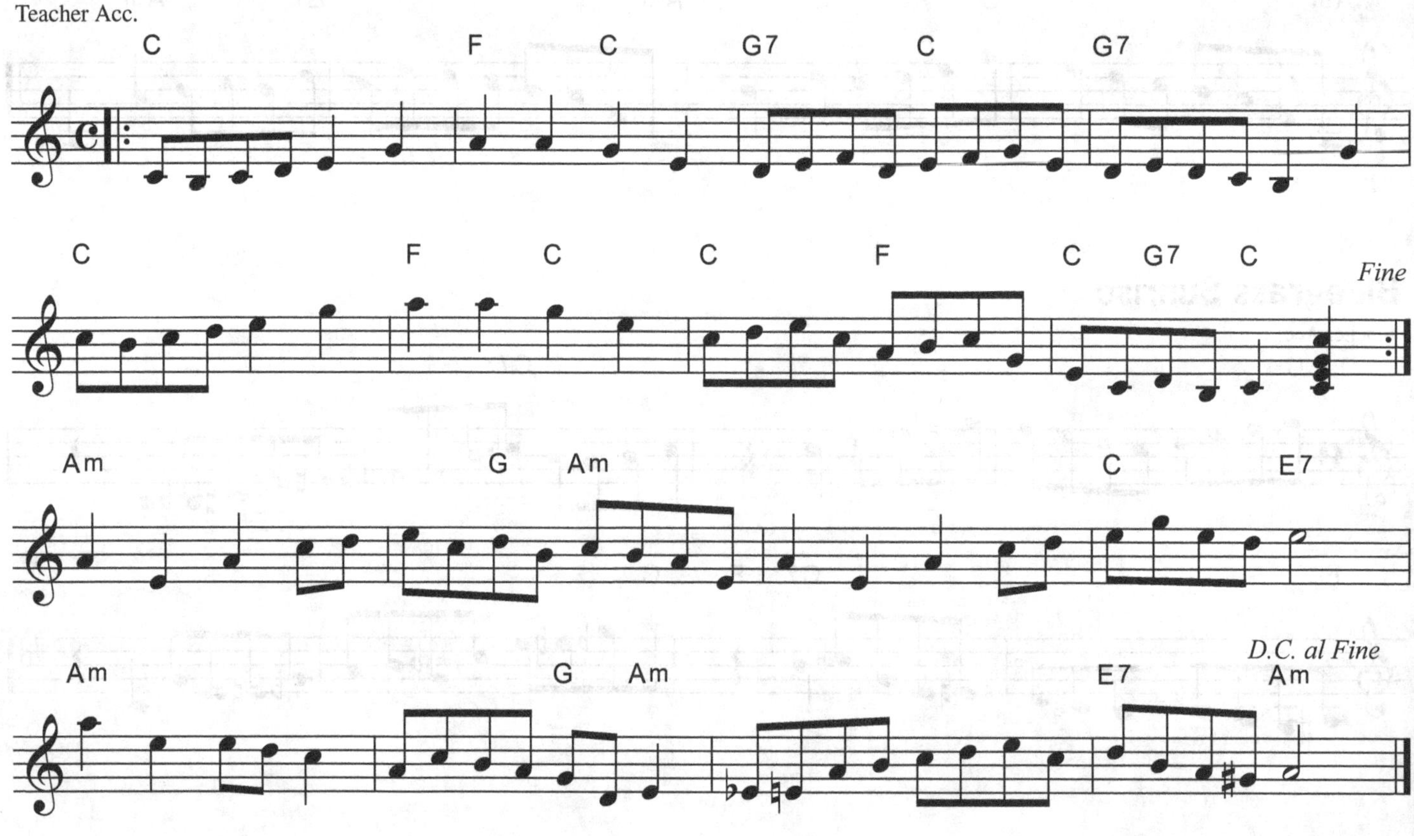

Words Indicating Variations of Tempo

Ritardando or ***Ritard (rit.)***...To grow slower — ***Accelerando (acc.)***...To increase the speed

Billy's Duet

Lafayette Square

Song Without Words

Guitar Duet

Arr. by Mel Bay

Terry's Tune

Mel Bay

The Key of G

The key of G will have one sharp (F♯). It will be identified by this signature:

The F notes will be played as shown:

6th String	4th String	1st String
2nd Fret	4th Fret	2nd Fret
2nd Finger.	4th Finger.	2nd Finger.

The G Scale

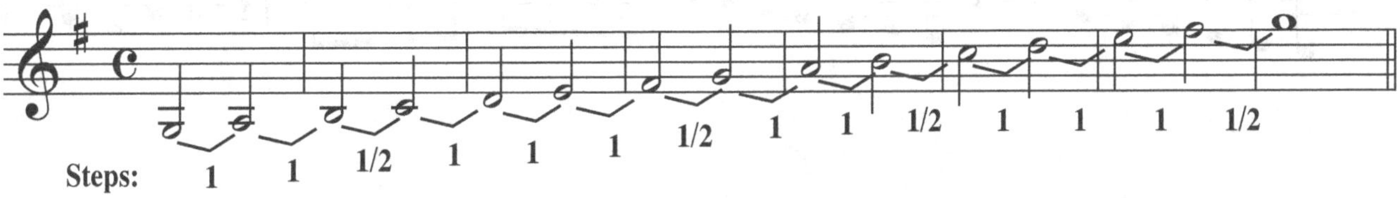

Note that, in order to have the half steps falling between the seventh and eighth degrees of the scale, the F must be sharped. Our major scale pattern is then correct (1-1-1/2-1-1-1-1/2 Steps).

A Daily Drill

Picking Studies in G

①

②

③

④

⑤

Chords in the Key of G

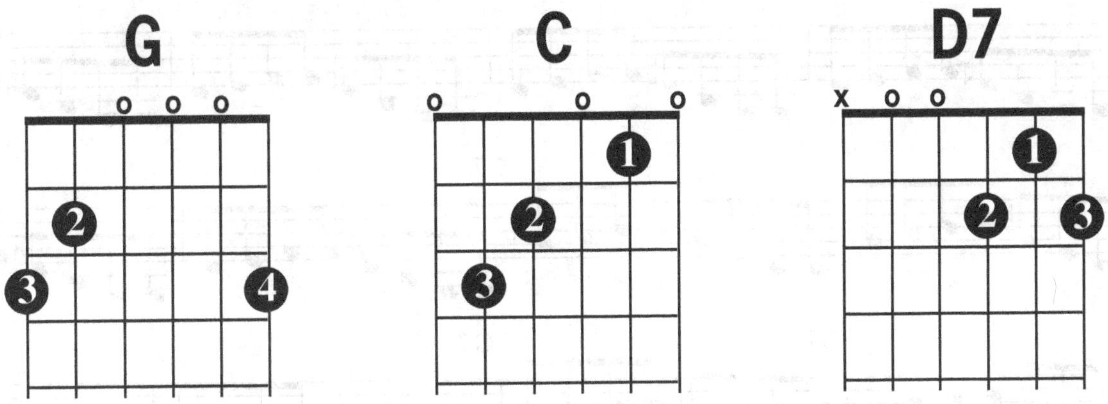

Accompaniment Styles in the Key of G

①

②

③

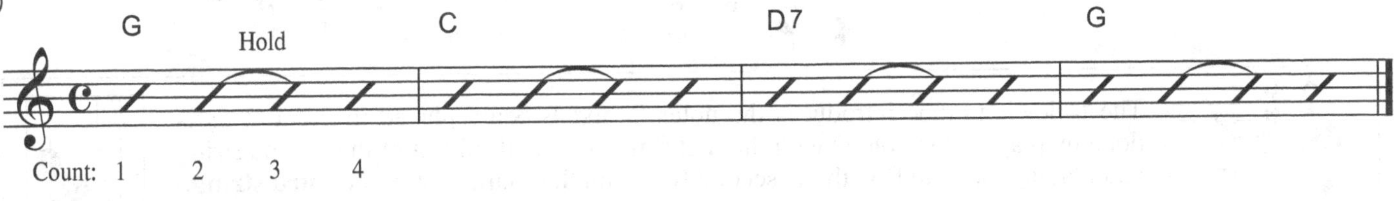

④

⑤

⑥

G Boogie

In the Evening by the Moonlight

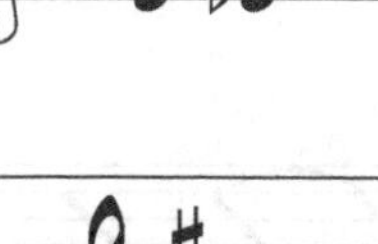

The following etude introduces the notes D and B being played together. This is done by playing the note D with the first finger on the third fret of the second string and playing the note B with the second finger on the fourth fret of the **third string.**

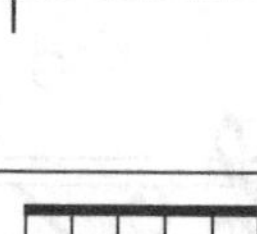

Etude

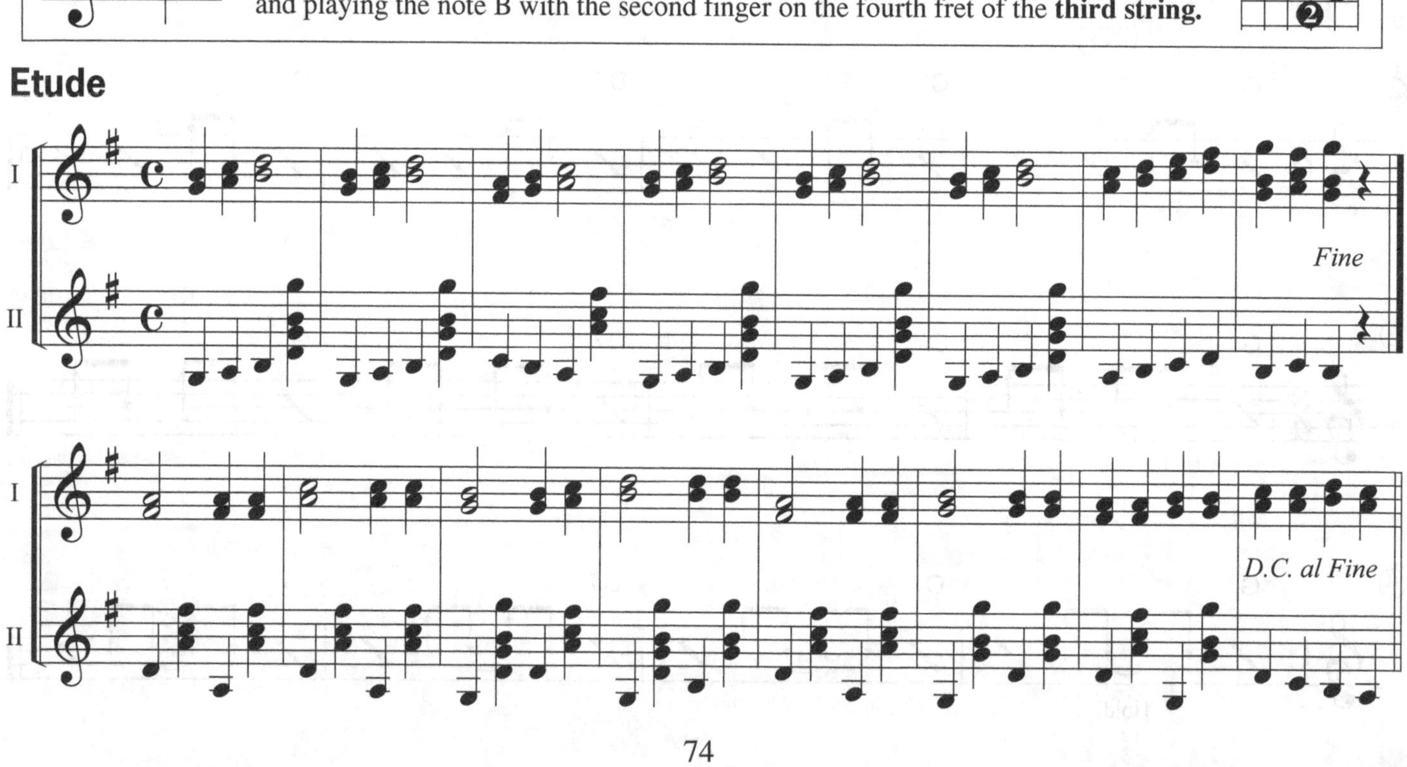

Two-Four Time

This sign  indicates **two-four** time.

2 – beats per measure.
4 – a quarter note receives one beat.

Two-four time will have two beats per measure with the quarter note receiving one beat.

The Old Mill

Guitar Duet

Two-Four Picking

Teacher Acc.

A Scale Study

Opening Day

A Serenade

Guitar Solo

Mel Bay

Moderato

Austrian Hymn

Guitar Duet

Haydn

Andante

Home on the Range

Guitar Solo

> = Accent

Andante

The Little Prince

Guitar Duet

Mazas
Arr. by Mel Bay

Andante

Carry Me Back to Old Virginny

Guitar Solo

Bland
Arr. by Mel Bay

Andante

* The wavy line before the last chord means to glide the pick slowly over the strings, producing a harp-like effect. The musical term for this is **Quasi Arpi**.

The Key of E Minor

(Relative to G Major)

The key of E minor will have the same key signature as G major.

Two E Minor Scales

Harmonic

Melodic

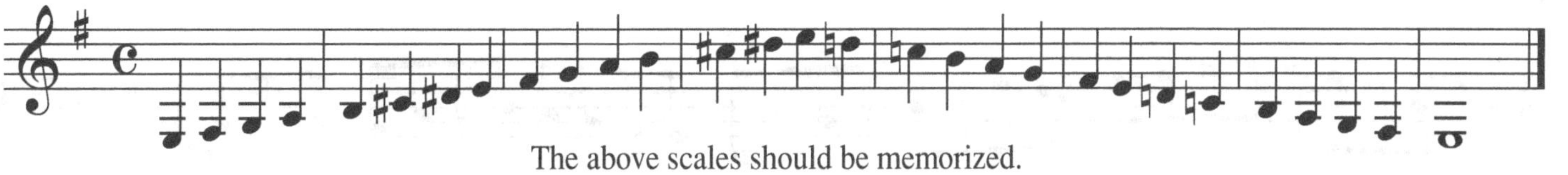

The above scales should be memorized.

Picking Studies

①

②

③

④

⑤

⑥

⑦

⑧

Chords in the Key of E Minor

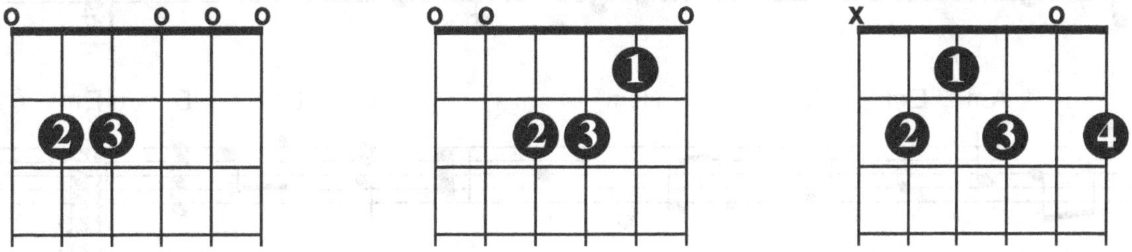

Accompaniment Styles in the Key of E Minor

* This sign (⁒) means that the previous measure is to be repeated.

Orchestration Styles

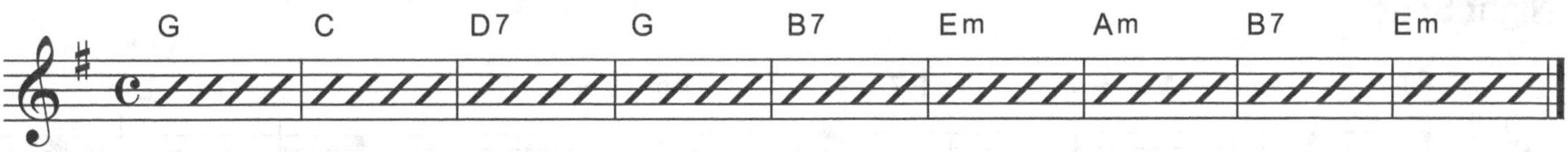

Chord Studies

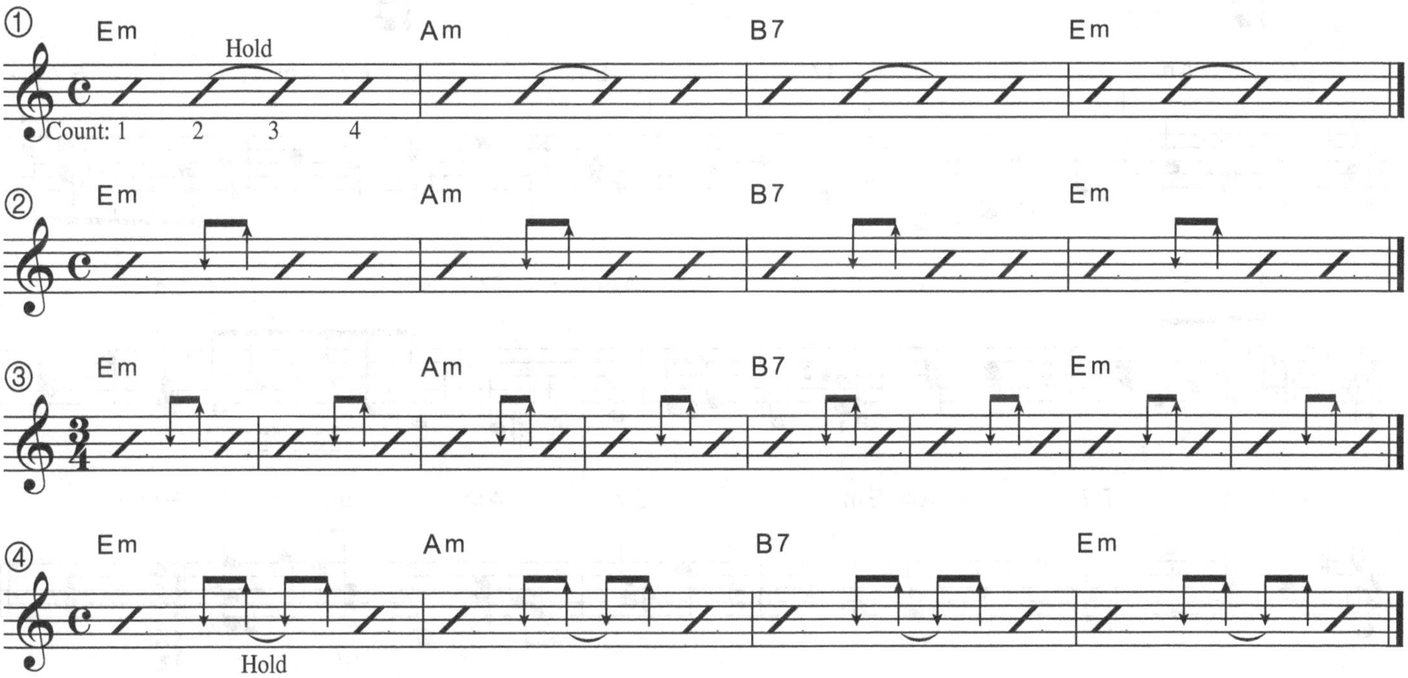

Morning Song

American Folk Hymn

Cindy

Night Song

Sor
Arr. by Mel Bay

East River

Teacher Acc.

Goblins

Teacher Acc.

A Chord Review

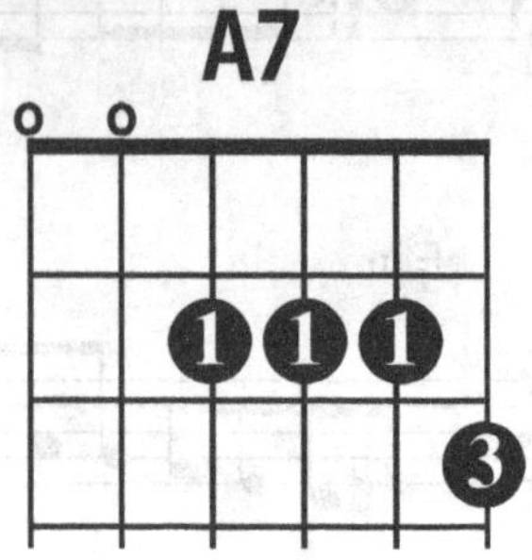

- The key of C has six chords. They are C, F, G7, Am, Dm, and E7.
- The latter three are in the relative minor key but use the key signature of C.
- All "outside" chords are **Accidental Chords**.
- The most commonly used of these chords are D7 and A7.
- The six chords found in the key of G are G, C, D7, Em, Am, and B7.
- The most common accidental chords found in the key of G are A7 and E7.

Spotting the accidentals in the various chords will facilitate the reading of them... for example:

- B7 will have a D♯ • E7 will have a G♯ • A7 will have a C♯ • D7 will have a F♯

In the following studies, you will see how they appear.

Lament

Guitar Solo

Mel Bay

Maytime

Guitar Duet

Wanhall-Bay

Tone

Music is composed of sounds pleasant to the ear.

Sound maybe made from **noise** or **tone.**

Noise is made by irregular vibrations such as would be caused by striking a table with a hammer, the shot of a gun, or slapping two stones together.

Tone is produced by regular vibrations as would be caused by drawing a bow over the strings of a violin, striking the strings of a guitar, or blowing through a wind instrument such as a trumpet.

A tone has four characteristics ... **pitch, duration, dynamics, and timbre**.

Pitch: the highness or lowness of a tone.
Duration: the length of a tone.
Dynamics: the force or power of a tone (loudness or softness).
Timbre: quality of the tone.

A note represents the pitch and duration of a tone.

Dynamics are indicated by words such as:

Pianissimo .... (***pp***) .... very soft
Piano .... (***p***) .... soft
Mezzo piano .... (***mp***) .... medium soft
Mezzo forte .... (***mf***) .... medium loud
Forte .... (***f***) .... very loud

Timbre depends upon the skill of the performer plus the quality of the instrument which is being played.

Rondo

Guitar Duet

Student should play both parts

Mazas, Op. 85
Arr. by Mel Bay

Sor's Waltz

Arr. by Mel Bay

Bluegrass Waltz

Mel Bay

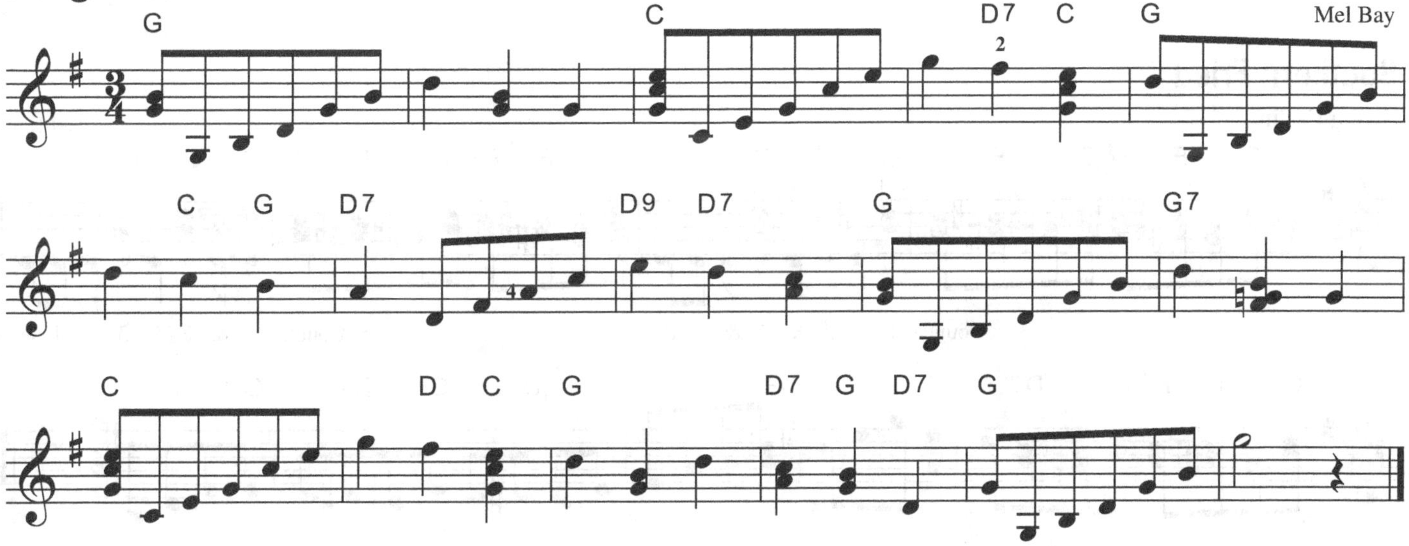

Running the Thirds in G

A Little Bit of Hanon

Mel Bay

Southern Fried

Swing Feeling

Mel Bay

THE MEL BAY MODERN GUITAR METHOD COMPLETE EDITION
Part 1/Grade 2

Online Audio

To access the online audio, scan the QR code above or go to:

www.melbay.com/30504

ONLINE AUDIO TRACKS FOR PART 1/GRADE 2

Audio #1 (75 min.)

1 Tuning
2 Etude, page 3
3 Picking Studies 1 & 2, page 3
4 Picking Studies 3 & 4, page 4
5 Picking Studies 5 & 6, page 4
6 Picking Studies 7 & 8, page 5
7 Picking Study 9, page 5
8 Leapfrog, page 6
9 Bull Durham, page 7
10 Frolic, page 7
11 Frog Junction, page 8
12 Catawissa Blues, page 8
13 Picking Studies 1 & 2, page 9
14 Picking Studies 3 & 4, page 9
15 Picking Studies 5 & 6, page 10
16 Picking Studies 7 & 8, page 10
17 Picking Studies 9 & 10, page 11
18 Picking Studies 11 & 12, page 11
19 Prelude in C/Am, page 12
20 C/Am Etude, page 12
21 Old Pail, page 13
22 Kuranda, page 13
23 Senorita, page 14
24 Nocturne, page 14
25 Valse, page 15
26 Russian Dance, page 15
27 Picking Studies 1 & 2, page 16
28 Picking Studies 3 & 4, page 16
29 Picking Studies 5 & 6, page 17
30 Picking Studies 7 & 8, page 17
31 Trekking, page 18
32 Lavender Waltz, page 18
33 The Gauchos, page 19
34 Poinsettia, page 19
35 Tarantelle, page 20
36 A Triple Play, page 20
37 Triplet Duet, page 21
38 Barcelona, page 21
39 Far from Home, page 22
40 The Teetotaler's Reel, page 22
41 Picking Studies 1 & 2, page 23
42 Picking Studies 3 & 4, page 23
43 Excursion, page 24
44 Jazz Etude, page 24
45 Forest Trail, page 25
46 Brighton Waltz, page 25
47 Razorback, page 26
48 The Hope, page 26
49 Wade in the Water, page 27
50 Coldwater Creek, page 27
51 A Daily Study, page 28
52 March Majestic, page 28
53 Picking Studies 1 & 2, page 29
54 Picking Studies 3 & 4, page 29
55 Picking Studies 5 & 6, page 30
56 Picking Studies 7 & 8, page 30
57 Picking Studies 9 & 10, page 31
58 Picking Studies 11 12, & 13, page 31
59 Melody in F, page 32
60 I Love Thee, page 33
61 Fargo, page 34
62 Silverheel's Shuffle, page 34
63 A Daily Study in F, page 35
64 The Carousel, page 35
65 The Recital, page 36
66 Triplet Etude, page 37
67 Happy Farmer, page 37
68 Bubba's Bounce, page 38
69 Soulard, page 38
70 Etude in Dm, page 39
71 Picking Study 1, page 39 & Picking Study 2, page 40
72 Picking Studies 3 & 4, page 40
73 Picking Studies 5 & 6, page 40
74 Picking Studies 7 & 8, page 41
75 Picking Studies 9, 10 & 11, page 41
76 Balkan Moon, page 42
77 Duet in Dm, page 43
78 Andante, page 44
79 March Slav, page 44
80 Invention in Dm, page 45
81 Bucharest, page 45
82 An Exercise in 3rds, page 46
83 Song in Dm, page 47
84 Swing Low Sweet Chariot, page 47
85 Valse in Dm, page 48
86 The Rights of Man, page 48

Audio #2 (63 min.)

1 3rds in the Key of F, page 49
2 Juanita, page 49
3 Delores, page 50
4 Romance, page 50
5 Trail Ridge, page 51
6 Manitou, page 51
7 Mesa Verde, page 51
8 Where You There, page 52
9 Now the Day is Over, page 52
10 Sonatina, page 53
11 Picking Studies 1 & 2, page 55
12 Picking Studies 3 & 4, page 55
13 Picking Studies 5 & 6, page 56
14 Picking Studies 7 & 8, page 56
15 Picking Study 9, page 56 & Picking Study 10, page 57
16 Picking Studies 11 & 12, page 57
17 Picking Studies 13 & 14, page 57
18 Rondo, page 58
19 Kirkwood Klucker, page 59
20 Hometown Waltz, page 59
21 Exercise, page 60
22 Cielito Lindo, page 60
23 2nd Position, Etude #1, page 61
24 He's Got the Whole World in His Hands, page 61
25 Turkey in the Straw, page 62
26 Soldier's Joy, page 62
27 Cascades, page 63
28 D Boogie, page 63
29 Etude, page 64
30 Freefall, page 64
31 Drink to Me Only with Thine Eyes, page 65
32 Caprice, page 65
33 A Speed Study in D, page 66
34 Brunswick Stew, page 67
35 The Clock, page 67
36 Drowsy Maggie, page 68
37 Bennett's Reel, page 68
38 Minuet in D, page 69
39 Etude in Bm, page 70
40 Aura Lee, page 70
41 Picking Studies 1 & 2, page 71
42 Picking Studies 3 & 4, page 71
43 Voyage, page 72
44 Quiet Thoughts, page 72
45 Waltz in Bm, page 73
46 Duet in Bm, page 74
47 Fifth Avenue Swing, page 75
48 Midnight Flight, page 75
49 Irish Washerwomen, page 76
50 6/8 Picking Studies 1 & 2, page 77
51 6/8 Picking Studies 3 & 4, page 77
52 6/8 Picking Studies 5 & 6, page 78
53 6/8 Picking Studies 7 & 8, page 78
54 6/8 Picking Study 9, page 78 & 6/8 Picking Studies 10 & 11, page 79
55 Dublin Dance, page 79
56 Swallowtail Jig, page 80
57 Territory Ahead, page 80
58 Minuet, page 81
59 A Spanish Dance, page 82
60 Prelude, page 84
61 Etude, page 84
62 The Plectrum Waltz, page 84
63 Skipping Along, page 85
64 Coronado, page 85
65 Country Gardens, page 86
66 Logan's Bluff, page 87
67 Blessed Quietness, page 87
68 Harvest Moon Strathspey, page 88
69 Alastair's Lament, page 88
70 Brighton Beach, page 88
71 Days of Lang Syne, page 88

The Notes on the First String

Notes	E	F	G	A	B	C	D	E	F
Fingers	0	1	3	1	3	4	1	3	4
Frets	0	1	3	5	7	8	10	12	13

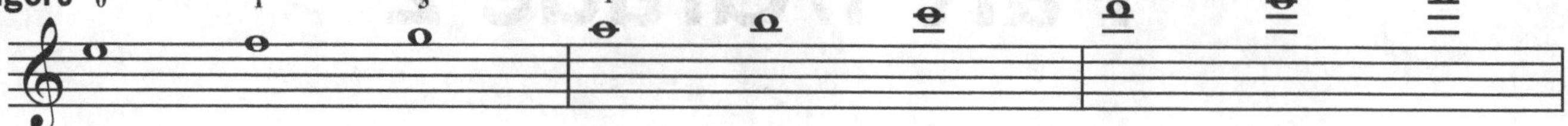

Scale of C Major
(Two Octaves)

Notes	C	D	E	F	G	A	B	C	D	E	F	G	A	B	C
Fingers	3 ⑤	0 ④	2	3	0 ③	2	0 ②	1	3	0 ①	1	3	1	3	4
Frets	3	0	2	3	0	2	0	1	3	0	1	3	5	7	8

A Rhythm Review

⓪

①

Accompaniment for the Above Exercises

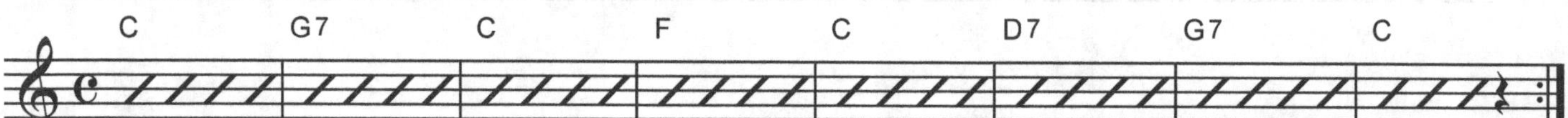

Alternate Picking

One of the most difficult things for the student is the mastery of the alternate stroke on diatonic passages.

To promote greater speed with proper accentuation, the alternate stroke should be developed.

The following study will seem difficult at first; but, by practicing slowly and placing the downstrokes on the beats followed by an upstroke, the desired result will be accomplished.

Key of C Review

Etude

CD 1 #2

Picking Studies

CD 1 #3

①

②

③ CD 1 #4

④

⑤ CD 1 #5

⑥

⑦ CD 1 #6

⑧

⑨ CD 1 #7

Leapfrog

Guitar Duet CD 1 #8

Arr. by Mel Bay

Allegro

Bull Durham

Swing Feeling

CD 1 #9

W. Bay

Frolic

Guitar Duet

CD 1 #10

Arr. by Mel Bay

Frog Junction

CD 1 #11

W. Bay

Swing Feeling

Catawissa Blues

CD 1 #12

W. Bay

Slowly

Key of A Minor Review

Picking Studies

① CD 1 #13

②

③ CD 1 #14

④

⑤ CD 1 #15

⑥

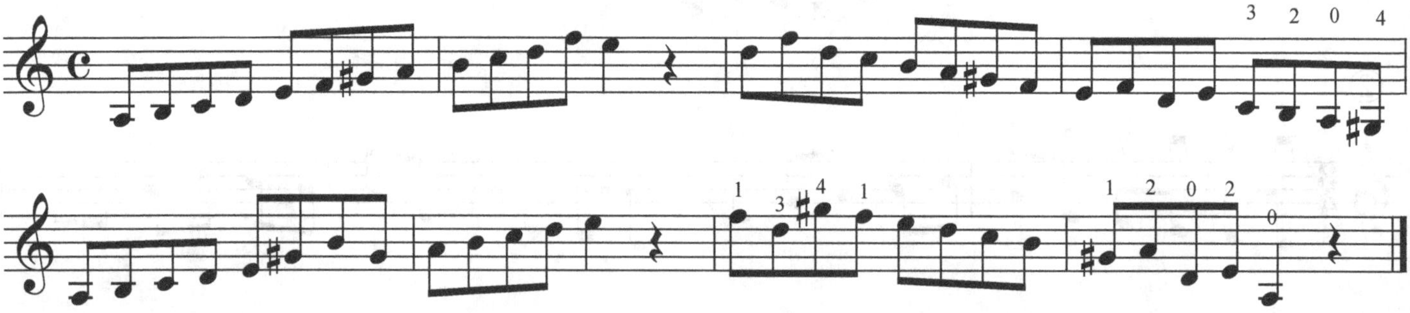

⑦ CD 1 #16

⑧

9 CD 1 #17

10

11 CD 1 #18

Let the first note of each measure ring.

12

Prelude in C/Am

CD 1 #19

Slowly

W. Bay

C/Am Etude

CD 1 #20

Moderately

W. Bay

Old Pail

CD 1 #21

Bluegrass

W. Bay

Kuranda

CD 1 #22

W. Bay

Señorita

Andante

CD 1 #23

Based on a Theme by Carcassi

Nocturne

Andante

CD 1 #24

W. Bay

Valse

CD 1 #25

Flowing Tempo

W. Bay

Russian Dance

CD 1 #26

Allegro

W. Bay

Key of G Review

Picking Studies

①

CD 1 #27

②

③

CD 1 #28

④

⑤ CD 1 #29

⑥

⑦ CD 1 #30

⑧

Trekking

CD 1 #31

Lively

W. Bay

Lavender Waltz

CD 1 #32

Slowly

W. Bay

Accidentals are effective only in the measures in which they are found. When that measure is passed, the accidentals become void.

In the following solo, *The Guachos*, the third part is in the key of C, which explains the natural on the fifth line in the signature.

The Gauchos

CD 1 #33

Guitar Solo

Carcassi - Bay

Poinsettia

CD 1 #34

Freely

W. Bay

How to Count Triplets

Q. What are ***triplets***?
A. A group of three notes played in the time span of two notes of the same kind.

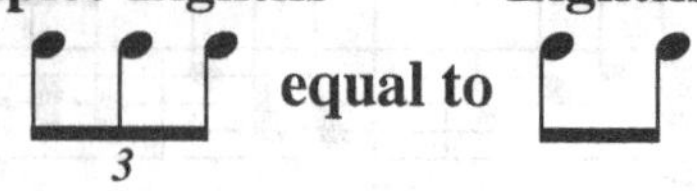

Tarantelle

Moderato CD 1 #35 All ⊓ stroke

A Triple Play

Guitar Solo Moderato CD 1 #36

Mel Bay

Triplet Duet

CD 1 #37

Barcelona

CD 1 #38

William Bay

Far From Home

CD 1 #39

Shetland Island Reel

The Teetotaler's Reel

CD 1 #40

E Minor Review

Picking Studies

① CD 1 #41

②

③ CD 1 #42

④

Excursion

CD 1 #43

Andante

W. Bay

Jazz Etude

Swing Feeling

CD 1 #44

W. Bay

Forest Trail

CD 1 #45

Moderately

W. Bay

Brighton Waltz

CD 1 #46

Slowly

W. Bay

Razorback

CD 1 #47

Rhythmically

W. Bay

The Hope (Hatikvoh)

CD 1 #48

Moderately

Hebrew Song

Wade in the Water

CD 1 #49

Moderately

Spiritual

Coldwater Creek

CD 1 #50

Swing Feeling

W. Bay

The Key of F

The key of F has one flat. All B notes will be played one half step lower as shown.

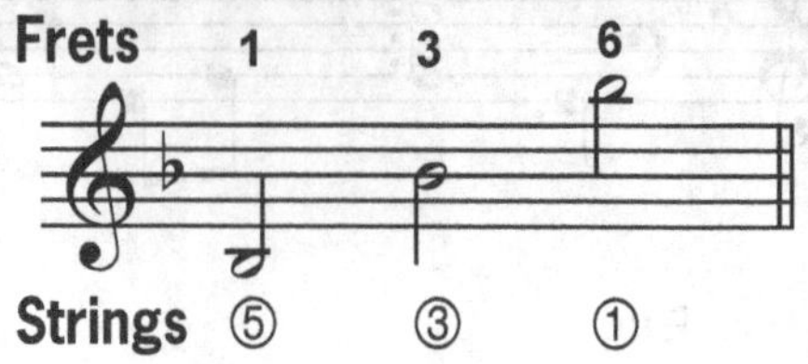

The F Major Scale

(Two Octaves)

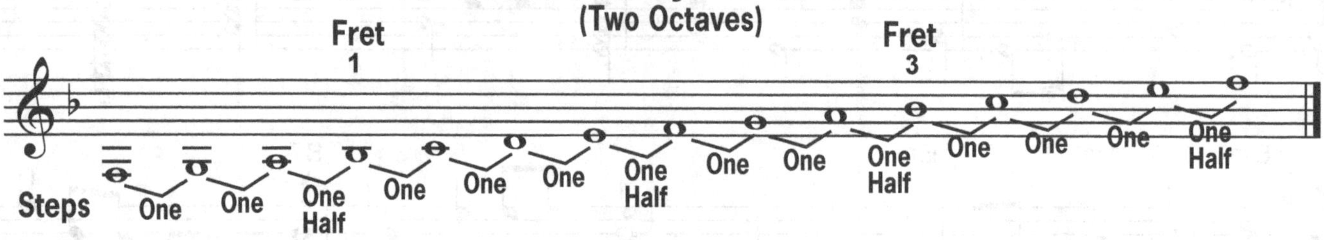

Practice the following exercise using the downstroke throughout. Later on, use the alternate stroking shown.

A Daily Study

CD 1 #51

March Majestic

Guitar Solo

CD 1 #52

Moderato

D.S. al Fine (Dal Segno al Fine): Go back to the sign 𝄋 and play to **Fine**, the end.

Key of F

Picking Studies

CD 1 #53

①

②

③ CD 1 #54

④

⑤ CD 1 #55

⑥

⑦ CD 1 #56

⑧

⑨ CD 1 #57

⑩

⑪ CD 1 #58

⑫

⑬

Chords in the Key of F

The three chords in the key of F are F, B-flat, and C7.

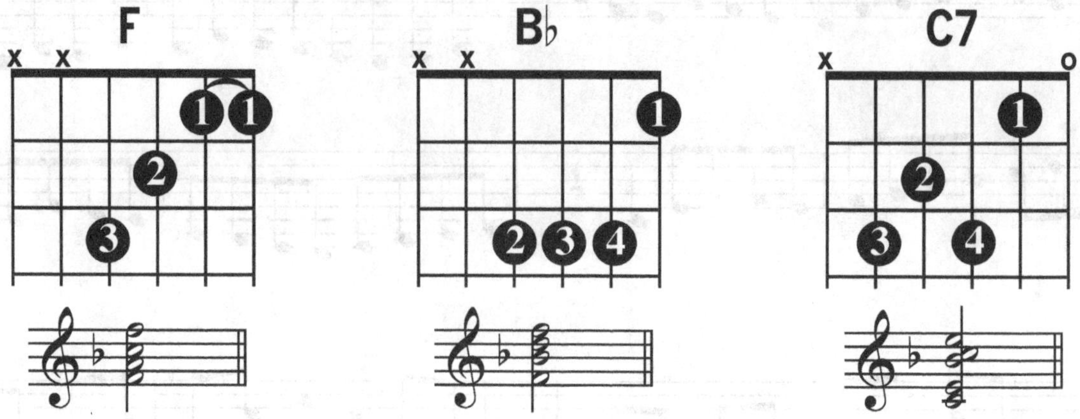

Accompaniment Styles

Common Time

Three-Four Time

Two-Four Time

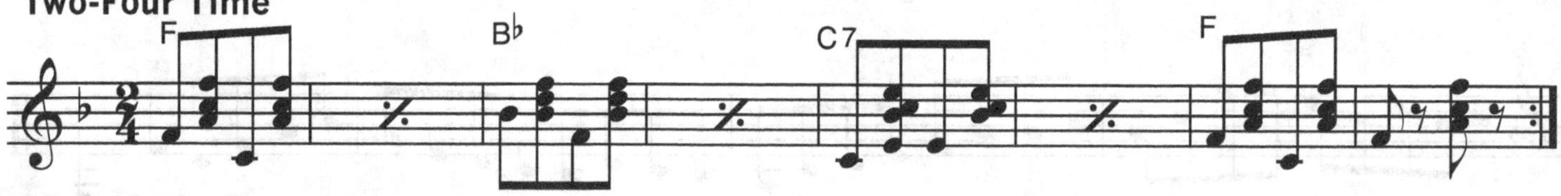

Melody in F

Guitar Solo

CD 1 #59

Moderato

Rubenstein-Bay

Musical Terms

Sforzando (*sfz*) – Forcing the tone suddenly loud
Ad libitum (a piacere) – At the liberty of the performer
A tempo – Back to the regular tempo
Animato – Lively
Cantabile – In a singing style
Crescendo (cresc.) – Gradually grow louder
Diminuendo (dim.) – Gradually grow softer
Sostenuto – Sustained
Dolce – Sweetly
Maestoso – Majestic
Morendo – Dying or fading away
Piu mosso – Quicker

I Love Thee

Guitar Duet CD 1 #60

Christian Hymn

Fargo

CD 1 #61

Moderato

W. Bay

Silverheel's Shuffle

CD 1 #62

Swing Feeling

W. Bay

Intervals

An **interval** is the distance between two tones or the difference in pitch between two tones when sounded.

Intervals are measured **upward** from the lower tone to the higher.

Intervals have **number** names and **type** names. For example, a 3rd could be major or minor depending upon the distance between the two notes.

The staff degree occupied by the lower note and the staff degree occupied by the higher note are **both included** when determining the number name in the interval.

Below are nine intervals from C to each note in the C scale.

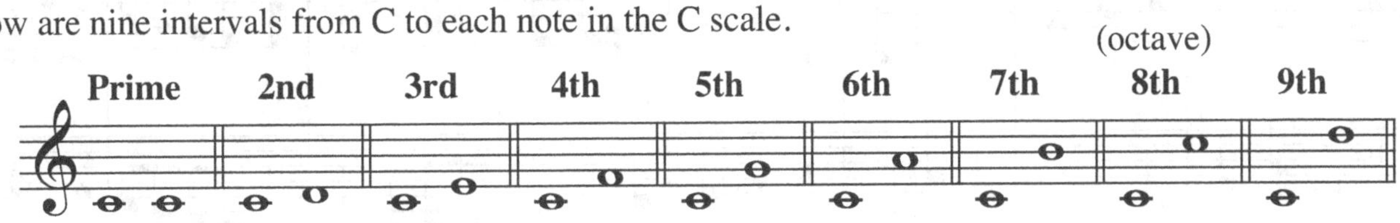

The **types** of intervals will be discussed in Grade 3 of *The Modern Guitar Method, Expanded Edition*.

A Daily Study in F

CD 1 #63

In the following solo, *The Carousel,* the second part is in the key of C.

The first line is repeated and, after the second line is played, the first line is played only once, ending at Fine. This will give the solo a total of 32 measures.

It should be practiced slowly at first and continued until a happy, spirited tempo is attained.

The Carousel

Guitar Solo

CD 1 #64

The Recital

CD 1 #65

Guitar Duet

Mazas
Arr. by Mel Bay

Moderato

Triplet Etude

CD 1 #66

All downstroke

The Happy Farmer

CD 1 #67

Guitar Solo

Robert Schumann
(Op. 68, No. 10)
Arr. by Mel Bay

Allegretto

Bubba's Bounce

Allegro, Swing Feeling

CD 1 #68

W. Bay

Soulard

Swing

CD 1 #69

W. Bay

The Key of D Minor

(Relative to F Major)

The D Minor Scales

Harmonic

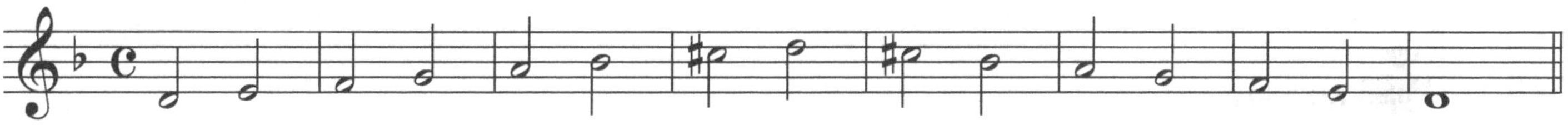

Melodic

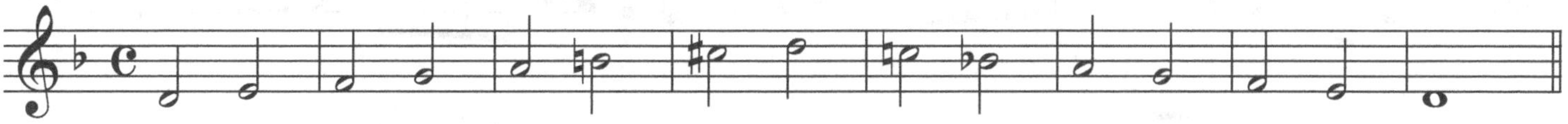

Etude in D Minor

CD 1 #70

Harmonic

Melodic

Picking Studies

CD 1 #71

①

②

③ CD 1 #72

④

⑤ CD 1 #73

⑥

⑦ CD 1 #74

⑧

⑨ CD 1 #75

⑩

⑪

The Chords in the Key of D Minor

The three principal chords in the key of D minor are:

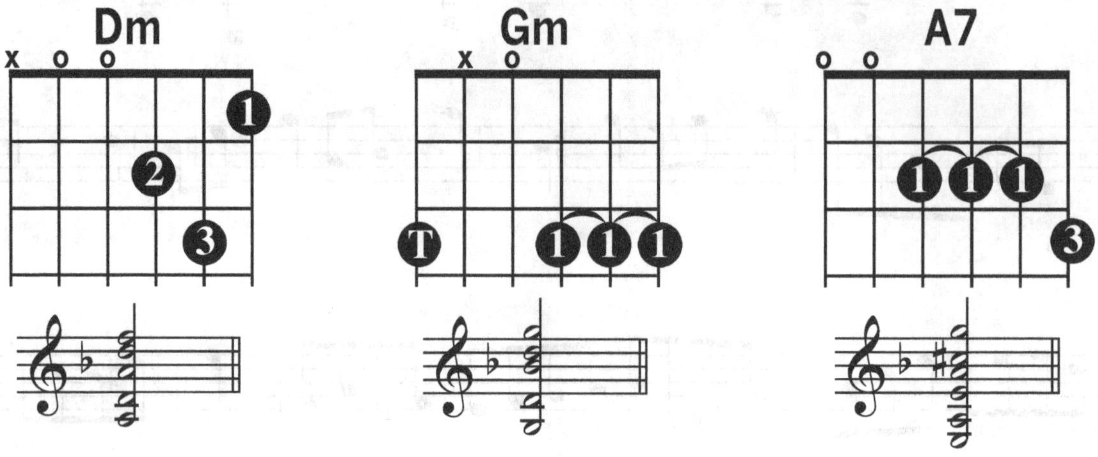

Accompaniment Styles

Common Time

Three-Four Time

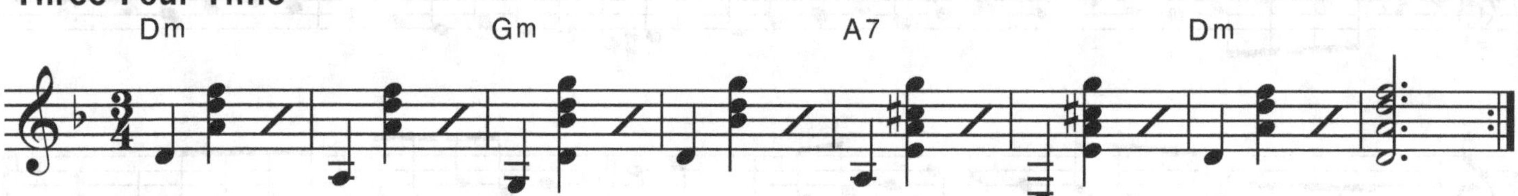

Two-Four Time

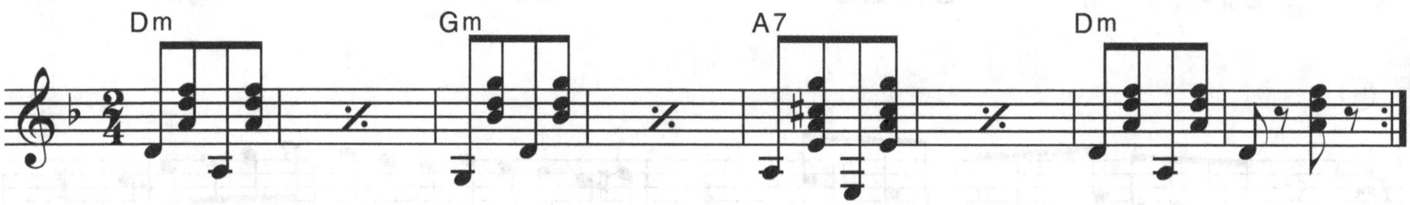

In the fifth and eighth measures of the guitar solo *Balkan Moon*, the note G should be played as shown in the example:
Place the third finger upon the fourth string behind the fifth fret.

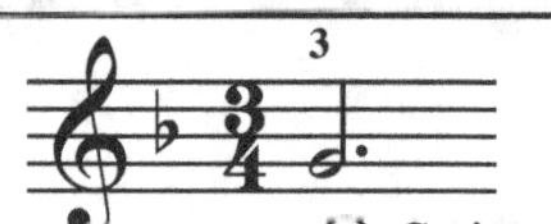

④ String
5th fret

Balkan Moon

Guitar Solo

CD 1 #76

Mel Bay

Finger Gymnastics

The following exercises have a two-fold purpose:

1. Training the individual fingers to perform independently of each other.
2. Acquainting the student with the technique of position playing that will be an important part of this course.

The first finger should be held down throughout these exercises.

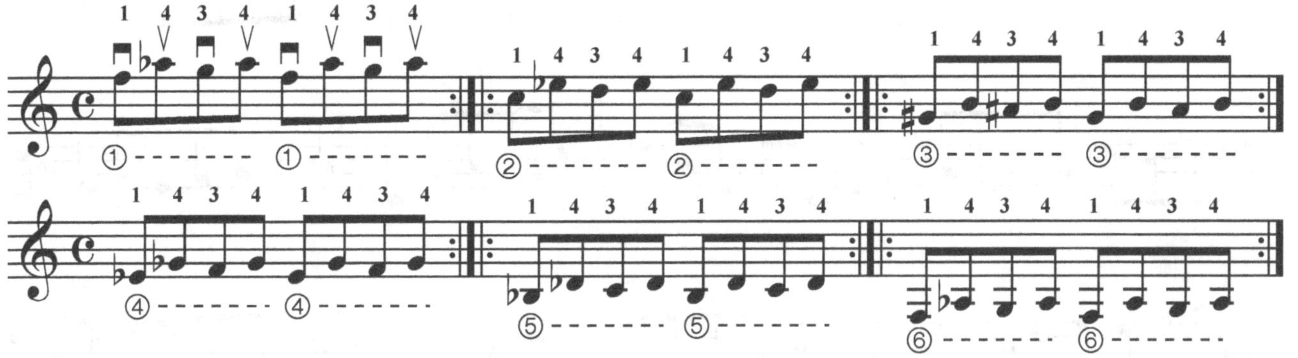

Duet in D Minor

CD 1 #77

Guitar Duet

Mazas
Arr. by Mel Bay

Moderato

* High B♭ – 1st string, 6th fret

Andante

CD 1 #78

W. Bay

March Slav

Guitar Solo

CD 1 #79

Tschaikowsky
Arr. by Mel Bay

Slow

Invention in Dm

CD 1 #80

W. Bay

Andante

Bucharest

Swing Feeling

CD 1 #81

W. Bay

The Notes on the Second String

Shown below are the notes on the second string.

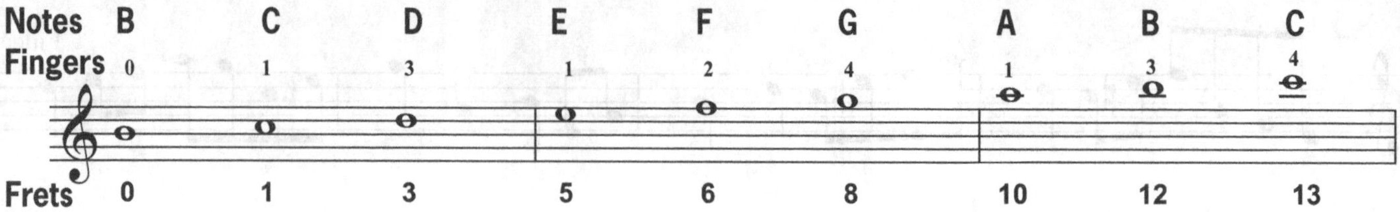

Any note played upon the first string may be played upon the second string **five frets higher** than its location on the first string.

In the diagram on the right you will see the notes on the first string and, directly below, the same notes played upon the second string. This is a very good aid in remembering the notes on the second string.

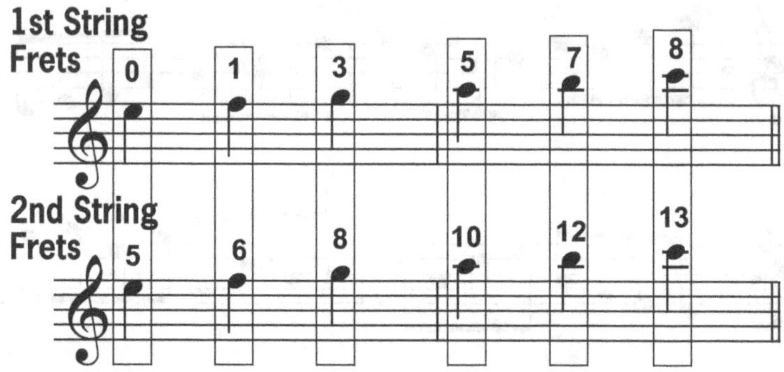

The C Scale in Thirds

The following study should be played upon the first and second strings.

The **top note will be on the first string** and the **bottom note on the second**.

To facilitate execution, it is better to let the fingers remain upon the strings as much as possible, gliding from fret to fret.

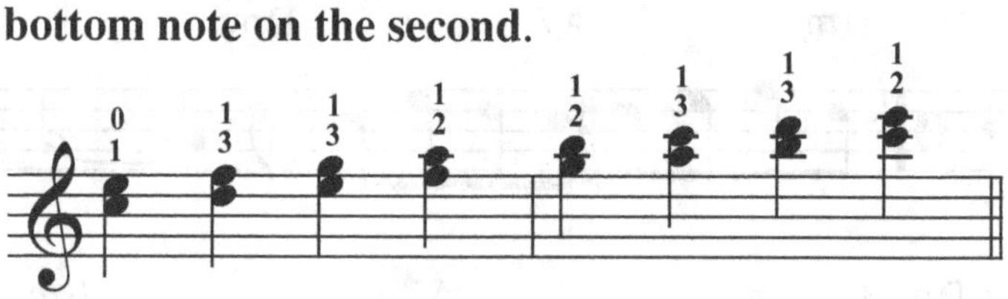

An Exercise in Thirds

CD 1 #82

Moderato

A Song in D Minor

CD 1 #83

Slow

Mel Bay

Swing Low Sweet Chariot

CD 1 #84

Slowly

Spiritual

Valse in Dm

CD 1 #85

W. Bay

The Rights of Man

CD 1 #86

Irish Reel

The Major Chord

The major chord is formed by combining the first, third, and fifth tones of the major scale.

The first tone of the scale is known as the **root** of the chord.

The major chord may be arranged in three positions called inversions.

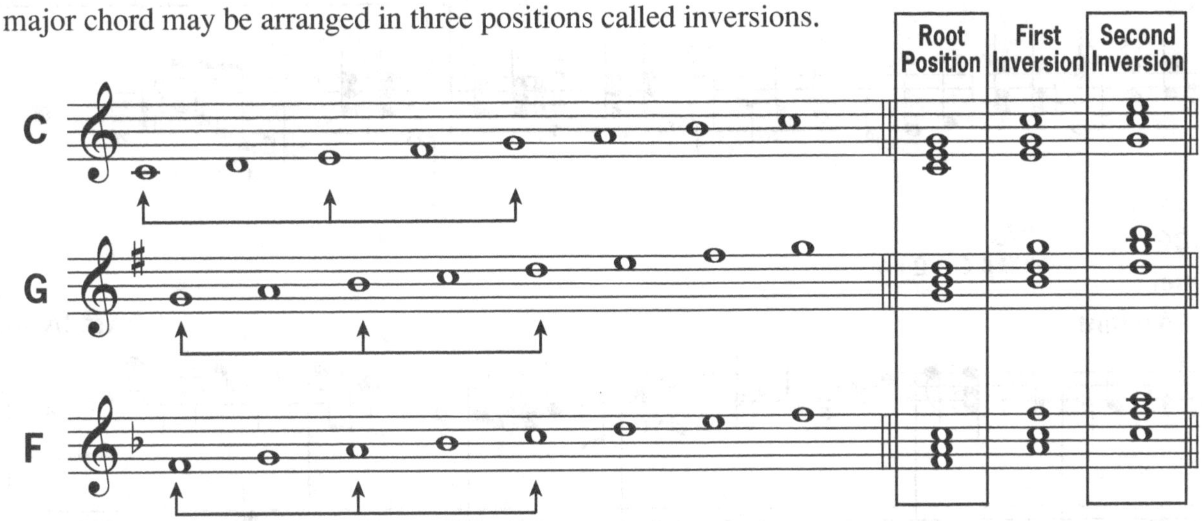

Thirds in the Key of F

CD 2 #1

Juanita

Guitar Solo **Moderato** CD 2 #2

Arr. by Mel Bay

Dolores

CD 2 #3

Waldteufel, Op. 170
Arr. by Mel Bay

Andantino

Romance

Guitar Duet

CD 2 #4

Mazas
Arr. by Mel Bay

Andante

Trail Ridge

Guitar Duet

CD 2 #5

Arr. Mel Bay

Andante

Manitou

Slowly

CD 2 #6

Arr. Mel Bay

Mesa Verde

Moderato

CD 2 #7

Arr. Mel Bay

Where You There?

CD 2 #8

Slowly

Spiritual

Now the Day is Over

Guitar Duet

CD 2 #9

Slowly

Hymn

Sonatina

Guitar Duet

CD 2 #10

Mazas

Arr. by Mel Bay

Andante

The Key of D Major

The key of D major has two sharps — F♯ and C♯.

To facilitate the fingering in the key of D major, it is necessary to move the first finger to the second fret, the second finger to the third fret, and the third finger to the fourth fret.

The D Major Scale

Exercise

The Chords in the Key of D Major

The chords in D major are D, G, and A7:

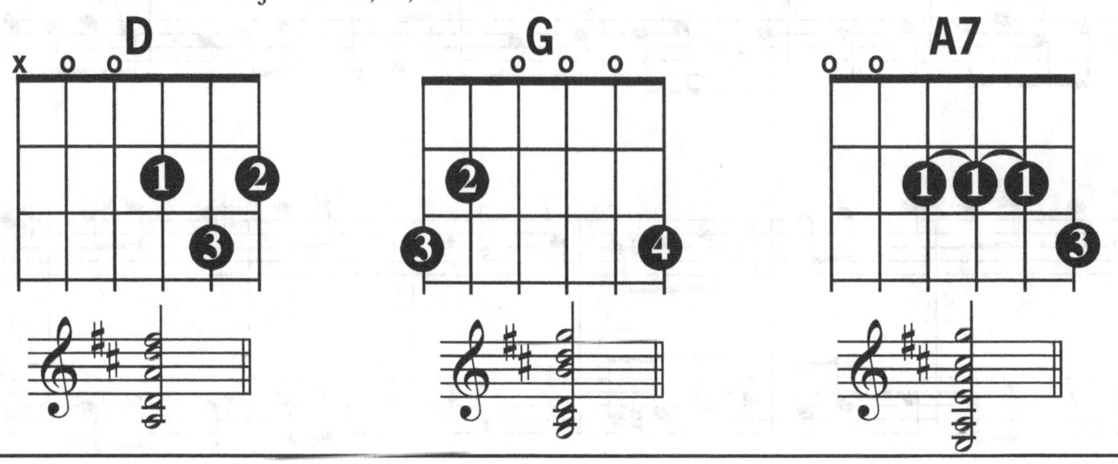

Accompaniment Styles

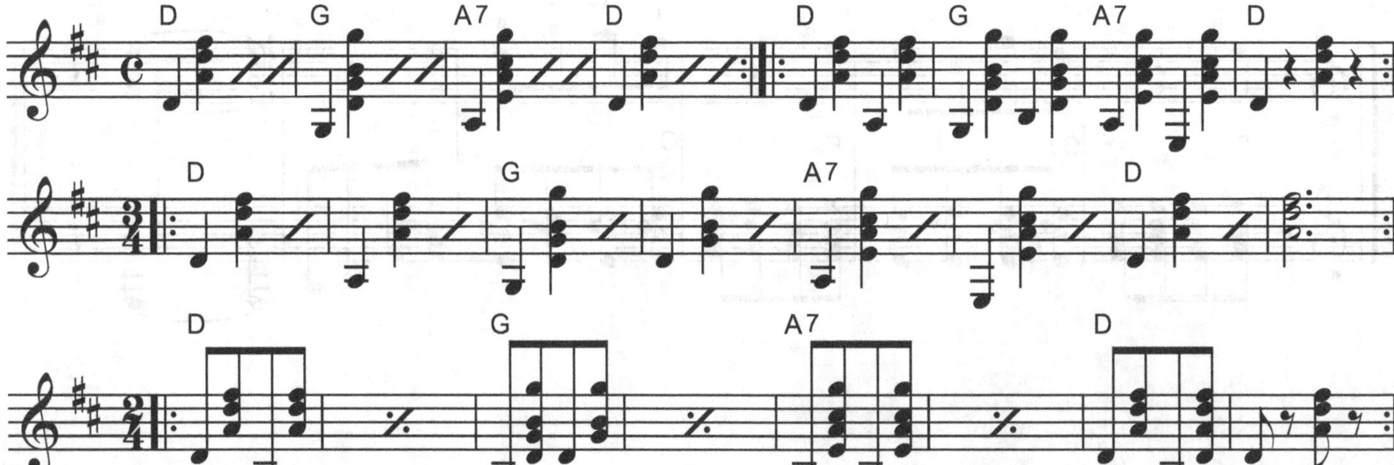

Key of D

Picking Studies

① CD 2 #11

②

③ CD 2 #12

④

⑤ CD 2 #13

⑥

⑦ CD 2 #14

⑧

⑨ CD 2 #15

⑩

⑪ CD 2 #16

⑫

⑬ CD 2 #17

⑭

Rondo

Guitar Duet

CD 2 #18

M. Gebauer, Opus 10
Arr. by Mel Bay

Allegretto

Kirkwood Klucker

CD 2 #19

Swing Feeling

W. Bay

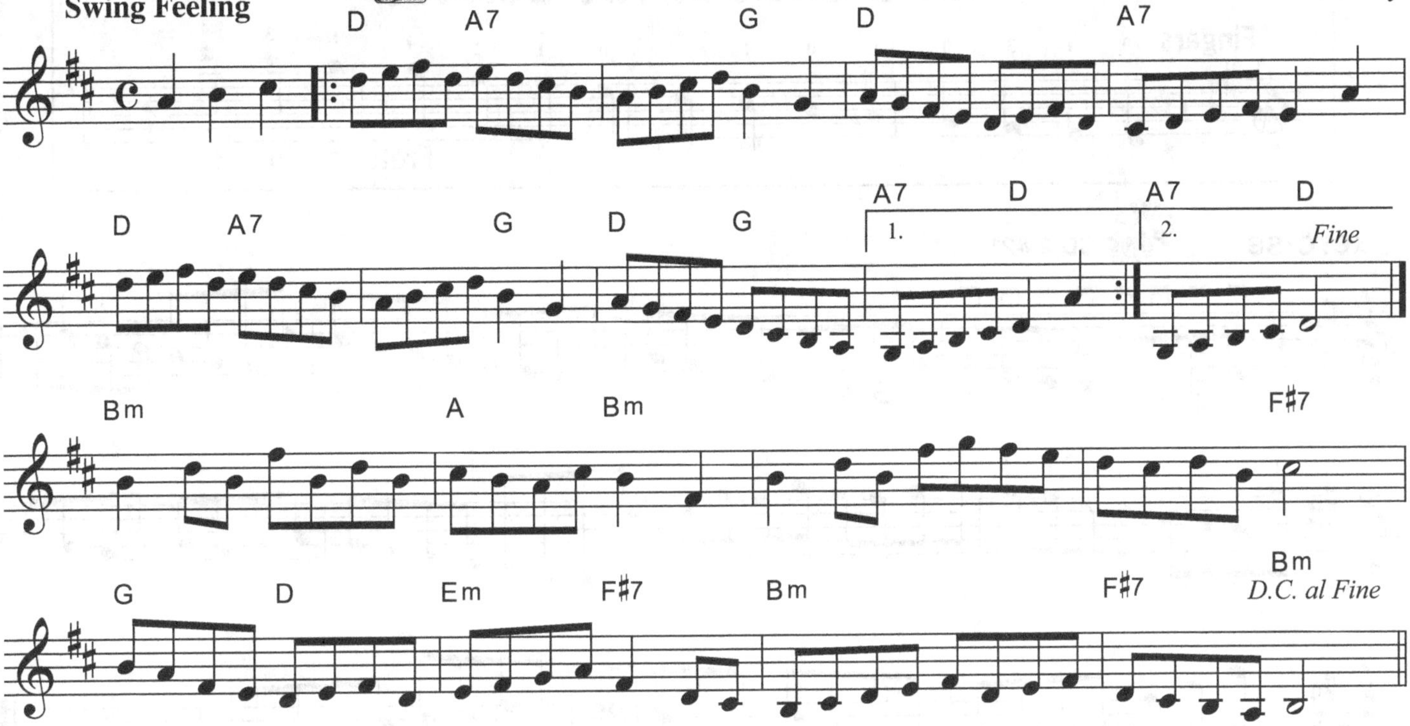

Hometown Waltz

CD 2 #20

Moderately

W. Bay

The D Scale in Two Octaves

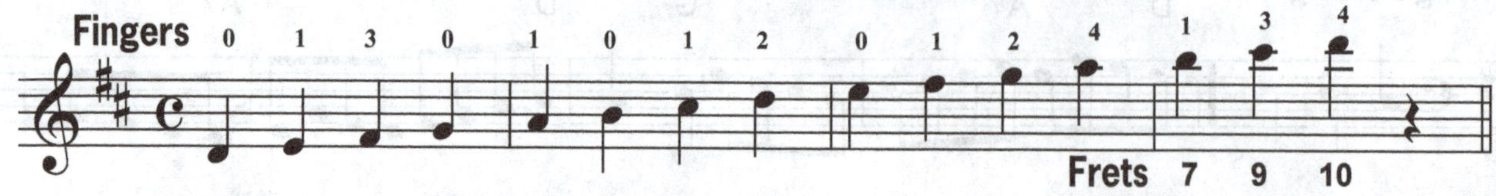

Exercise

CD 2 #21

Cielito Lindo

Guitar Solo

CD 2 #22

Allegretto

Arr. by Mel Bay

Second–Position Etude No. 1 CD 2 #23

(Key of D)

He's Got the Whole World in His Hands CD 2 #24

(Second Position)

The following selections should be played entirely in the second position. Please observe fingering.

Turkey in the Straw

(Second Position)

CD 2 #25

Soldier's Joy

(Second Position)

CD 2 #26

Cascades
(Second Position)

CD 2 #27

Moderately

W. Bay

D Boogie
(Second Position)

CD 2 #28

Etude
(Second Position)

CD 2 #29

W. Bay

Freefall
(Second Position)

CD 2 #30

Moderately

W. Bay

Thirds in the Key of D

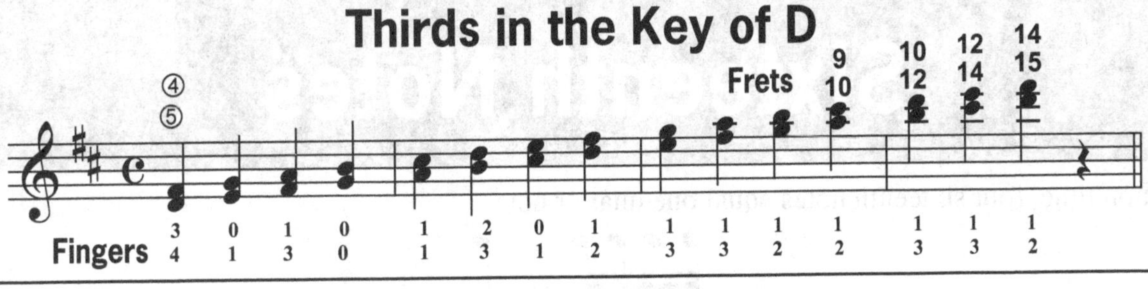

Drink to Me Only with Thine Eyes

CD 2 #31

Guitar Solo

Arr. by Mel Bay

Andante

Caprice

CD 2 #32

Guitar Duet

Mazas, Opus 38
Arr. by Mel Bay

Allegretto

Sixteenth Notes

In common time, four sixteenth notes equal one quarter note.

They may be counted in this manner:

1-six-teenth-notes, 2-six-teenth-notes, 3-six-teenth-notes, 4-six-teenth-notes

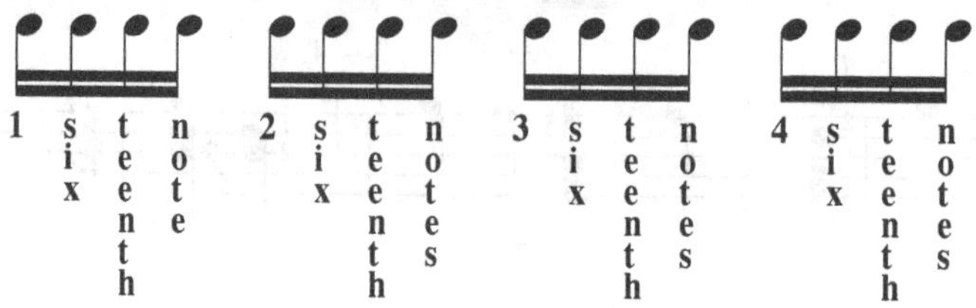

Table of Notes and Rests

Whole Note		**A Whole Measure Rest**
Half Notes	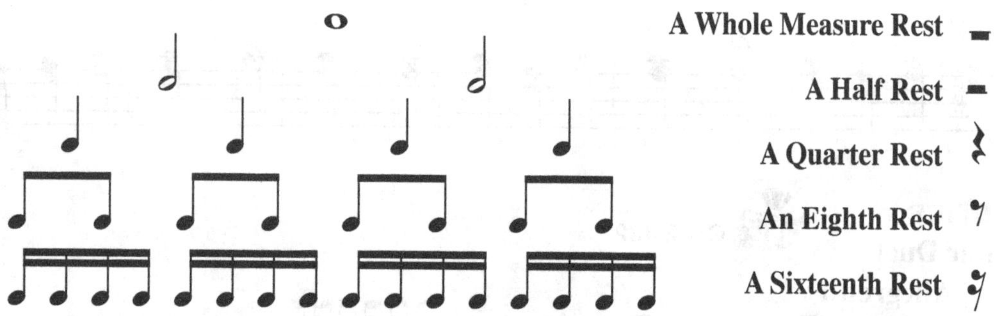	**A Half Rest**
Quarter Notes		**A Quarter Rest**
Eighth Notes		**An Eighth Rest**
Sixteenth Notes		**A Sixteenth Rest**

In the fifth and ninth measures of the following study, an eighth note is followed by two sixteenth notes. ( )

They may be counted in this manner:

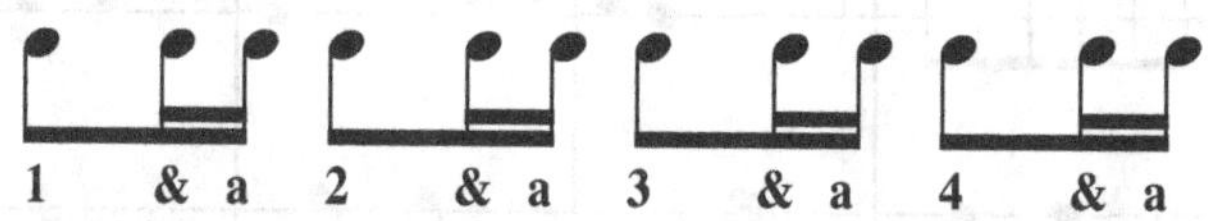

A Speed Study in D (Second Position)

CD 2 #33

Brunswick Stew

CD 2 #34

Allegro

W. Bay

The Clock

CD 2 #35

W. Bay

Drowsy Maggie

CD 2 #36

Lively Tempo

Irish

Bennett's Reel

CD 2 #37

Allegro

Fiddle Tune

Minuet in D

Guitar Duet

CD 2 #38

Arr. by Mel Bay

The Key of B Minor

(Relative to D Major)

The B Minor Scales

Harmonic

Melodic

Etude in B Minor

CD 2 #39

Harmonic

Melodic

Aura Lee

CD 2 #40

Arr. by Mel Bay

Slow

Guitar Solo

Picking Studies

①

CD 2 #41

②

③

CD 2 #42

④

Voyage

CD 2 #43

W. Bay

Andante

Quiet Thoughts

CD 2 #44

W. Bay

Andante

The Chords in the Key of B Minor

The principal chords in the key of B minor are Bm, Em and F♯7.

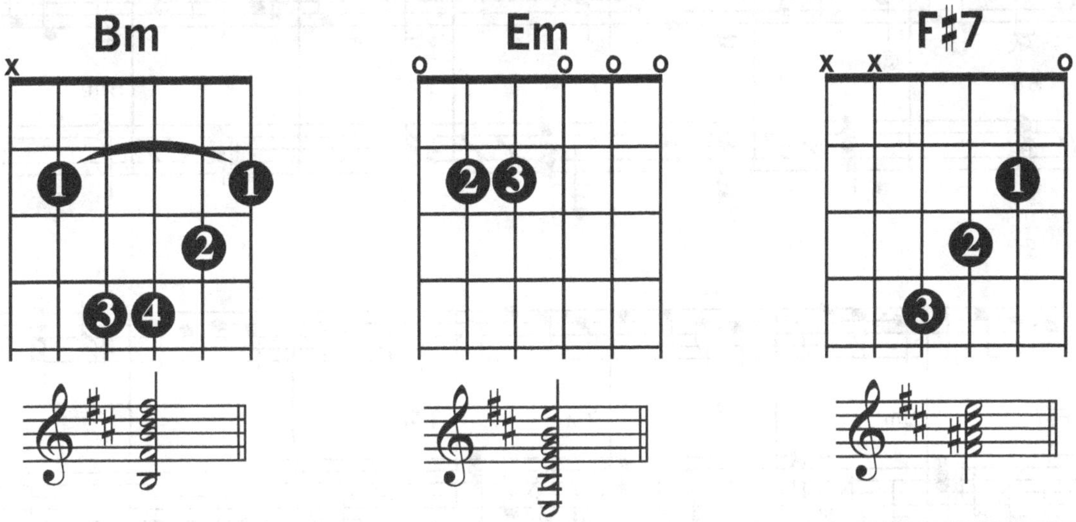

Accompaniment Styles

Waltz in B Minor

Guitar Solo **Andante**

CD 2 #45

W. Bay

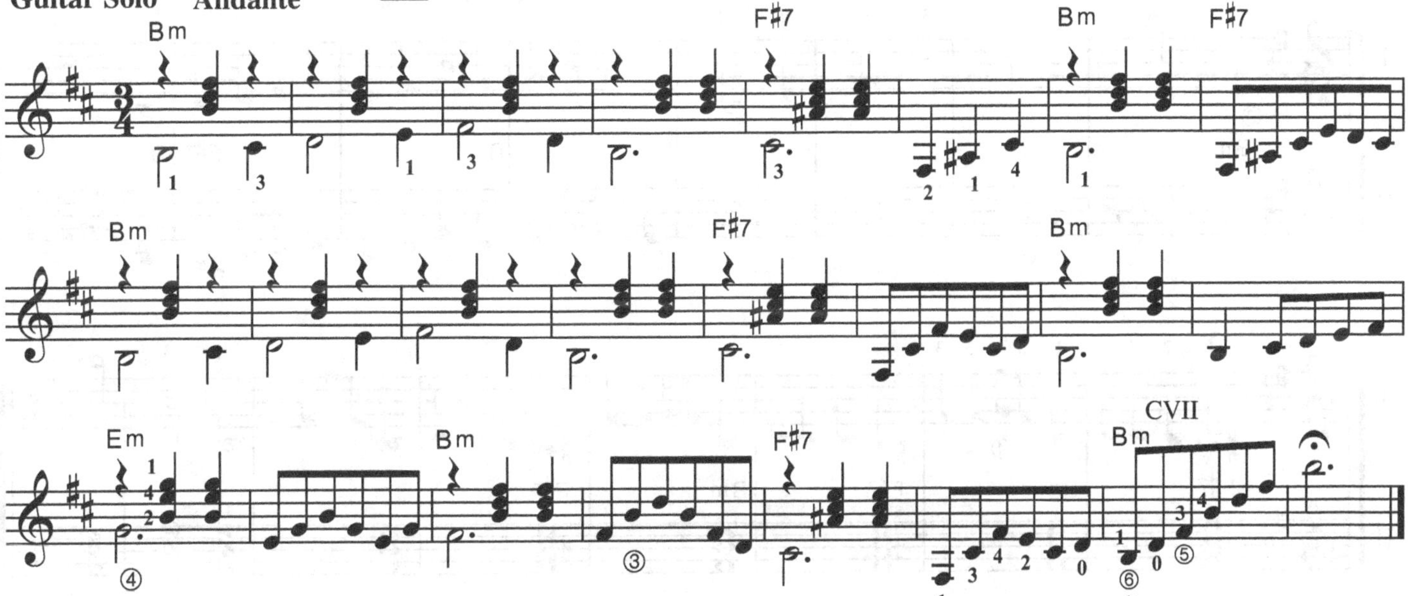

Duet in B Minor

CD 2 #46

Guitar Duet

Gebauer–Bay

Allegro

5th Avenue Swing

CD 2 #47

Swing Feeling

W. Bay

Midnight Flight

CD 2 #48

(Second Position)

W. Bay

The Technical Names of the Chords

As we learned earlier, each degree of the scale has a technical name.

Chords built upon a scale degree will bear the technical name of that degree.

The three principal chords in any key are the **tonic, subdominant,** and the **dominant seventh**.

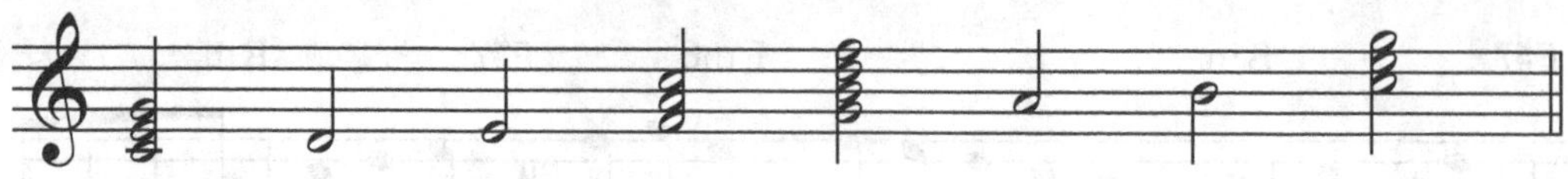

Note that the chords are built upon the tonic, subdominant, and the dominant degrees of the scale.

The lowest tone of a chord is called the **root** and the remaining tones are numbered according to their distance from that root.

Six-Eight Time

This sign  indicates **six-eight** time.

6 – beats per measure.
8 – type of note receiving one beat.

An eighth note ♪ = one beat, a quarter note ♩ = two beats, a dotted quarter note ♩. = three beats, and a sixteenth note = 1/2 beat.

Six-eight time consists of two units containing three beats each.

It will be counted:  with the accents on beats one and four.

The Irish Washerwomen

CD 2 #49

Guitar Solo **Allegro**

Arr. by Mel Bay

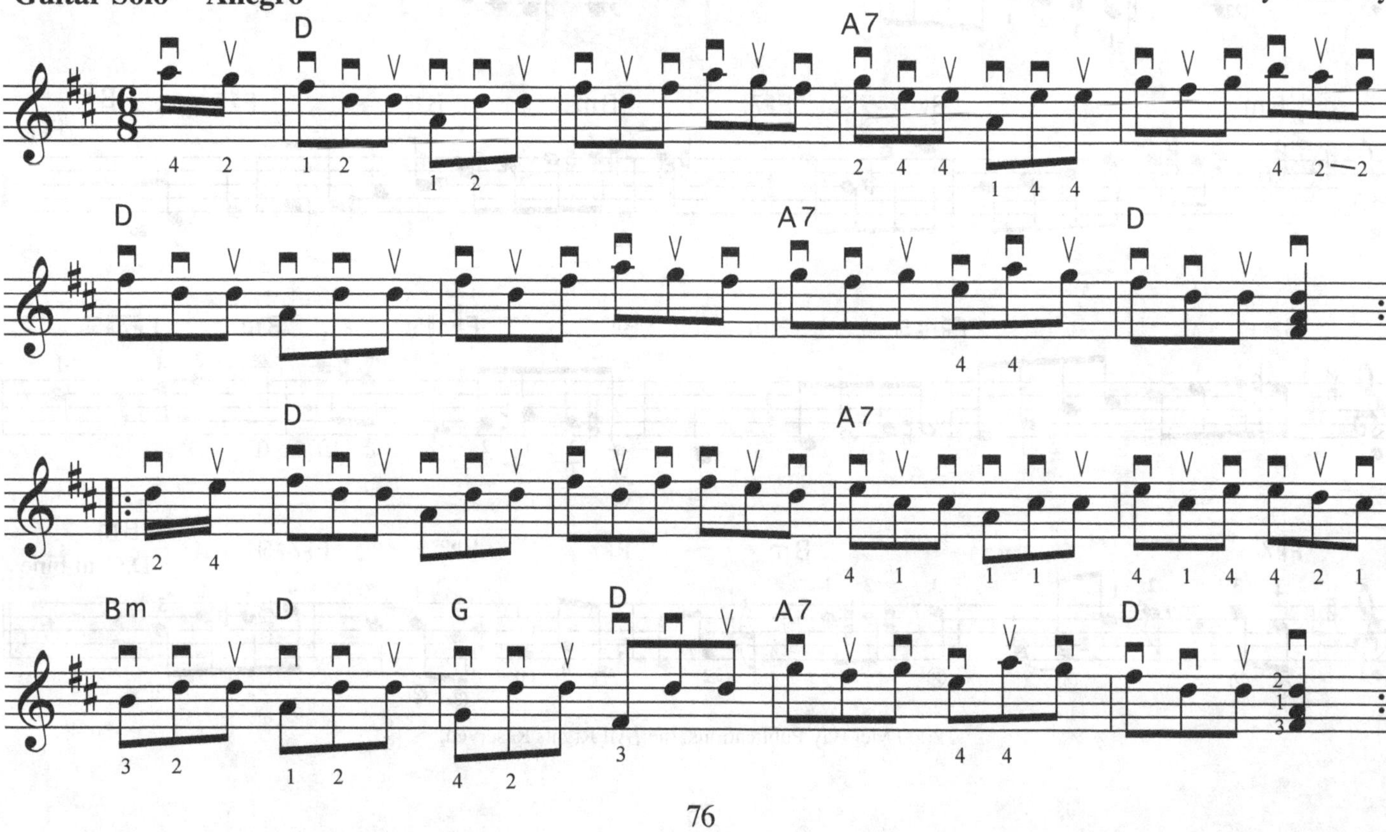

6/8 Picking Studies

① CD 2 #50

②

③ CD 2 #51

④

⑤ CD 2 #52

⑥

⑦ CD 2 #53

⑧

⑨ CD 2 #54

⑩

⑪

Dublin Dance

CD 2 #55

W. Bay

Lively

Swallowtail Jig

CD 2 #56

Territory Ahead

CD 2 #57

Minuet

CD 2 #58

Guitar Duet

J. S. Bach
Arr. by Mel Bay

Andante ④③

Three-Eight Time

This sign 𝄞 3/8 indicates **three-eight** time.

3 – beats per measure.
8 – type of note receiving one beat.

An eighth note ♪ = one beat, a quarter note ♩ = two beats, a dotted quarter note ♩. = three beats, and a sixteenth note 𝅘𝅥𝅯 = 1/2 beat.

A Spanish Dance

CD 2 #59

Arr. by Mel Bay

Guitar Duet

Lively

A Spanish Dance (cont.)

Plectrum Technique

The following studies are excellent for the development of plectrum technique. Follow the stroking carefully and play slowly at first, increasing speed gradually.

Prelude

CD 2 #60

Etude

CD 2 #61

The Plectrum Waltz

CD 2 #62

Carcassi - Bay

Skipping Along

CD 2 #63

Guitar Solo

Allegretto

Carcassi-Bay

Coronado

CD 2 #64

Guitar Solo

Carcassi-Bay

Dotted Eighth Note

A dotted eighth note is equal to an 8th note tied to a 16th note:

Example:

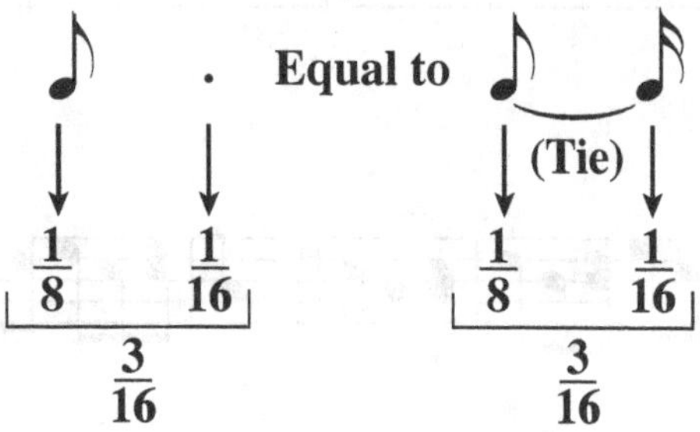

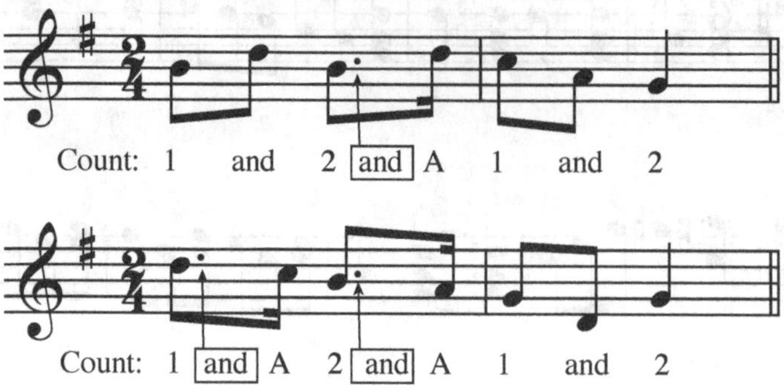

Country Gardens

Guitar Duet

Moderato

CD 2 #65

English Folk Dance
Arr. Mel Bay

Logan's Bluff

CD 2 #66

Moderately

W. Bay

Blessed Quietness

CD 2 #67

Slowly

Gospel Song

Harvest Moon Strathspey

CD 2 #68

Moderately

W. Bay

Alastair's Lament

CD 2 #69

Slow, march-like tempo

W. Bay

Brighton Beach

CD 2 #70

Spirited tempo

W. Bay

Days of Lang Syne

CD 2 #71

Scottish

THE MEL BAY MODERN GUITAR METHOD COMPLETE EDITION

Part 1/Grade 3

Online Audio

To access the online audio, scan the QR code above or go to:

www.melbay.com/30504

ONLINE AUDIO TRACKS FOR PART 1/GRADE 3

Audio #1 (61 min.)

1 Tune Up [1:37]
2 Daily Drill [:22]
3 A Scale Studies #1 [:17]
4 A Scale Studies #2 [:21]
5 A Scale Studies #3 [:20]
6 A Scale Studies #4 [:22]
7 A Study #1 - Open Position [:54]
8 Taranto [:39]
9 A Scale Study #5 [:20]
10 Maria [1:25]
11 Red Haired Boy [:56]
12 Bill Cheathum [:58]
13 Steep Levee [:55]
14 Mere Point [:49]
15 Emerald Shores [1:31]
16 Romance [2:08]
17 The Speedway - 2nd Position [:36]
18 A Scale Study #1 - 2nd Position [:19]
19 A Scale Study #2 - 2nd Position [:19]
20 A Study #3 - 2nd Position [:30]
21 Festival Waltz - 2nd Position [:36]
22 Spanish Dance - 2nd Position [:52]
23 Crazy Creek [:59]
24 Venetian Nights [1:42]
25 Country Life [1:47]
26 Prelude [:44]
27 Souvenirs [1:22]
28 Happy Guitarist [:44]
29 F♯m Study #1 - 2nd Position [:24]
30 F♯m Study #2 - 2nd Position [:21]
31 F♯m Study #3 - 2nd Position [:26]
32 F♯m Study #4 - 2nd Position [1:07]
33 Lark in the Morning [:52]
34 Ode for Guitar - 2nd Position [1:33]
35 Hymn [:50]
36 Chord Solo [:28]
37 Walking Chords [:35]
38 Polish Dance [1:09]
39 C Study #1 - 2nd Position [:21]
40 C Study #2 - 2nd Position [:21]
41 C Study #3 - 2nd Position [:19]
42 Poem - 2nd Position [:53]
43 Spring Break - 2nd Position [:49]
44 Shuckin' - 2nd Position [:39]
45 C Boogie - 2nd Position [:29]
46 Lonely Journey [:48]
47 Quiet Moments [:37]
48 Dance [:29]
49 Chimes [:34]
50 Am Picking Study [:21]
51 A Minor Study #1 - 2nd Position [:22]
52 A Minor Study #2 - 2nd Position [:23]
53 A Minor Study #3 - 2nd Position [:18]
54 Sierra Dawn [:40]
55 Noche [:38]
56 Black Stallion - 2nd Position [:41]
57 Salisbury Waltz - 2nd Position [:52]
58 Song [:33]
59 Anthem [:42]
60 G Picking Study [:19]
61 Ballad [:33]
62 Silver Threads among the Gold [1:02]
63 G Study #1 - 2nd Position [:18]
64 G Study #2 - 2nd Position [:18]
65 G Study #3 - 2nd Position [:17]
66 Billy in the Low Ground [:58]
67 Thunder in the Valley 2nd Position [:37]
68 Molly O'Hare - 2nd Position [:33]
69 The Downfall of Paris [:34]
70 Melancholy Mood [1:00]
71 Slur Song [:34]
72 Slide Song [:33]
73 Gondola [:27]
74 Neopolitan [:28]
75 Alma Mater [:55]
76 Memories [:50]
77 Walking Triads [:32]
78 Abide with Me [:54]
79 The Snapper [:22]
80 Slur Jig [:35]
81 Train to Tulsa [:20]
82 Chanson Triste [1:13]
83 Glissando Study [:36]
84 Autumn [:52]
85 Soliliquy [:38]

Audio #2 (60 min. 37 sec.)

1 Bm Scale Study #1 [:28]
2 Bm Scale Study #2 [:30]
3 Bm Scale Study #3 [:32]
4 Luckie Bawdins' Reel [:56]
5 Postlude [:47]
6 Etude in Bm [1:48]
7 Lilac [:50]
8 Air by Mozart [:47]
9 Study #1 [:25]
10 Study #2 [:20]
11 Study #3 [:20]
12 Serenade [1:33]
13 Minuet in D minor [1:19]
14 Largo [:36]
15 Lucy's Waltz [:24]
16 Crystal Sea [:36]
17 F Picking Study [:19]
18 A Daily Scale Study in B Flat [:25]
19 Study #1 [:19]
20 Study #2 [:19]
21 Skylark [:52]
22 Gasconade Waltz [:32]
23 Odyssey [:55]
24 Russian Easter [:29]
25 Song [:23]
26 Waltz from the Poet and Peasant Overture [:54]
27 Holiday [1:09]
28 G Minor Study #1 - Open Position [:36]
29 Gm Picking Study [:19]
30 Gm Study [:20]
31 Equation [1:07]
32 Bucharest [1:06]
33 Broken Bottle [:32]
34 Slippery Slope [:35]
35 Sultana [:58]
36 Coventry Carol [:52]
37 Early Christmas Morn [:43]
38 An Adventure in B Flat [2:57]
39 Third-Position Etude No. 1 [:29]
40 Third-Position Etude No. 2 [:24]
41 Hi Pointe [:51]
42 Shady Oak [:51]
43 Galleria [:39]
44 Westfield [:39]
45 The Arkansas Traveler [:53]
46 Beautiful Dreamer [1:34]
47 Esquire [2:24]
48 C Minor Etude in the Third Position [:26]
49 Cm Study #2 [:49]
50 Cm Study #3 [:23]
51 Vyaltsevo [:56]
52 Tocatta [:49]
53 Summer Nights [:45]
54 Dialogue [:40]
55 Prelude in Cm [:40]
56 Sarabande [:52]
57 Syncopation Etude [1:34]
58 A♭ Study #2 [:23]
59 A♭ Study #3 [:22]
60 A♭ Study #4 [:24]
61 A♭ Scale in Open Position [:25]
62 Wyoming Trail/A♭ in Open Position [1:06]
63 Sudden Voyage/A♭ in 3rd Position [1:01]
64 A♭ Scale Study #5 [:30]
65 A♭ Review Etude [1:05]
66 Triplet Etude in A Flat [:23]
67 Elsie's Walk [:22]
68 The Cavalcade [3:19]
69 Fm Study #1 [:24]
70 Fm Study #2 [:23]
71 Fm Study #3 [:25]
72 Descent [:55]
73 Fm Prelude [:24]
74 Hawthorne [:40]
75 Dundee's Dilemma [:45]
76 Sedona [:25]
77 Opus 1 [1:24]

The Key of A

The key of A has three sharps (F♯, C♯, and G♯).

It is identified by this signature:

The notes affected by the above signature are played as shown:

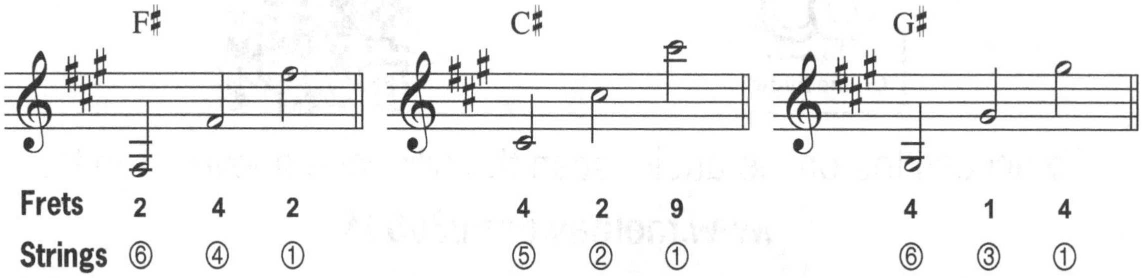

A Scale — Open Position

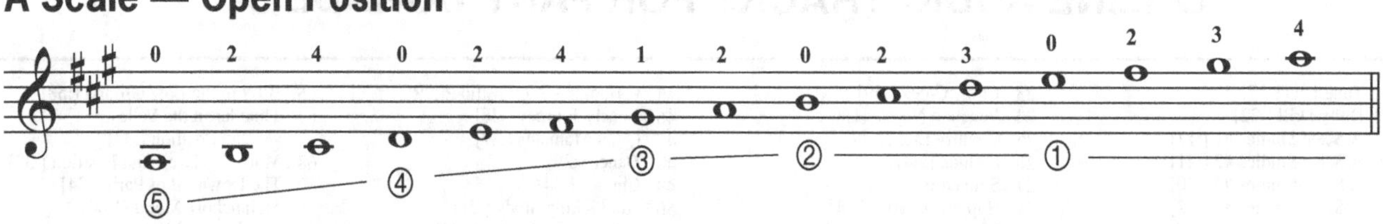

A Arpeggio — Open Position

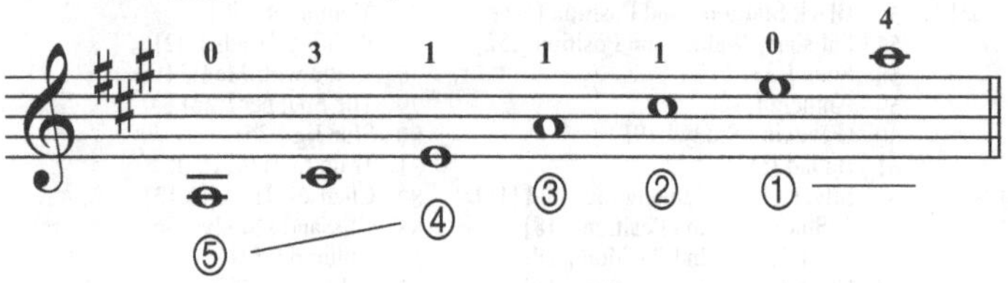

Daily Drill

CD 1 Track #2

A Scale Studies

① CD 1 Track #3

② CD 1 Track #4

③ CD 1 Track #5

④ CD 1 Track #6

A Study #1 — Open Position

CD 1 Track #7

Taranto

CD 1 Track #8

Guitar Solo

Carcassi
Arr. by Mel Bay

A Scale Study #5

CD 1 Track #9

The Chords in the Key of A

The three principal chords in the key of A are A, D, and E7.

tonic	subdom.	dom. 7th
A	D	E7

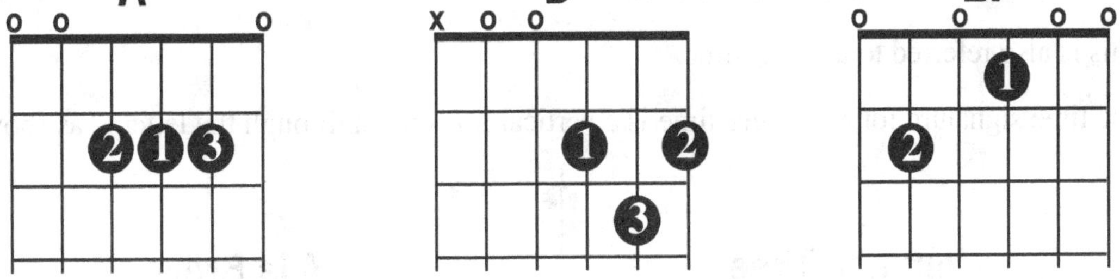

The Musical Notation of the Chords

Accompaniment Styles

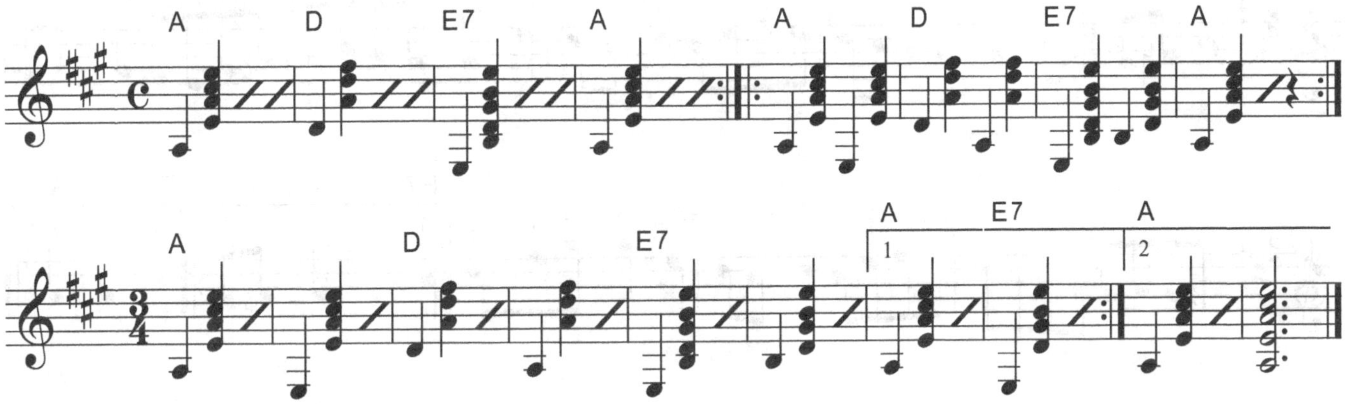

Maria CD 1 Track #10

Guitar Solo

Arr. by Mel Bay

Alla Breve Time

When common time is to be played in a tempo too fast to count four beats conveniently, it is then best to count only two beats to each measure.

Each half measure will receive one beat.

This is also referred to as "cut" time.

The time signature for *alla breve* time is a vertical line drawn through the letter C as shown:

¢

Common Time

Count: 1 2 3 4

Alla Breve

1 2

Red Haired Boy CD 1 Track #11

Swing Feeling

Bill Cheatham CD 1 Track #12

Swing Feeling

Steep Levee CD 1 Track #13

Swing Feeling

W. Bay

Mere Point

CD 1 Track #14

Swing Feeling

W. Bay

Emerald Shores

CD 1 Track #15

Lyrically, slowly

W. Bay

* High C♯ — 1st string, 9th fret.

Romance CD 1 Track #16

Guitar Duet

Mazas - Bay

A in Second Position

A Scale – 2nd Position

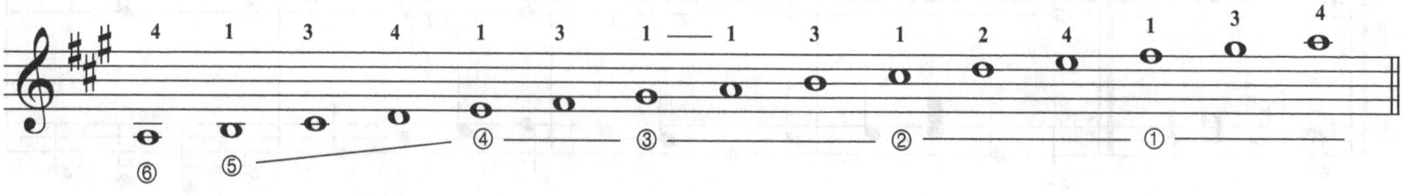

A Arpeggio – 2nd Position

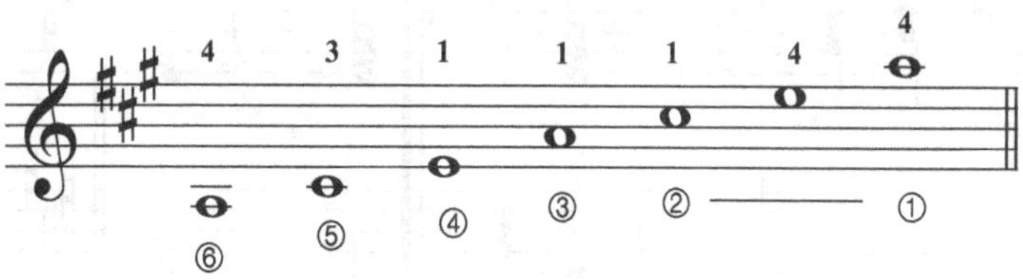

The Speedway – 2nd Position

CD 1 Track #17

A Scale Study #1 – 2nd Position

CD 1 Track #18

A Scale Study #2 – 2nd Position

CD 1 Track #19

A Study #3 – 2nd Position

CD 1 Track #20

Festival Waltz – 2nd Position

CD 1 Track #21

W. Bay

Spanish Dance – 2nd Position

CD 1 Track #22

Allegro

W. Bay

Crazy Creek

CD 1 Track #23

Swing Feeling

2nd Position

The Notes on the Third String

The notes on the third (G) string are located as shown:

The G chromatic scale will be played on the third string as follows:

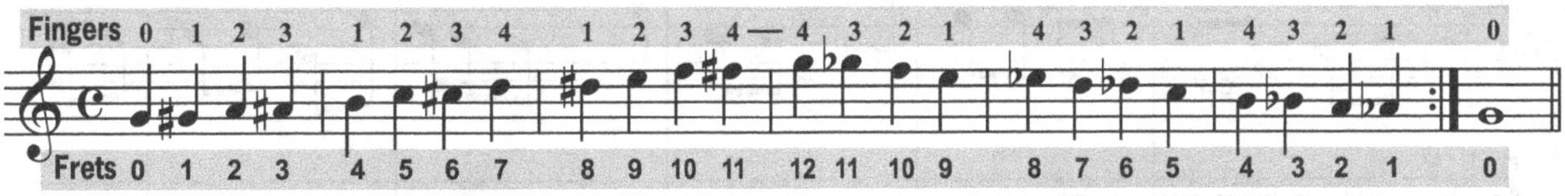

The G Scale

The A Scale

Hold fingers down as indicated

G String Etude

Venetian Nights

CD 1 Track #24

Guitar Solo

M. Carcassi
Arr. by Mel Bay

Country Life CD 1 Track #25

Guitar Duet

Mazas, Opus 38
Arr. by Mel Bay

Allegretto

I
II
C♯7
F♯m
Bm F♯m
Bm G♯7
C♯7
F♯m
C♯7
C♯7
F♯m
F♯m
Bm Bm
F♯m C♯7
F♯m
E7
A Am

The Notes on the Fourth String

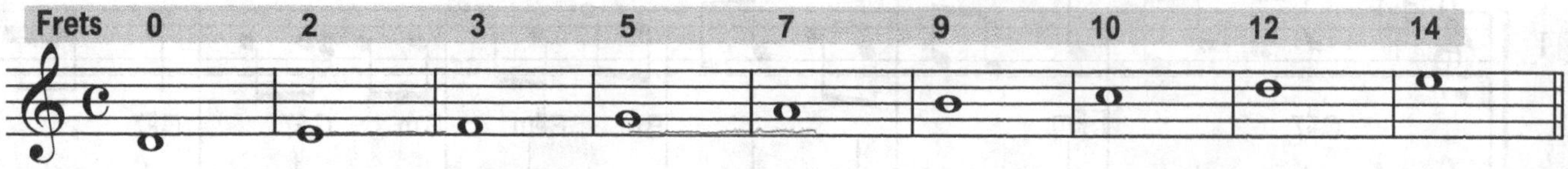

A Table of Notes on the First, Second, Third, and Fourth Strings

It is important that the student thoroughly understand the above chart before proceeding.

Prelude

Guitar Solo

CD 1 Track #26

F. Chopin, Opus 28, No. 7
Arr. by Mel Bay

Souvenirs

CD 1 Track #27

Guitar Solo

Andante

The Happy Guitarist

CD 1 Track #28

Guitar Solo

Arr. by Mel Bay

Allegretto

The Key of F Sharp Minor

(Relative to A Major)

Two F Sharp Minor Scale

Harmonic

Melodic

The Chords in the Key of F Sharp Minor

The chords in the key of F♯ minor are F♯m, Bm and C♯7.

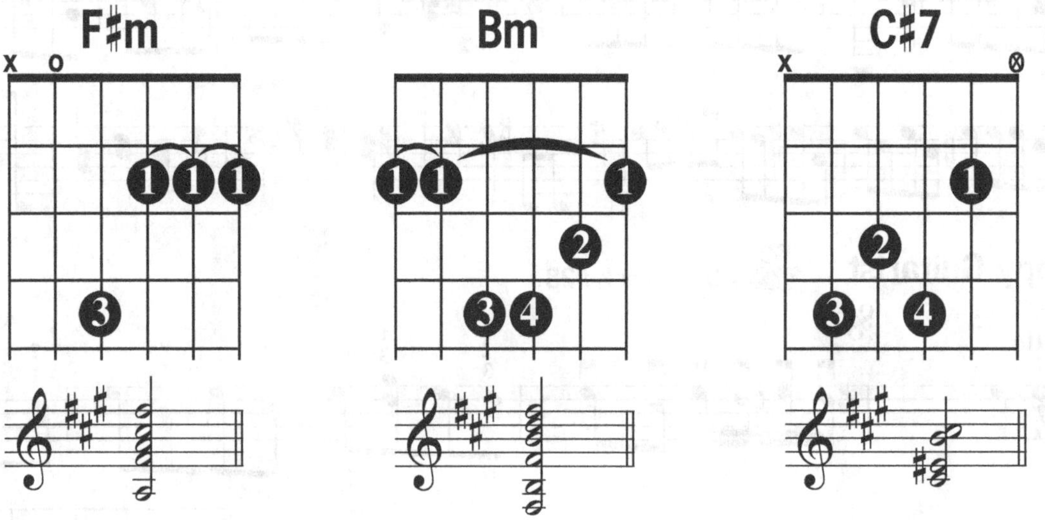

⊗ = ***deadened string*** — kill the sound of the string with unused part of the left hand.
(See the *Mel Bay's Melody Chord Playing System* for further explanation.)

Accompaniment Styles

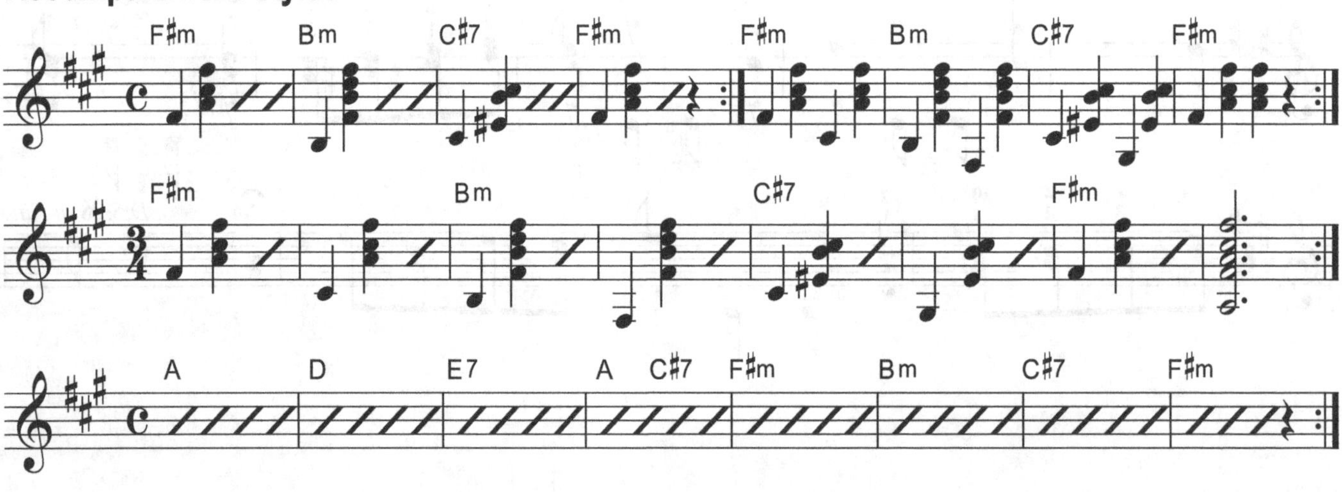

More Chromatic Signs

Up to this point we have studied and used the sharp (♯), the flat (♭), and the natural (♮). The student is familiar by now with their functions. We now introduce the ***double sharp*** and the ***double flat***.

𝄪 = double sharp. A double sharp raises the sound of a tone **two frets**.

𝄫 = double flat. A double flat lowers the sound of a tone **two frets**.

A natural cancels all sharps, flats, double sharps and double flats. If a note has been double sharped or double flatted, the return to one sharp or flat will require a natural sign followed by the desired sharp or flat.

Example:

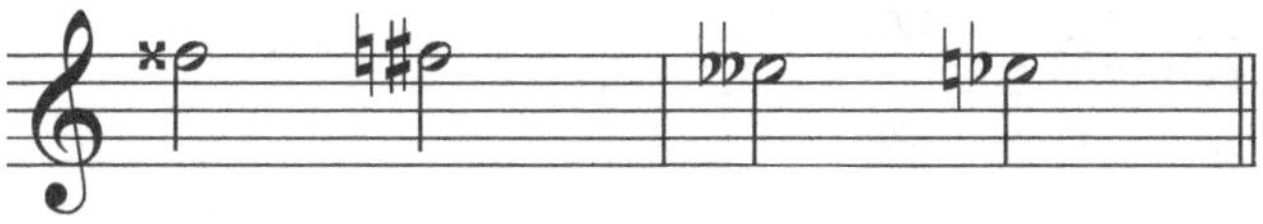

Major to Relative Minor Etude

A Major

F♯ Minor (Harmonic)

Melodic

A Major

Key of F Sharp Minor

F Sharp Minor Scale / Harmonic Mode – 2nd Position

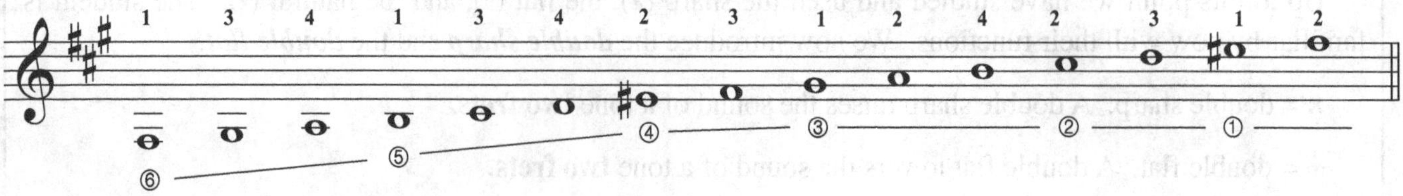

F Sharp Minor Arpeggio – 2nd Position

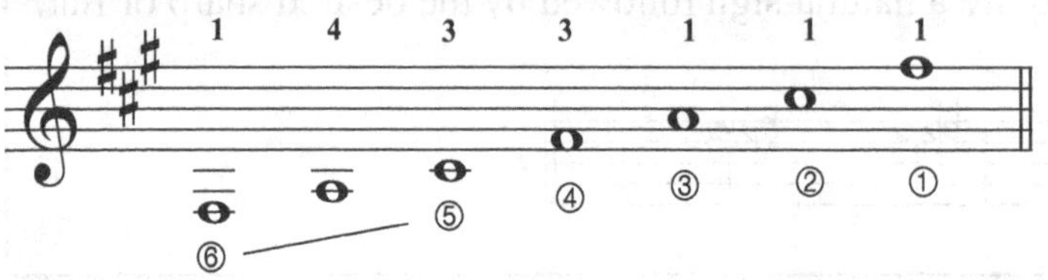

F♯m Study #1 – 2nd Position

CD 1 Track #29

F♯m Study #2 – 2nd Position

CD 1 Track #30

F♯m Study #3 – 2nd Position

CD 1 Track #31

F♯m Study #4 – 2nd Position

CD 1 Track #32

Andante

W. Bay

Lark in the Morning

CD 1 Track #33

Moderately

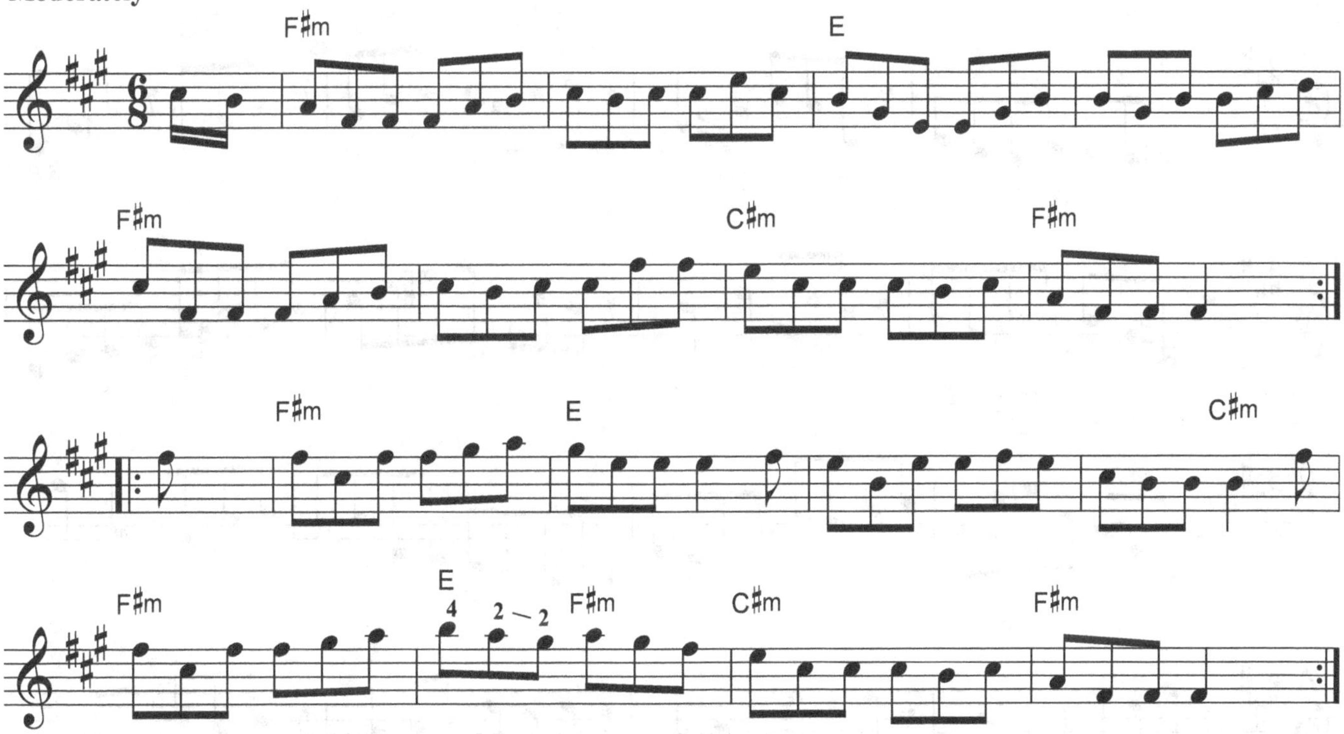

Key of F Sharp Minor Review

Ode for Guitar – 2nd Position

CD 1 Track #34

Slowly

W. Bay

Harmonized Scales

Practice the following harmonized scales until a smooth technique and clear tone have been developed.

Carefully note the fingering.

The C Scale

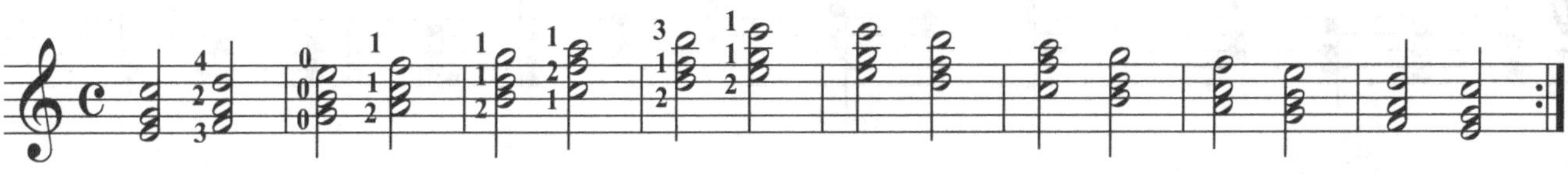

Hymn

CD 1 Track #35

W. Bay

Chord Solo

CD 1 Track #36

W. Bay

Walking Chords
CD 1 Track #37

Slowly

Polish Dance (Kuiawak)
CD 1 Track #38

Wieniawski
Arr. by Mel Bay

Allegretto

C Scale - 2nd Position

C Scale - 2nd Position

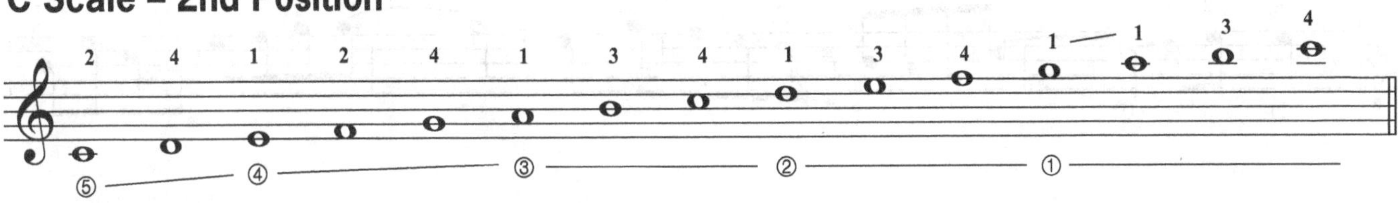

C Arpeggio - 2nd Position

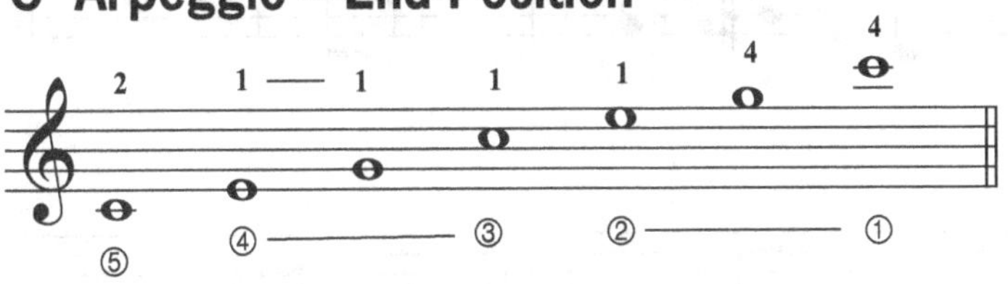

C Study #1 - 2nd Position

CD 1 Track #39

C Study #2 - 2nd Position

CD 1 Track #40

C Study #3 - 2nd Position

CD 1 Track #41

Poem – 2nd Position   CD 1 Track #42

Moderately

W. Bay

Spring Break – 2nd Position   CD 1 Track #43

Moderately

W. Bay

Shuckin' – 2nd Position

CD 1 Track #44

Swing Feeling

W. Bay

C Boogie – 2nd Position

CD 1 Track #45

The Slide

The slide is performed by one finger of the left hand sliding over the frets from the first to the second note. The first note is struck, and the second note is sounded by the slide.

The slide is indicated by the following sign:

Slide Etude

The A Minor Scale
(Harmonic Mode)

Lonely Journey

CD 1 Track #46

Guitar Solo

Mel Bay

Quiet Moments

CD 1 Track #47

W. Bay

Dance

CD 1 Track #48

W. Bay

Chimes

CD 1 Track #49

W. Bay

Am Picking Study

CD 1 Track #50

Swing Feeling

Key of A Minor – 2nd Position

A Minor Scale / Harmonic Mode – 2nd Position

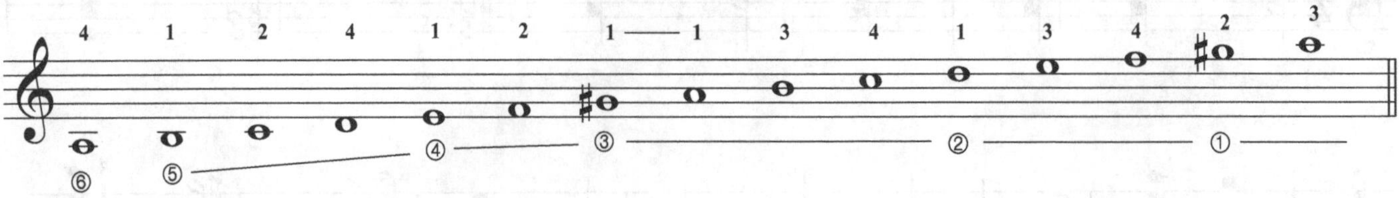

A Minor Arpeggio – 2nd Position

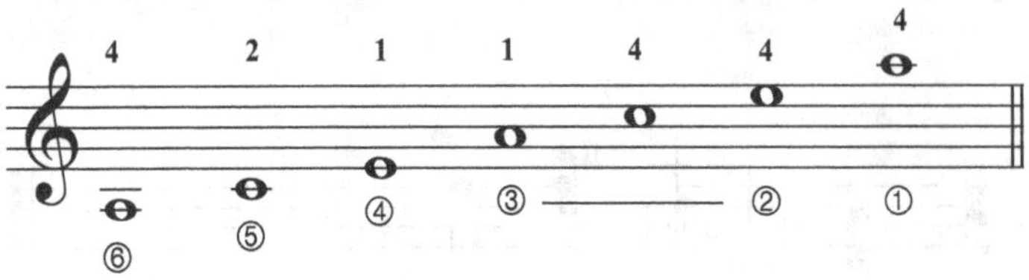

A Minor Study #1 – 2nd Position

CD 1 Track #51

A Minor Study #2 – 2nd Position

CD 1 Track #52

A Minor Study #3 – 2nd Position

CD 1 Track #53

Sierra Dawn

CD 1 Track #54

Moderately

W. Bay

Noche

CD 1 Track #55

Slowly

W. Bay

Black Stallion – 2nd Position

CD 1 Track #56

Swing Feeling

W. Bay

Salisbury Waltz – 2nd Position

CD 1 Track #57

Moderately

W. Bay

The Triads Built on the G Scale

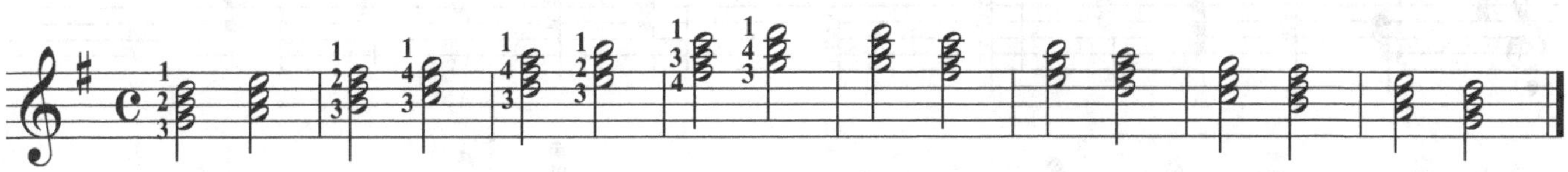

Song CD 1 Track #58

W. Bay

Anthem CD 1 Track #59

W. Bay

G Picking Study CD 1 Track #60

Swing Feeling

Ballad
CD 1 Track #61

To obtain the proper effect, the following solo should be memorized. Play it slowly in a cantabile or smooth "song-like" manner.

Silver Threads among the Gold
CD 1 Track #62

Guitar Solo

H. P. Danks
Arr. by Mel Bay

Slow

The Slur

To execute ***ascending slurs*** of two notes, the lower note is played and the finger of the left hand descends hammer-like upon the higher note, creating the tone desired.

Descending slurs are executed by first fingering the notes to be played with the left hand. Strike the higher note by drawing the finger sideways off the string; the lower note will automatically sound. Slurred notes are connected by a curved line (⌒) and are sometimes called "pull-offs."

Ascending Slurs

Descending Slurs

Key of G

G Scale – 2nd Position

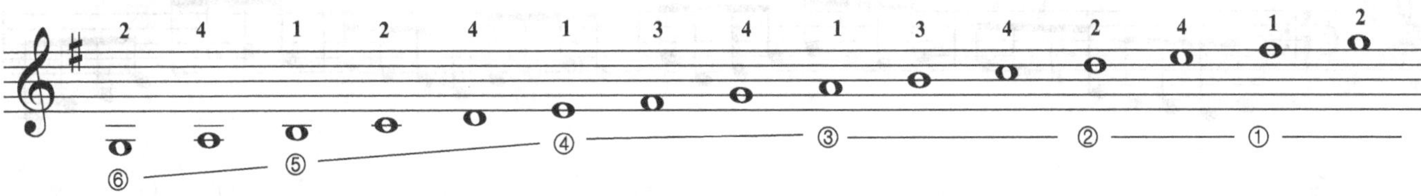

G Arpeggio – 2nd Position

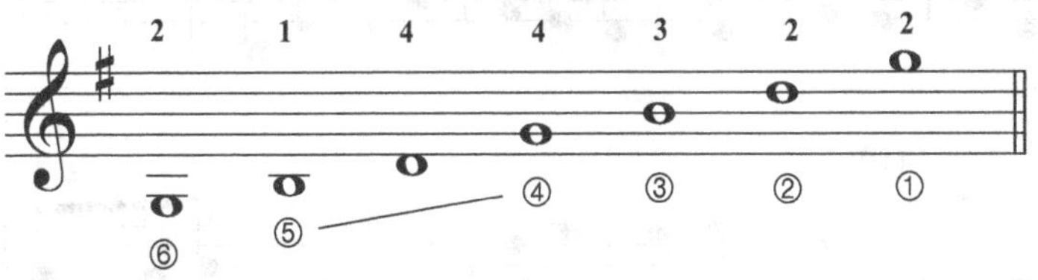

G Study #1 – 2nd Position

CD 1 Track #63

G Study #2 – 2nd Position

CD 1 Track #64

G Study #3 – 2nd Position

CD 1 Track #65

Billy in the Low Ground – 2nd Position

CD 1 Track #66

Lively Tempo

Thunder in the Valley – 2nd Position

CD 1 Track #67

W. Bay

Molly O'Hare – 2nd Position

CD 1 Track #68

Lively

W. Bay

The Downfall of Paris

CD 1 Track #69

Moderately

Set Dance

The E Minor Scale

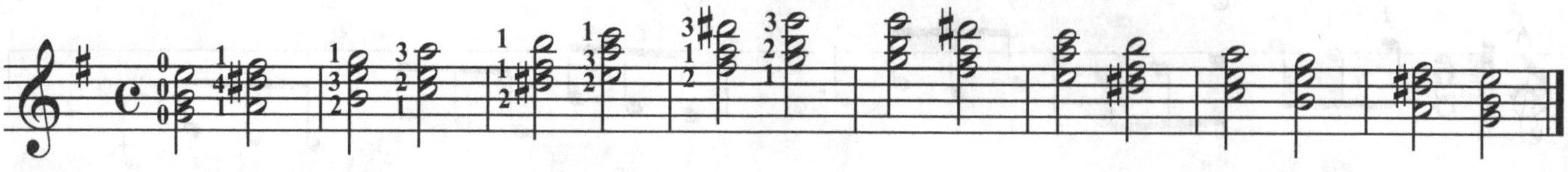

Melancholy Mood

CD 1 Track #70

Guitar Solo

Mel Bay

The Tremolo

This sign (≡) indicates the ***tremolo***.

The tremolo is a rapid succession of alternate down and up strokes.

The student should start slowly with a relaxed wrist, averaging four alternate strokes per quarter beat. The speed of the tremolo should be gradually increased until one continuous sound is produced.

The fourth finger of the right hand may rest upon the guard if the student has difficulty in properly gauging the pick.

A Tremolo Study

Whole Notes

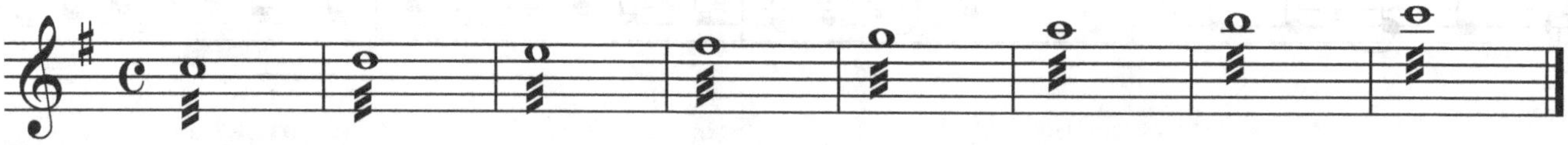

Half Notes

Slur Song

CD 1 Track #71

W. Bay

Slowly

Slide Song

CD 1 Track #72

W. Bay

Slowly

Gondola

CD 1 Track #73

W. Bay

Slowly

Neopolitan

CD 1 Track #74

W. Bay

Slowly

Triads

The ***triad*** is the smallest chord. All chords are based on the triad.

The triad (from *tri,* meaning *three*) is built of two thirds placed over each other.

The tones of a triad are the root (the tone from which the triad is built), the third above and fifth above.

Triads in the major scale are as follows:

Major Minor Minor Major Major Minor Dim. Major

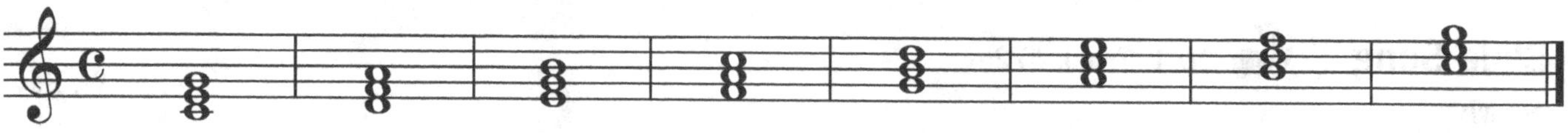

I II III IV V VI VII Octave

A **major** third consists of two whole steps (2).

A **minor** third consists of one and a half steps (1 1/2).

A **major** triad contains a major third plus a minor third (reading upward).

A **minor** triad contains a minor third plus a major third.

A **diminished** triad is composed of a minor third plus a minor third.

An **augmented** triad is composed of a major third plus a major third.

An analysis of the triads built on the major-scale degrees shows the following results:

1. Tonic	Major	C-E-G	2 + 1 1/2 Steps
2. Super-tonic	Minor	D-F-A	1 1/2 + 2 Steps
3. Mediant	Minor	E-G-B	1 1/2 + 2 Steps
4. Sub-dominant	Major	F-A-C	2 + 1 1/2 Steps
5. Dominant	Major	G-B-D	2 + 1 1/2 Steps
6. Sub-mediant	Minor	A-C-E	1 1/2 + 2 Steps
7. Leading	Diminished	B-D-F	1 1/2 + 1 1/2 Steps

The triads in the minor scale are as follows:

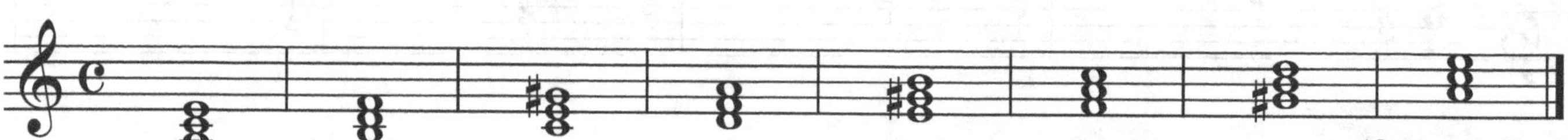

(Octave or First)

Minor Dim. Aug. Minor Major Major Dim. Minor

Ma. = Major mi. = Minor Aug. = Augmented Dim. = Diminished

The D Scale Harmonized

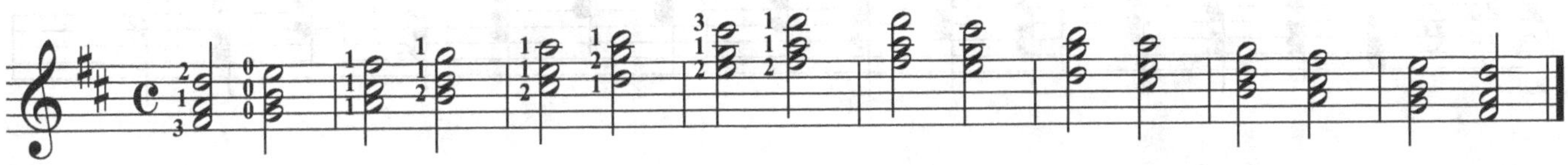

Alma Mater

CD 1 Track #75

W. Bay

Memories

CD 1 Track #76

W. Bay

Walking Triads

CD 1 Track #77

Abide with Me

CD 1 Track #78

Guitar Solo

W. H. Monk
Arr. by Mel Bay

Adagio

The Snap

The *snap* is similar to the slur in execution. The second note of the snap is usually an open string.

The first note is played, and immediately the left-hand finger pulls the string sideways as it slides off the fingerboard.

When snapping a note to a closed note, both notes should be held before executing the snap effect.

Example One

Example Two

The Snapper

CD 1 Track #79

Moderately

W. Bay

Slur Jig

CD 1 Track #80

W. Bay

Lively Tempo

Train to Tulsa

CD 1 Track #81

W. Bay

Swing Feeling

The B Minor Scale

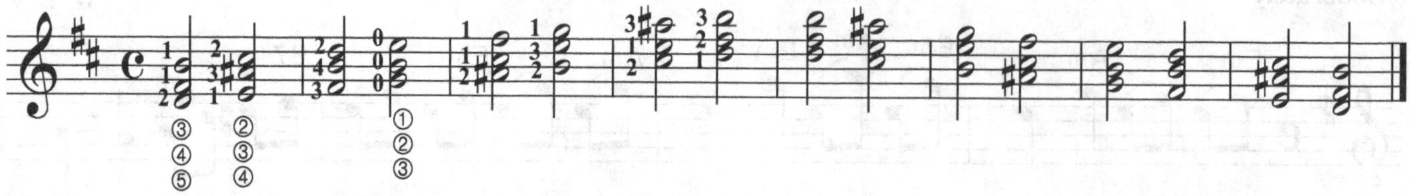

Chanson Triste

CD 1 Track #82

Guitar Solo

Tschaikowsky-Bay

Slow

The Glissando

The ***glissando*** will be designated by a wavy line with or without the abbreviation *Gliss* above it.

The glissando is performed by combining the slide and tremolo.

The first note will be tremoloed while sliding to the second.

Chords may be glissandoed with a very pleasant effect.

The glissando should be used sparingly.

Glissando of Single Notes

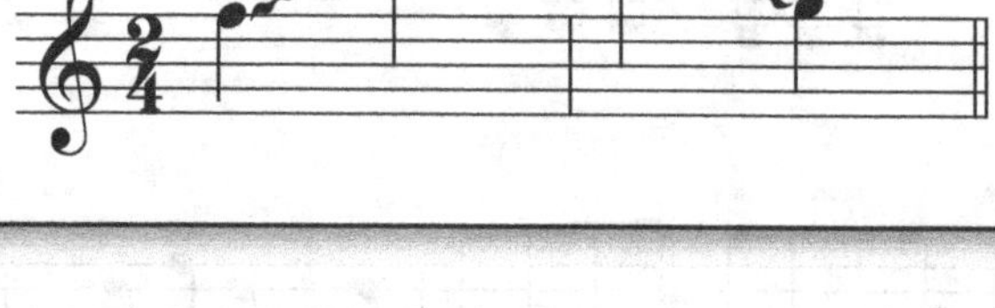

Glissando of Chords

Glissando Study

CD 1 Track #83

Slowly

W. Bay

Autumn

CD 1 Track #84

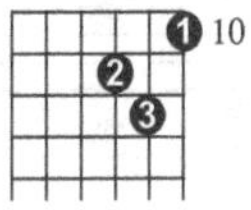

Slowly

W. Bay

Soliliquy

CD 1 Track #85

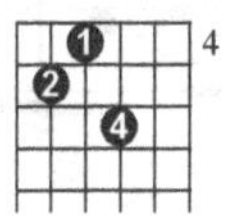

Slowly

W. Bay

Key of B Minor Review

B Minor Scale / Harmonic Mode – 2nd Position

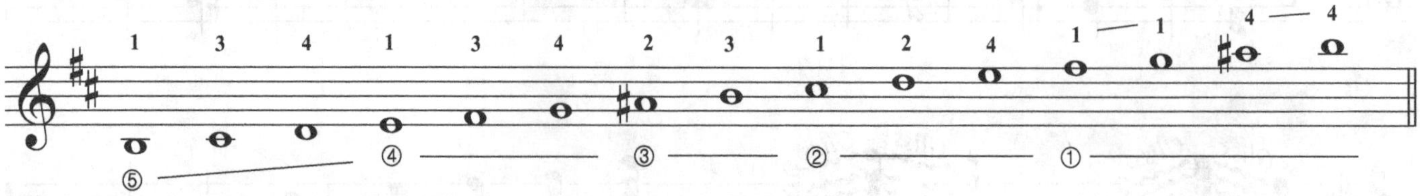

B Minor Arpeggio – 2nd Position

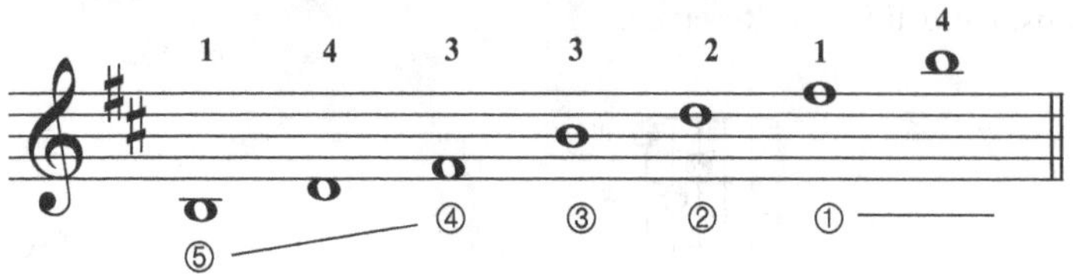

Bm Scale Study #1

CD 2 Track #1

Bm Scale Study #2

CD 2 Track #2

Bm Scale Study #3

CD 2 Track #3

Luckie Bawdins' Reel

CD 2 Track #4

Moderately

Scottish

Postlude

CD 2 Track #5

Andante

W. Bay

Etude in Bm

CD 2 Track #6

Signs Pertaining to Expression and Phrasing

The *staccato* (or) indicates staccato. Tones designated in this manner are played in a disconnected style with emphasis.

: Short lines over notes indicate emphasis and individuality.

: Every tone marked this way should be emphasized individually and slightly separated.

: Accent with sudden force.

Legato ( ) : All tones are connected and played in a flowing style.

: Gradual increase of intensity or volume.

: Gradual diminishing of intensity.

The ***swell*** ( ) : Increase and diminish volume.

Tenuto (∧) : Hold the tone its full value.

Luft pause (//) : An exaggerated pause. Usually follows a note that is held by a hold sign (fermata).

Example: //

The ***comma*** (❜) is used sometimes to indicate an interruption in the flow of tone.

The F Scale Harmonized

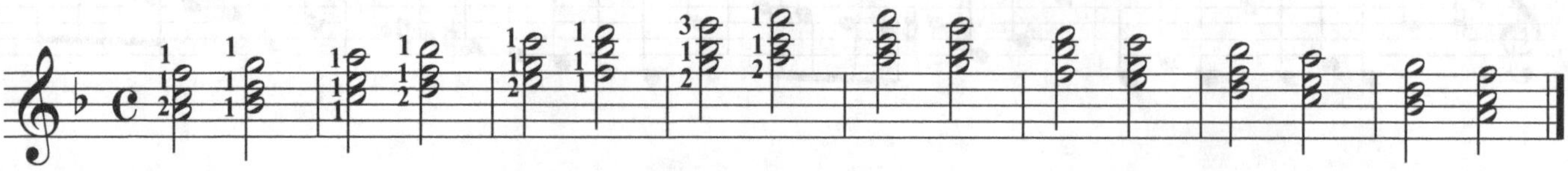

Lilac

CD 2 Track #7

Slowly

W. Bay

Air by Mozart

CD 2 Track #8

Guitar Solo

Arr. by Mel Bay

Key of D Minor – 2nd Position

D Minor Scale / Harmonic Mode – 2nd Position

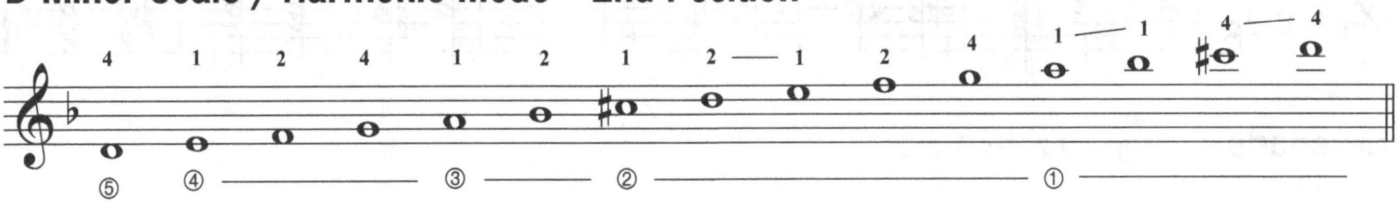

D Minor Arpeggio – 2nd Position

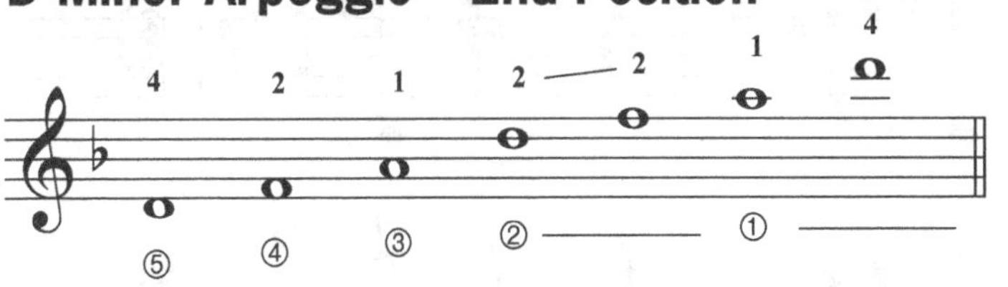

Study #1 CD 2 Track #9

Study #2 CD 2 Track #10

Study #3 CD 2 Track #11

The D Minor Scale

Serenade

CD 2 Track #12

Guitar Solo

Schubert-Bay

With expression

Minuet in D minor

CD 2 Track #13

Guitar Duet

J. S. Bach

Arr. by Mel Bay

Largo
CD 2 Track #14

Slowly

W. Bay

Lucy's Waltz
CD 2 Track #15

Moderately

W. Bay

Crystal Sea
CD 2 Track #16

Slowly

W. Bay

F Picking Study
CD 2 Track #17

Swing Feeling

The Key of B Flat

The key of B flat has two flats. All B and E notes are lowered 1/2 step.

The B Flat Scale

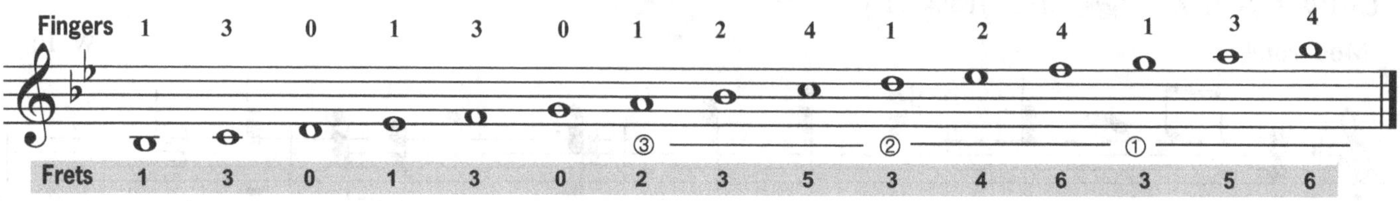

Etude

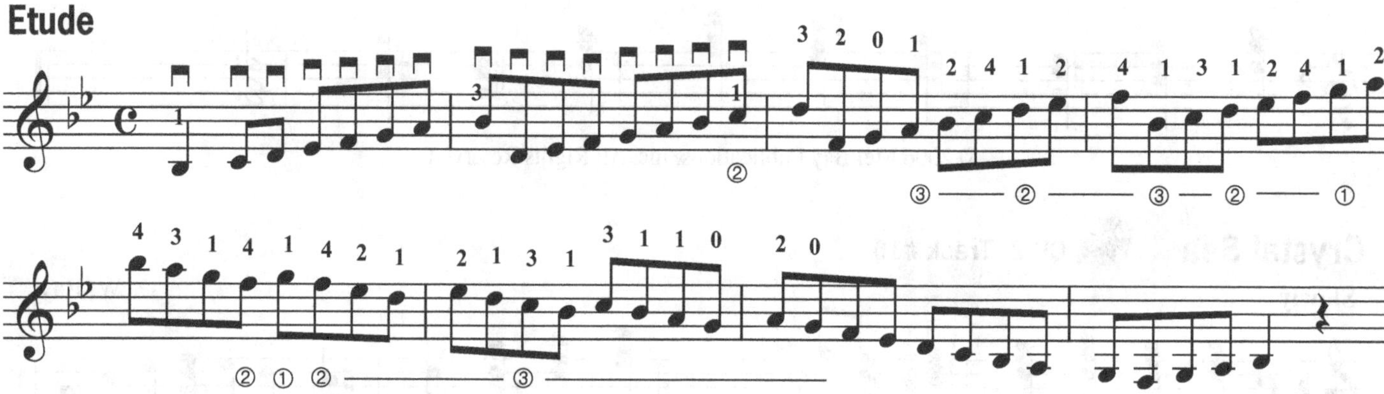

Triplet Etude in B Flat Major

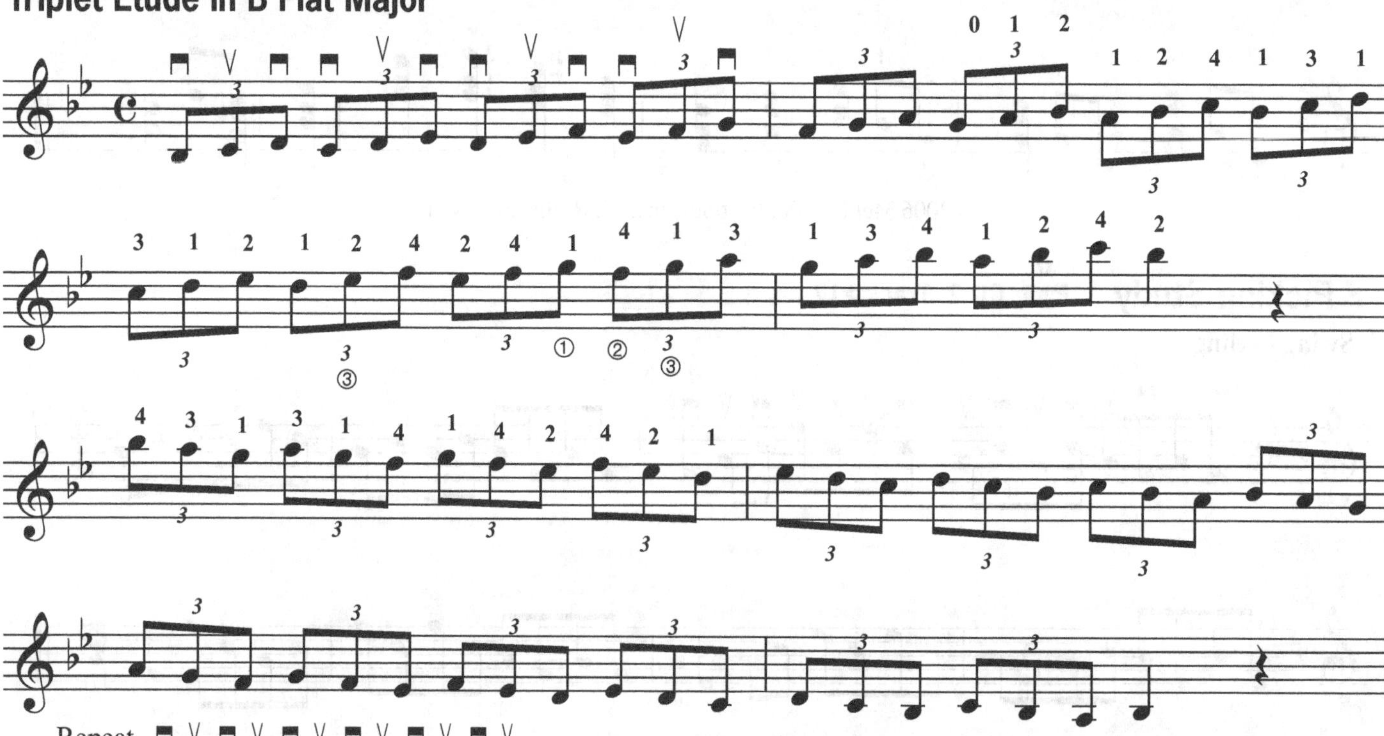

Repeat

A Daily Scale Study in B Flat

CD 2 Track #18

Study #1

CD 2 Track #19

Study #2

CD 2 Track #20

Skylark

CD 2 Track #21

Moderately

W. Bay

Gasconade Waltz

CD 2 Track #22

W. Bay

Odyssey

CD 2 Track #23

W. Bay

The Quarter-Note Triplet

This group of notes (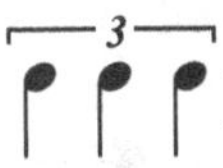) is used extensively in modern music. Three quarter notes will be played in the same time required by two. In playing this type of triplet employ the *alla breve* type of count.

Harmonized Scale

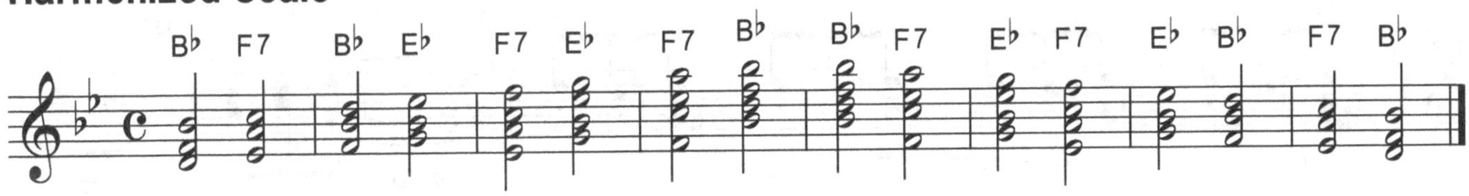

Accompaniment Etudes

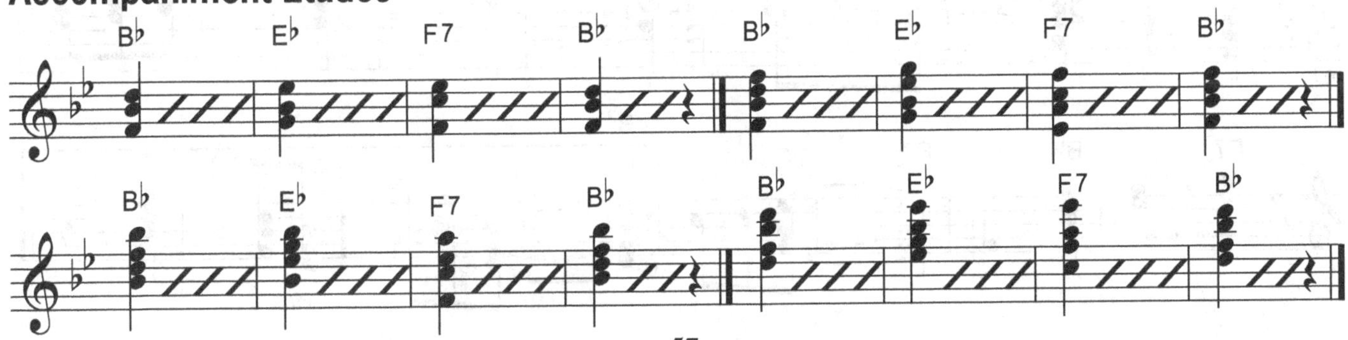

Russian Easter

CD 2 Track #24

W. Bay

Song

CD 2 Track #25

W. Bay

Waltz from the Poet and Peasant Overture

CD 2 Track #26

F. von Suppe
Arr. by Mel Bay

Holiday

Guitar Duet

CD 2 Track #27

Mazas-Bay

Allegretto

The Key of G Minor

(Relative to B Flat Major)

The key of G minor has the same key signature as B flat major

The G Minor Scales

Harmonic

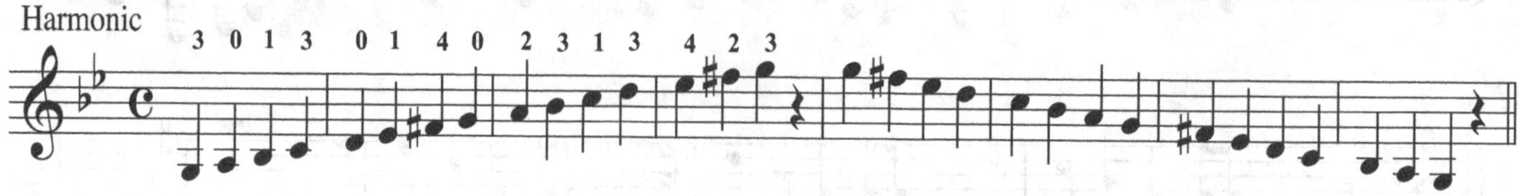

Melodic

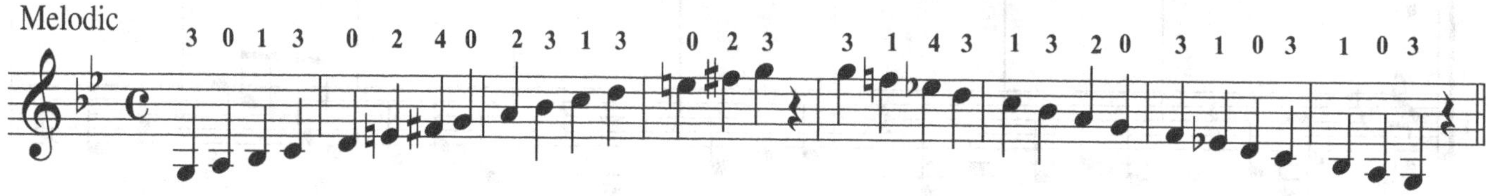

Mixed

Gypsy

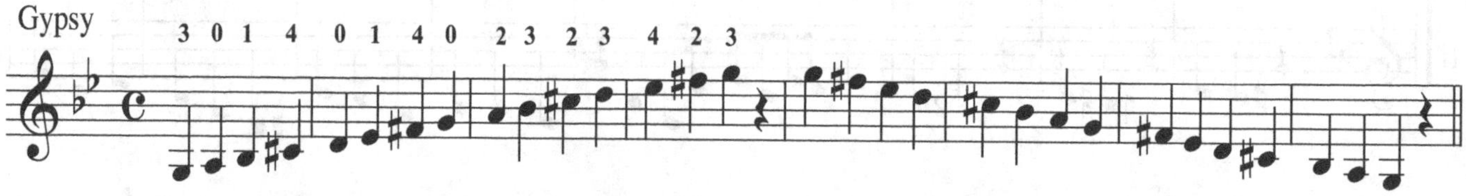

Accompaniment Styles

The Mixed Minor Scales

The **mixed** minor scale will ascend in the **melodic mode** but descend **harmonic.**

The Gypsy Minor Scale

This colorful and widely used scale is created by raising the fourth and seventh degrees half step.

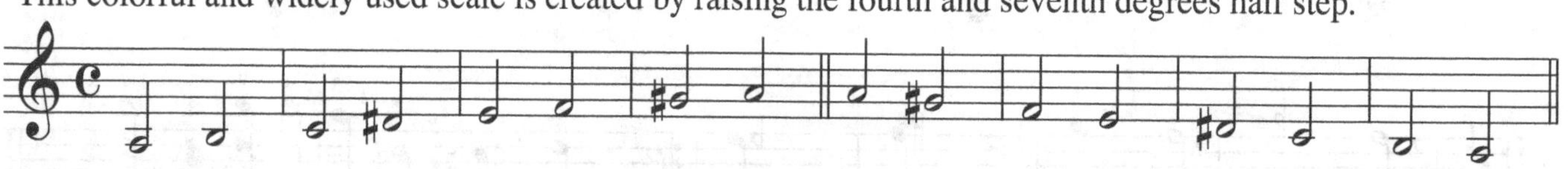

The Tonic Minor Scale

Lowering the third and sixth degrees of a major scale will create a harmonic minor scale. This is done extensively by composers.

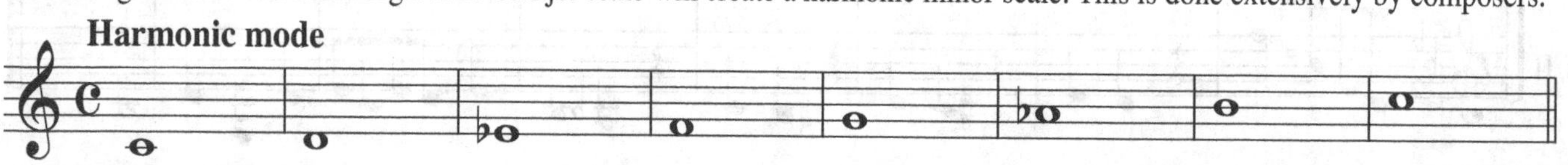

Key of G Minor

G Minor Scale / Harmonic Mode – Open Position

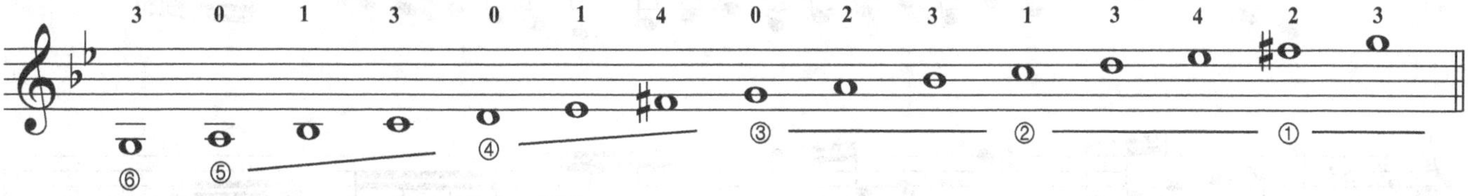

G Minor Arpeggio – Open Position

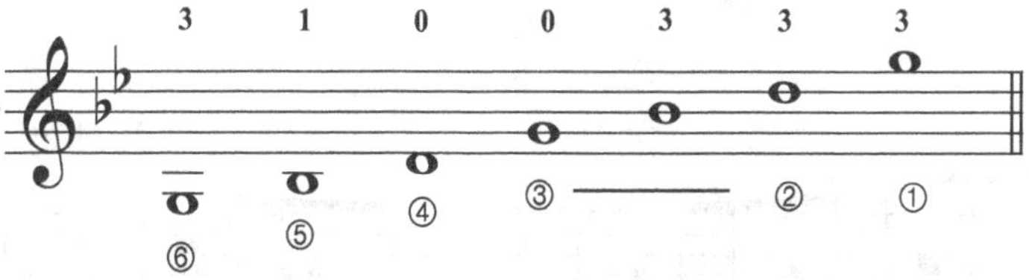

G Minor Study #1 – Open Position

CD 2 Track #28

W. Bay

Gm Picking Study

CD 2 Track #29

Swing Feeling

Gm Study

CD 2 Track #30

W. Bay

Equation

CD 2 Track #31

W. Bay

Bucharest

CD 2 Track #32

Slowly

W. Bay

Broken Bottle

CD 2 Track #33

Lively

W. Bay

Slippery Slope

CD 2 Track #34

Medium, with a beat

W. Bay

Sultana

CD 2 Track #35

Guitar Duet

Arr. by Mel Bay

Harmonized Scale

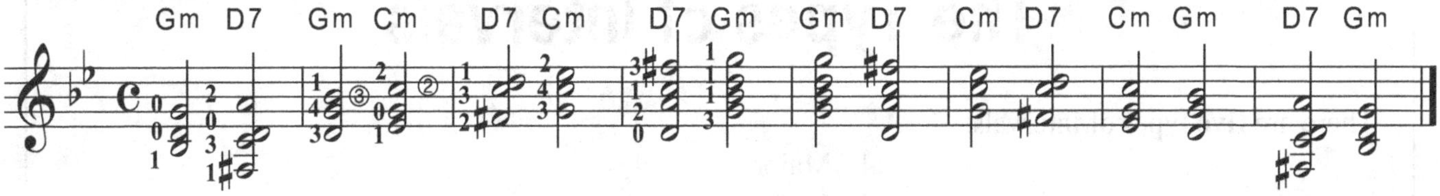

Coventry Carol

CD 2 Track #36

English Carol
Arr. by W. Bay

Slowly

Early Christmas Morn

CD 2 Track #37

13th Century Tune
Arr. by W. Bay

Slowly

The Types of Intervals

There are **five** types of intervals:

1. Major
2. Perfect
3. Minor
4. Diminished
5. Augmented

The Major Intervals

The interval is **major** if the upper tone belongs to the key of the lower tone.

The **number names** of the major intervals are 2nd, 3rd, 6th, and 7th.

The Perfect Intervals

The interval is **perfect** if the upper tone belongs to the key of the lower tone and **the lower tone belongs to the key of the upper tone**.

The **number names** of the major intervals are primes, 4th, 5th, and octave.

Perfect Prime or Unison	Major 2nd	Major 3rd	Perfect 4th	Perfect 5th	Major 6th	Major 7th	Perfect Octave

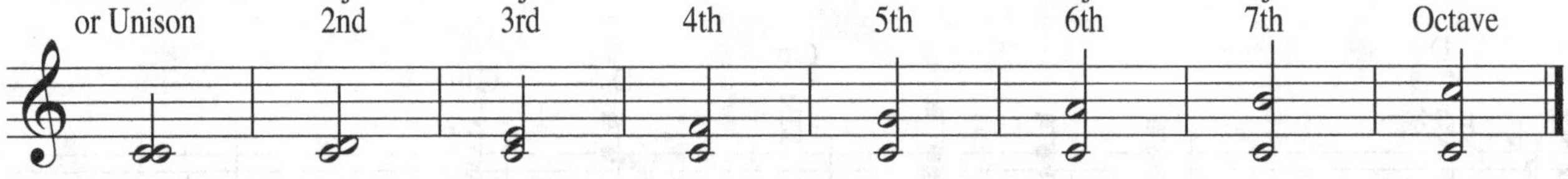

Distance: 0	1 Step	2 Steps	2 1/2 Steps	3 1/2 Steps	4 1/2 Steps	5 1/2 Steps	6 Steps

Note that in the example above the upper note in the major 2nd (D) is in the key of C, the key of the lower tone; but the lower note (C) is **not** in the key of the upper tone. (The note C is sharped in the key of D.)

The same situation arises intervals C-E, C-A, and C-B.

The above mentioned intervals will be **major.**

In the interval C-F, observe that the upper note (F) is in the key of the lower note (C), and the lower note (C) is in the key of the upper note (F). The same thing occurs in the interval C-G and C-C.

These intervals will be **perfect.**

Interval Measurement

Unisons or Primes	0 (No distance)
Major 2nd	1 Step
Major 3rd	2 Steps
Perfect 4th	2 1/2 Steps
Perfect 5th	3 1/2 Steps
Major 6th	4 1/2 Steps
Major 7th	5 1/2 Steps
Perfect Octave	6 Steps

It is advisable to check the distances of the above intervals on a piano or any keyboard instrument.

The distance of each interval should be memorized.

An Adventure in B Flat

CD 2 Track #38

Guitar Duet

Arr. by Mel Bay

Adventure (cont.)

*a tempo – resume original tempo

I
II
F7 B♭ Cm F7
B♭ F7 B♭
Ⓓ
E7 F7 E7 F7
E7 F7 E7 F7 F7
B♭ E♭ B♭ C° F7 B♭ F7
B♭ F7 B♭ Bar 3- - - ② ① B♭ B♭

The Key of E Flat

The key of E♭ has three flats. They are B♭, E♭, and A♭.

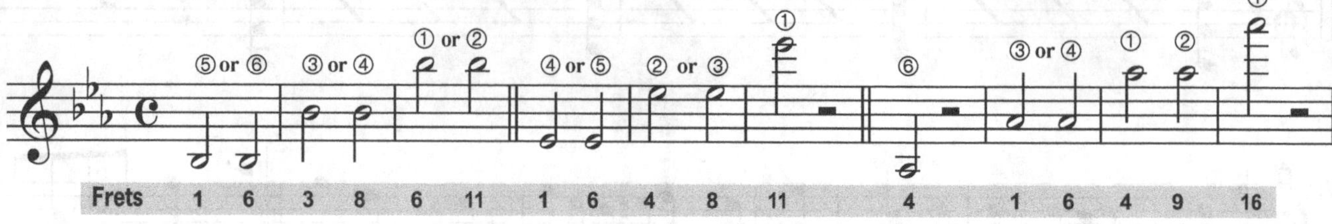

The E Flat Major Scale

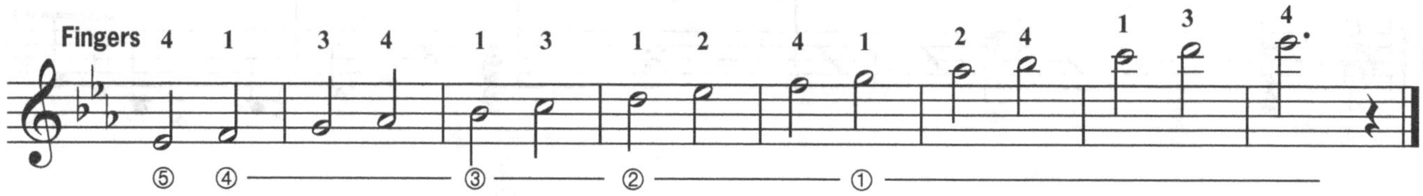

The Third Position

The **third position** extends from the third to the sixth frets.

Third-Position Etude No. 1

CD 2 Track #39

The Types of Intervals

Play the following example until chord changing is accomplished without loss of rhythm.

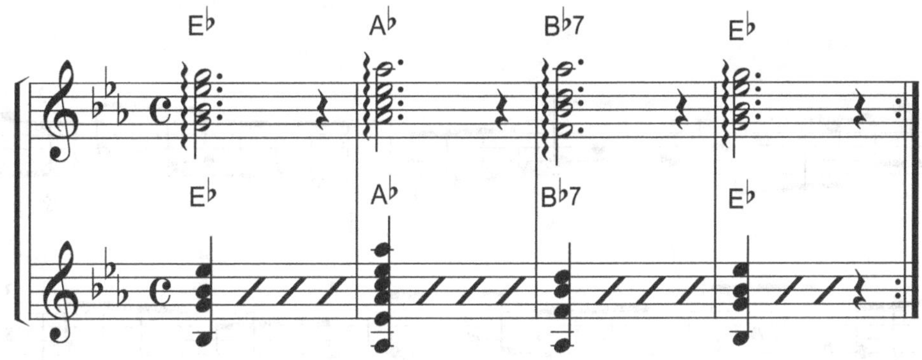

Third-Position Etude No. 2

CD 2 Track #40

While Shepherds Watched Their Flocks

(Third Position)

George F. Handel

Hi Pointe

CD 2 Track #41

W. Bay

Shady Oak

CD 2 Track #42

W. Bay

Galleria

CD 2 Track #43

W. Bay

Westfield

CD 2 Track #44

W. Bay

The Arkansas Traveler (Third Position)

CD 2 Track #45

Guitar Duet

Arr. by Mel Bay

Beautiful Dreamer

CD 2 Track #46

Guitar Solo

Stephen C. Foster
Arr. by Mel Bay

Esquire

CD 2 Track #47

Guitar Duet

Pleyel

Arr. by Mel Bay

Esquire (cont.)

The Minor Intervals

A minor interval is a half step smaller than a major.

Only major intervals may become minor.

Minor 2nd	1/2 Step
Minor 3rd	1 1/2 Steps
Minor 6th	4 Steps
Minor 7th	5 Steps

Interval Inversion

Intervals may be inverted by raising the lower tone an octave or by lowering the upper tone an octave.

Example:

When Inverted:

A major interval becomes minor.
A minor interval becomes major.
A perfect interval remains perfect.

A perfect prime becomes a perfect octave.
A major 2nd becomes minor 7th.
A major 3rd becomes minor 6th.
A perfect 4th becomes a perfect 5th.
A perfect 5th becomes a perfect 4th.
A major 6th becomes minor 3rd.
A major 7th becomes minor 2nd.
A perfect prime becomes a perfect octave.

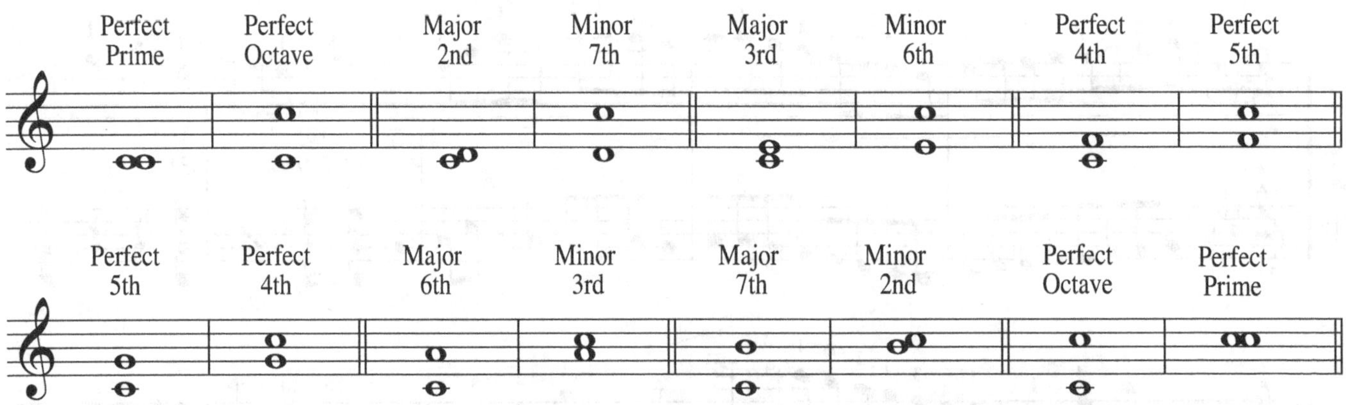

There should be a thorough drill in the recognition of intervals both through sight and sound.

The intervals should be played separately for sound recognition, then played together as the student improves in recognizing the tones.

The Key of C Minor

(Relative to E♭ Major)

The C minor scales will be played in the third position of the higher notes which will be played as shown.

The C Minor Scales

Harmonic

Melodic

The following etude is in *alla breve* or cut time.
When playing the quarter-note triplets, divide the measure into two beats, giving each set of triplets one beat.

Etude in C Minor (Third Position)

Melodic

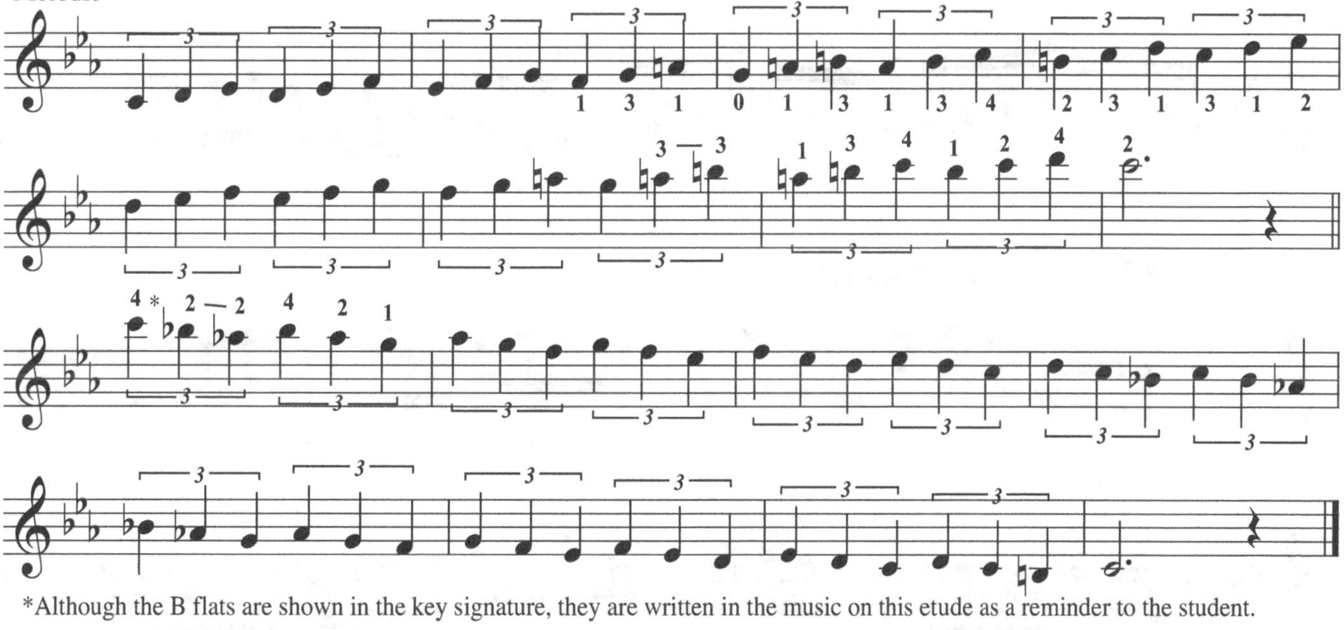

*Although the B flats are shown in the key signature, they are written in the music on this etude as a reminder to the student.

The C Minor Chords in the Third Position

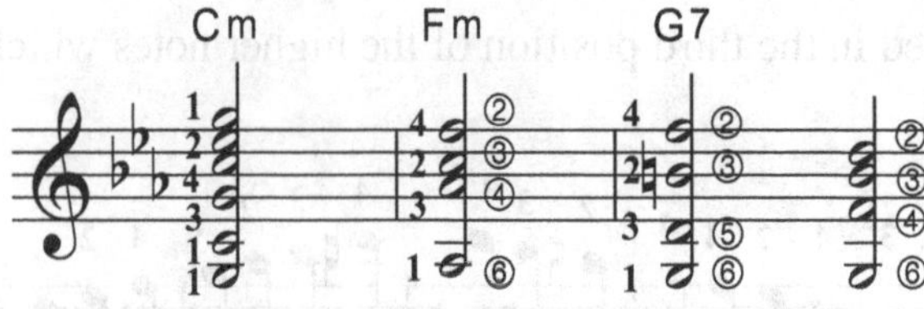

C Minor Etude in the Third Position

CD 2 Track #48

Cm Study #2

CD 2 Track #49

Cm Study #3

CD 2 Track #50

Vyaltsevo

CD 2 Track #51

W. Bay

Moderately

Tocatta

CD 2 Track #52

W. Bay

Moderately

Summer Nights CD 2 Track #53

Flowing Tempo

W. Bay

Dialogue CD 2 Track #54

W. Bay

Prelude in Cm

CD 2 Track #55

W. Bay

Sarabande

CD 2 Track #56

Handel
Arr. by W. Bay

Very Slow

Syncopation

Syncopation means irregularity of rhythm. The accent falls on the beats not naturally accented.

The scale studies below introduce three types of syncopation.

The major scale will be counted:

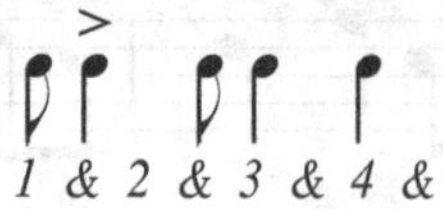

Melodic:

Harmonic:

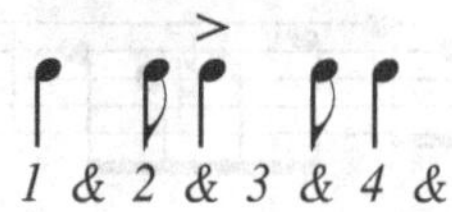

Syncopation Etude CD 2 Track #57

Major

Harmonic

Melodic

The Key of A Flat

The key of A flat has four flats. All B, E, A, and D notes are lowered 1/2 step. The flatted notes are easy to remember by spelling b-e-a-d.

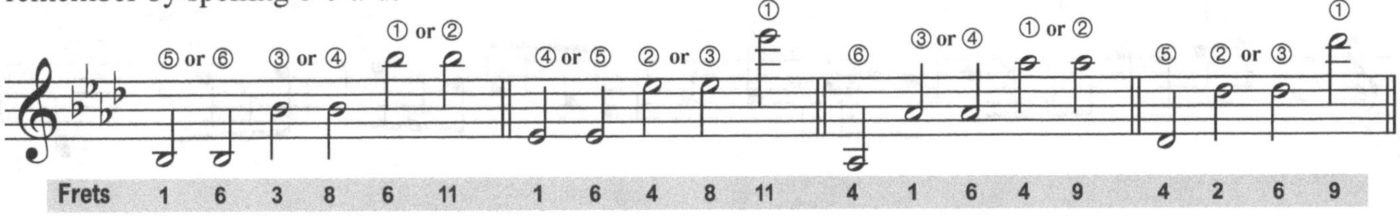

The A Flat Scale in the Third Position

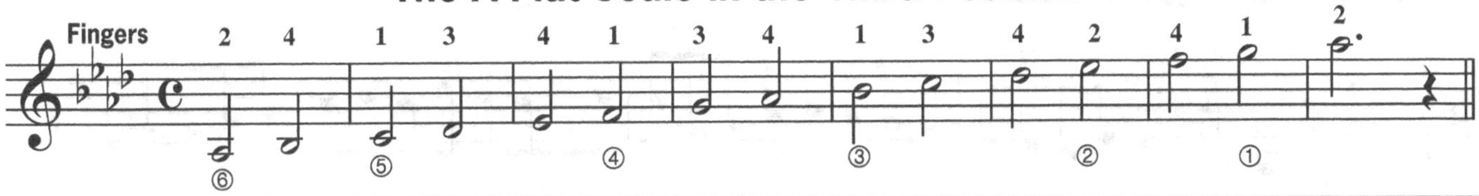

A Daily Scale Study in A Flat (Third Position)

The following daily study is an excellent etude for developing finger strength, speed, and good position playing. It should be played daily. The number of times should increase as the fingers become stronger. It is played entirely in the third position.

A♭ Study #2 CD 2 Track #58

A♭ Study #3 CD 2 Track #59

A♭ Study #4 CD 2 Track #60

A♭ Scale in Open Position CD 2 Track #61

Wyoming Trail/A♭ in Open Position

CD 2 Track #62

W. Bay

Sudden Voyage/A♭ in 3rd Position

CD 2 Track #63

W. Bay

A♭ Scale Study #5

CD 2 Track #64

A♭ Review Etude

CD 2 Track #65

Open Position

W. Bay

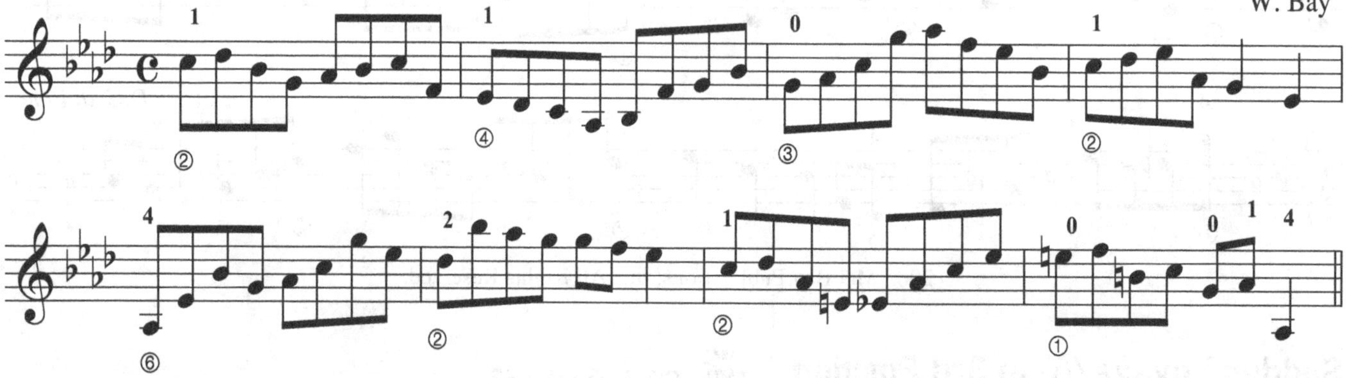

3rd Position

The Chords in the Key of A Flat

The three principal chords in the key of A♭ are A♭, D♭, and E♭7.

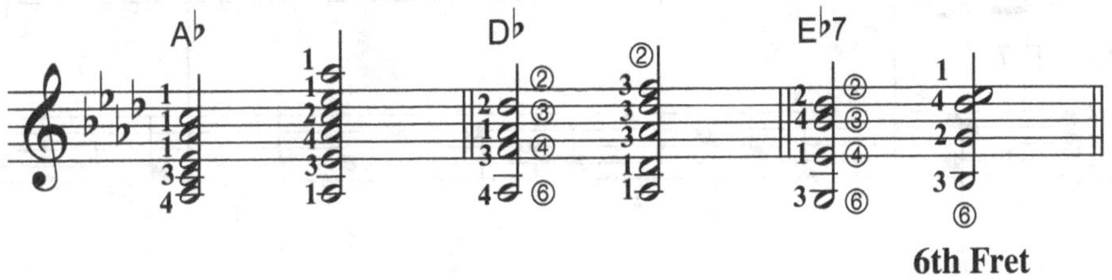

Triplet Etude in A Flat (Third Position) CD 2 Track #66

Allegro

Elsie's Walk CD 2 Track #67

W. Bay

Moderately

The Cavalcade (Third Position) CD 2 Track #68

Guitar Duet

Mazas, Opus 38
Arr. by Mel Bay

Note: Both parts should be played in the third position.

The Cavalcade (cont.)

*Change fingers on the same note.

The Cavalcade (cont.)

The Key of F Minor

(Relative to A♭ Major)

The F Minor Scales

Harmonic

Melodic

The Chords in the Key of F Minor

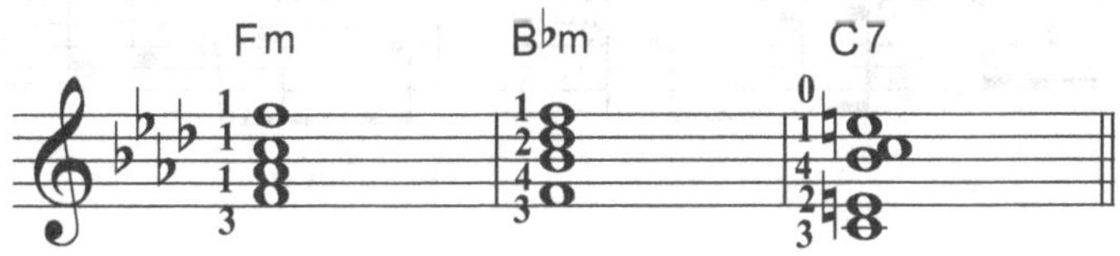

Fm Study #1 CD 2 Track #69

Fm Study #2 CD 2 Track #70

Fm Study #3

CD 2 Track #71

Descent

CD 2 Track #72

W. Bay

Moderately

Fm Prelude

CD 2 Track #73

W. Bay

Hawthorne

CD 2 Track #74

W. Bay

Moderately

Dundee's Dilemma

CD 2 Track #75

W. Bay

Allegro

Sedona

CD 2 Track #76

Allegro

W. Bay

Opus 1

CD 2 Track #77

Slowly, with expression

W. Bay

THE MEL BAY MODERN GUITAR METHOD COMPLETE EDITION
Part 1/Grade 4

Online Audio

To access the online audio, scan the QR code above or go to:

www.melbay.com/30504

ONLINE AUDIO TRACKS FOR PART 1/GRADE 4

AUDIO CONTENTS

CD 1

1 Etude in E Major
2 E Scale Studies Ex. 1
3 E Scale Studies Ex. 2
4 E Scale Studies Ex. 3
5 E Scale Studies Ex. 4
6 E Scale Studies Ex. 5
7 E Scale Studies Ex. 6
8 Prairie Sunset
9 Epigram
10 Picking Studies Ex. 1
11 Picking Studies Ex. 2
12 Picking Studies-C Picking
13 Picking Studies-G Picking
14 Picking Studies-D Picking
15 Picking Studies-A Picking
16 Picking Studies-E Picking
17 Fourth-Position Etude #1
18 Etude #2
19 Starburst
20 Eclipse
21 I Gave My Love a Cherry
22 Cheyenne Wells-4th Pos.
23 Study #3-4th Pos.
24 Waltz
25 Italian Air (Multi-Pos. Study)
26 A Triplet Etude
27 A Study #2-4th Pos.
28 Fourth-Position Etude
29 A Study #3-4th Pos.
30 Stuck in the Kitchen-4th Pos.
31 Exhilaration-4th Pos.
32 Rose O Sharon-4th Pos.
33 Morning Dance-4th Pos.
34 A Scale Study #4-4th Pos.
35 Key of A Review
36 C♯ Minor Studies-4th Pos. Ex. 1
37 C♯ Minor Studies-4th Pos. Ex. 2
38 C♯ Minor Studies-4th Pos. Ex. 3
39 C♯ Minor Studies-4th Pos. Ex. 4
40 C♯ Minor Studies-4th Pos. Ex. 5
41 Bering Sea-4th Pos.
42 Portrait-4th Pos.
43 Nocturne-4th Pos.
44 Images-4th Pos.
45 Reflection-4th Pos.
46 Sarabande (Duet in C♯ Minor)
47 Ivy Leaf Reel
48 Little House Round the Corner
49 Minueto
50 Lyric Moment-4th Pos.
51 Daydreams-4th Pos.
52 Star of Bethlehem-4th Pos.
53 Schooner-4th Pos.
54 St. Clair's Hornpipe-4th Pos.
55 Fifth-Position Etude #1
56 Fifth-Position Etude #2
57 The Court Jester (Fifth Position)
58 Woodlands-5th Pos.
59 Narcissus-5th Pos.
60 Sonatina in F Major-5th Pos.
61 The Commentator
62 Fifth-Position Etude #3
63 Stallion at Daybreak-5th Pos.
64 Riley McGurk-5th Pos.
65 Levelland by Night-5th Pos.
66 Jonquil-5th Pos.
67 Sundance-5th Pos.
68 Clare Waltz-5th Pos.
69 High Five-5th Pos.
70 Traverse Bay-5th Pos.
71 Shadows
72 Ballad-5th Pos.
73 River Glen-5th Pos.
74 Sailors Hornpipe-5th Pos.
75 Meramec Echoes-5th Pos.
76 Buena Vista-5th Pos.
77 Suffolk-5th Pos.
78 Shamrock-5th Pos.
79 Ruby-5th Pos.

CD 2

1 Key of Am-5th Pos. Ex. 1
2 Key of Am-5th Pos. Ex. 2
3 Key of Am-5th Pos. Ex. 3
4 Leipzig - 5th Pos.
5 J.S.-5th Pos.
6 Dance-5th Pos.
7 Silouette-5th Pos.
8 Starling-5th Pos.
9 Mirage-5th Pos.
10 B♭ Scale Etude
11 B♭ Studies-5th Pos.
12 Song-5th Pos.
13 Exploration-5th Pos.
14 Etude-5th Pos.
15 Minuetto
16 Triplet Etude in the Fifth Pos. #1
17 Triplet Etude in the Fifth Pos. #2
18 DeSoto-5th Pos.
19 Dora's Waltz-5th Pos.
20 Erin's Waltz-5th Pos.
21 Cross Country-5th Pos.
22 Snapshop-5th Pos.
23 Poem
24 Seventh-Position Etude
25 Waterfall-7th Pos.
26 Joplin-7th Pos.
27 Kreutzer's Etude-7th Pos.
28 Seventh-Pos. Etude in G
29 Sor's Song-7th Pos.
30 Breathe on me, Breath of God
31 Lucky Seven-7th Pos.
32 Rondo
33 Scale Study-7th Pos.
34 Gardenia-7th Pos.
35 Gypsy Rondo-7th Pos.
36 Portrait-7th Pos.
37 Discovery-7th Pos.
38 Dawn-7th Pos.
39 Passage-7th Pos.
40 Misty Night-7th Pos.
41 Sierra-7th Pos.
42 Vista-7th Pos.
43 Workout-7th Pos.
44 Glasgow-7th Pos.
45 Sunset-7th Pos.
46 Autumn-7th Pos.
47 Nightfall-7th Pos.
48 Cruising-7th Pos.
49 Muse-7th Pos.
50 Snowfall-7th Pos.
51 Panorama-7th Pos.
52 Natasha-7th Pos.
53 Farewell-7th Pos.
54 Ninth-Position Etude #1
55 Ninth-Position Etude #2
56 The Ninth Inning-9th Pos.
57 Maze-9th Pos.
58 Susan Lynn - Multiple Pos.
59 The Golden Wedding (La Cinquantaine)
60 Carcassi's Etude (A Major)
61 Norwegian Dance
62 Excursion (A Position Review)

The Key of E Major

The key of E has four sharps. All F, C, G, and D notes are sharped.

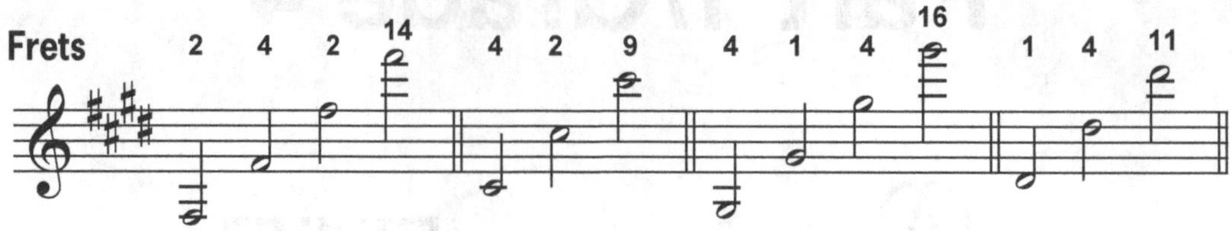

The E Major Scale

(Three Octaves)

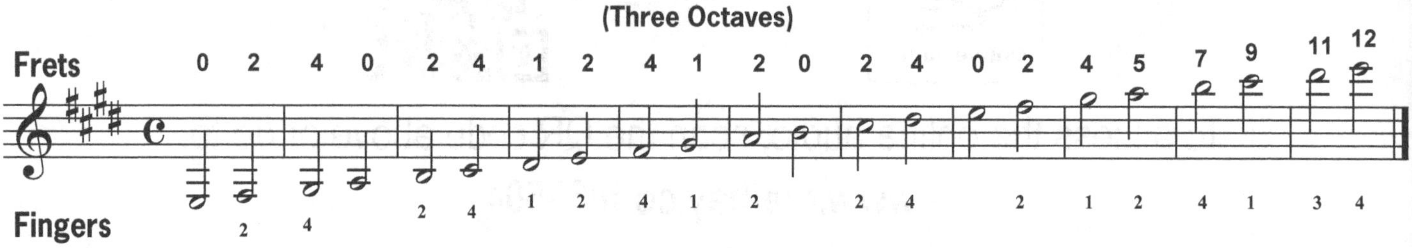

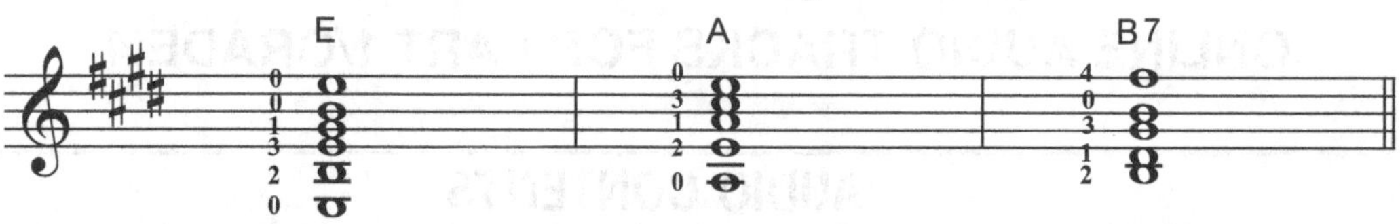

Etude in E Major

TRACK 1

Allegro

Mel Bay

E Scale Studies

TRACK 2

①

② TRACK 3

③ TRACK 4

④ TRACK 5

⑤ TRACK 6

⑥ TRACK 7

Prairie Sunset

TRACK 8

Medium tempo

Epigram

Picking Studies

①

②

Picking Studies

TRACK 12

C Picking

G Picking

TRACK 13

D Picking

TRACK 14

A Picking

TRACK 15

E Picking

TRACK 16

The Fourth Position

E Scale – 4th Position

Fourth-Position Etude #1

TRACK 17

Etude #2

TRACK 18

Starburst

TRACK 19

Eclipse

TRACK 20

I Gave My Love a Cherry

TRACK 21

Ballad

Slowly

Cheyenne Wells – 4th Pos.

TRACK 22

Study #3 – 4th Pos.

TRACK 23

Waltz

With the exception of the open B note, designated by the zero (0), the entire selection is in the 4th position.

Italian Air (Multi-Position Study)

Guitar Solo

Matteo Carcassi
Arr. by Mel Bay

A in Fourth Position

Key of A

A Scale – 4th Position

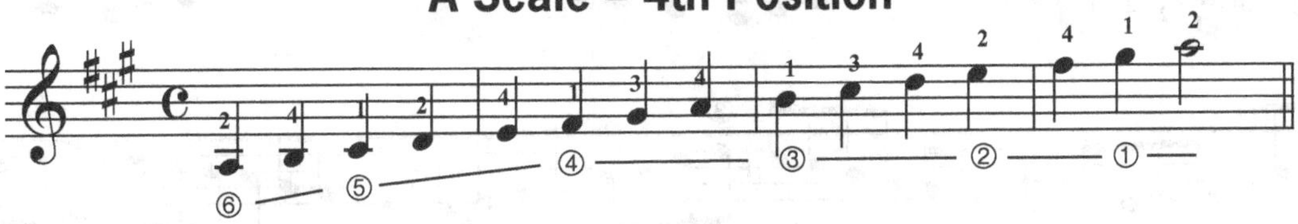

A Arpeggio – 4th Position

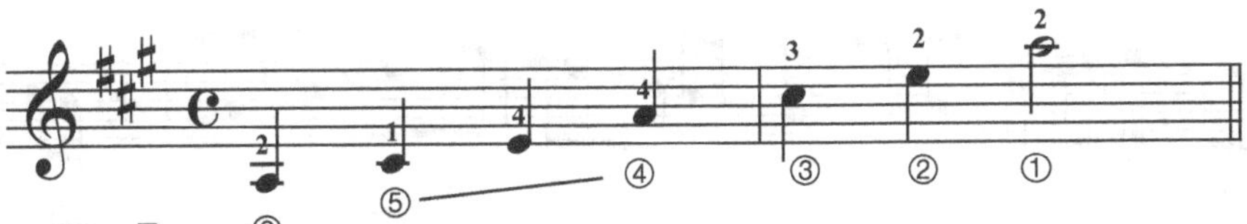

A Triplet Etude

TRACK 26

A Study #2 – 4th Position

TRACK 27

Fourth-Position Etude

TRACK 28

Allegro

A Study #3 – 4th Position

TRACK 29

Andante

Stuck in the Kitchen – 4th Position

W. B.

Exhilaration – 4th Position

Rose O Sharon – 4th Position

TRACK 32

Moderately

W. B.

Morning Dance – 4th Position

TRACK 33

Allegro

W. B.

A Scale Study #4 – 4th Position

TRACK 34

Key of A Review

TRACK 35

Slowly

W. B.

Open Position

The Key of C Sharp Minor

(Relative to E Major)

The C sharp minor scales are played in the fourth position except where shown.

Harmonic

Melodic

Chords in the Key of C Sharp Minor

C♯ Minor Studies – 4th Position

TRACK 36

①

② TRACK 37

③ TRACK 38

④ TRACK 39

⑤ TRACK 40

Bering Sea – 4th Position

TRACK 41

Slowly

W. B.

Portrait – 4th Position

Track 42

Slowly

W. B.

Nocturne – 4th Position

Track 43

Slowly

W. B.

Images – 4th Position

TRACK 44

Largo

W. B.

Reflection – 4th Position

TRACK 45

Slowly

W. B.

Grace Notes

Grace notes are small notes which subtract their value from the note they precede. The technical term for the grace note is "appoggiatura." The grace note is crossed at the end and is played the same as slurs. When the grace note is on a different string from the principal note, pick it separately.

Examples 1 & 2

Sarabande (Duet in C# Minor)

TRACK 46

Slowly

Corelli

Ivy Leaf Reel

Little House Round the Corner

Irish Jig

Minueto (from the Sonata Op. 25)

TRACK 49

F. Sor
Arr. by Mel Bay

Moderato

* Pick the first note and slur the remaining three

Key of D in Fourth Position

D Scale – 4th Position

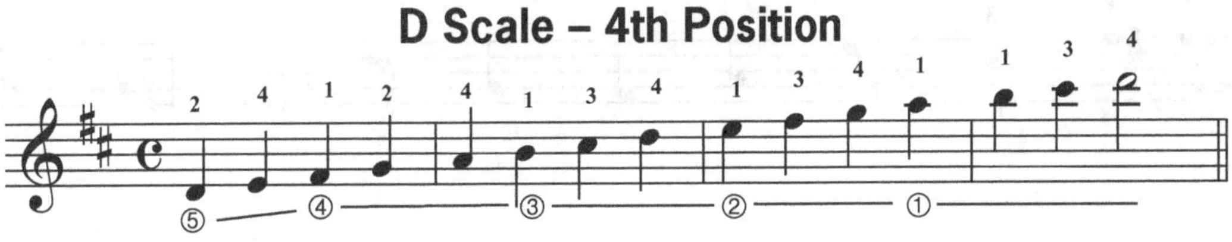

D Arpeggio – 4th Position

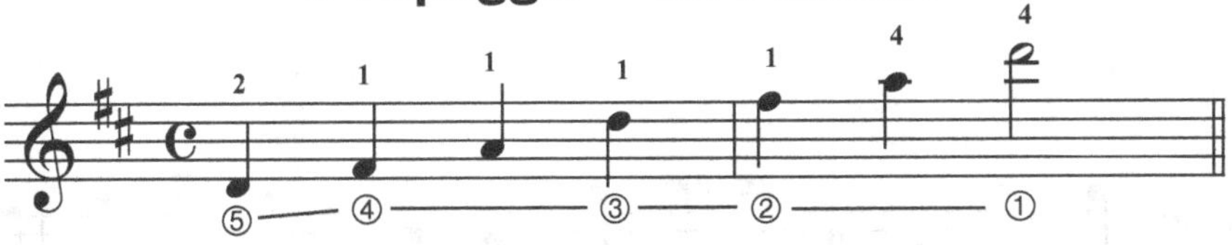

Lyric Moment – 4th Position

TRACK 50

W.B.

Andante

Daydreams – 4th Position

TRACK 51

Star of Bethlehem – 4th Position

TRACK 52

Schooner – 4th Position

TRACK 53

Moderately

W.B.

St. Clair's Hornpipe – 4th Position

TRACK 54

The Major Chords

Three chord forms are used to produce the major chords. The forms are movable and should be practiced from the first to the tenth frets on the first four strings of the guitar. The forms are numbered I, III, and V, corresponding to the chord interval, namely root (I), third (III), and fifth (V).

The top note of the chords is on the first string. The top note of any chord will be the note highest in pitch. The top note of form I is the root of the chord. The top note of form III is the third, and the top note of form V is the fifth interval of the major chord.

Playing the forms chromatically up the fingerboard produces the following major chords:

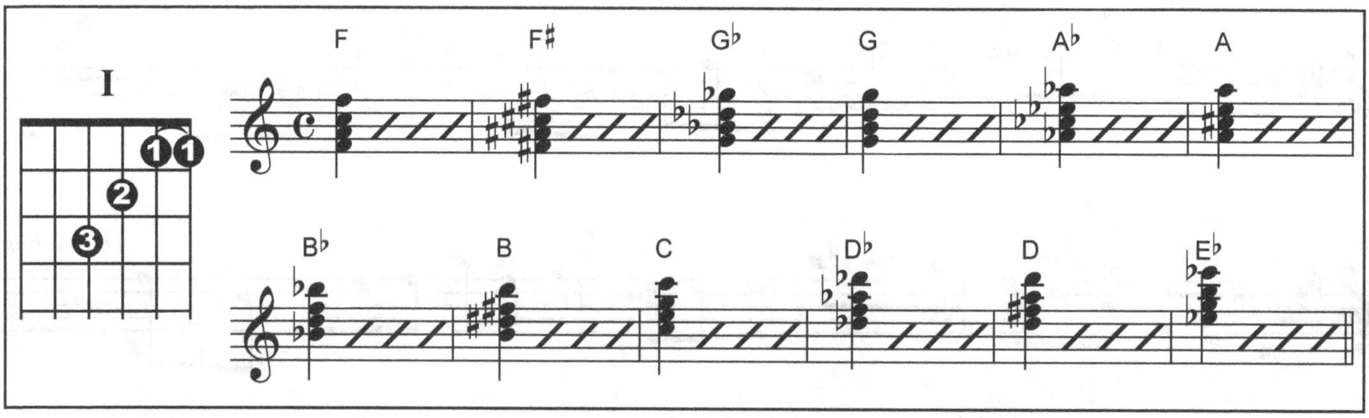

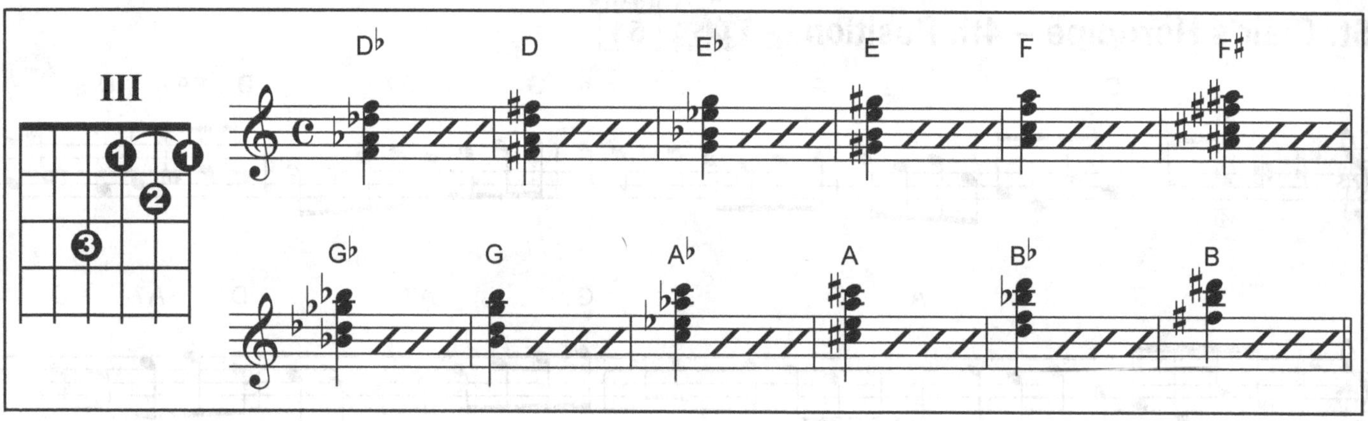

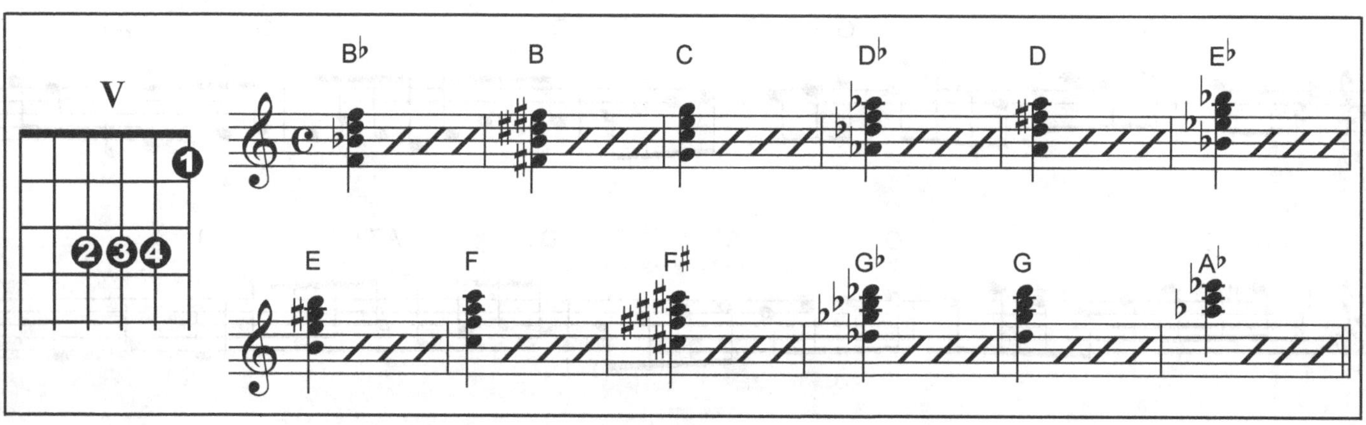

Note: This page should be memorized

The Fifth Position

Key of F

F Scale – 5th Position

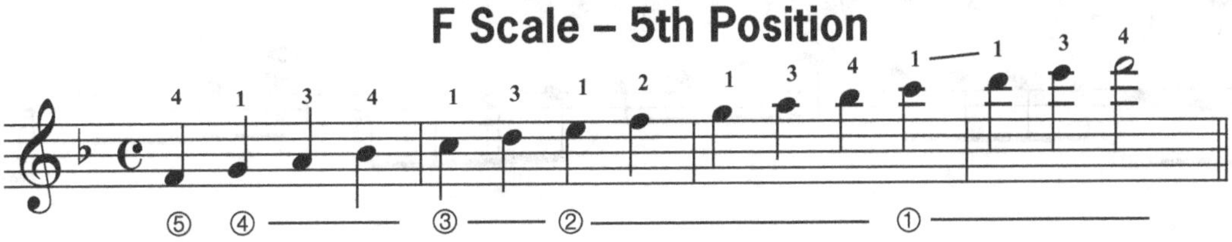

F Arpeggio – 5th Position

Fifth-Position Etude #1

TRACK 55

Our First Major Chord Etude

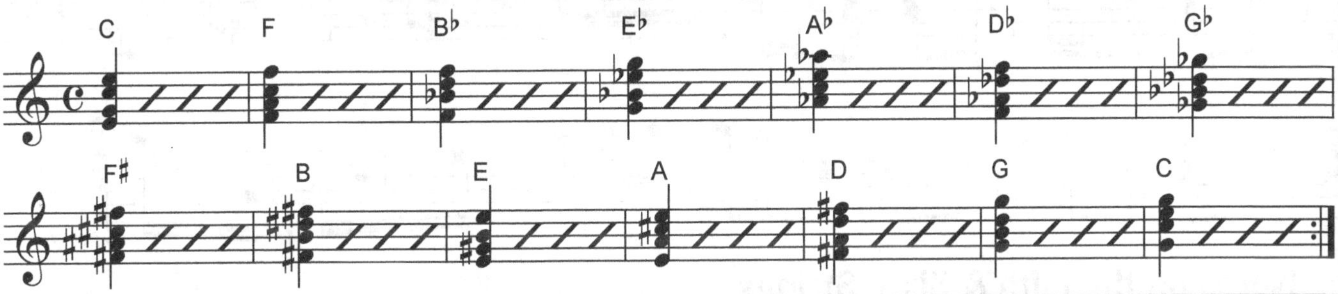

The Note-Spelling of the Major Chords

C (C-E-G) F (F-A-C) B♭ (B♭-D-F) E♭ (E♭-G-B♭) A♭ (A♭-C-E♭)
D♭ (D♭-F-A♭) G♭ (G♭-B♭-D♭) F♯ (F♯-A♯-C♯) B (B-D♯-F♯) E (E-G♯-B)
A (A-C♯-E) D (D-F♯-A) G (G-B-D)

Memorize

Fifth-Position Etude No. 2

TRACK 56

The Court Jester (Fifth Position)

TRACK 57

Guitar Solo

Carcassi

The Notes on the Fifth & Sixth Strings

Woodlands – 5th Position

TRACK 58

Moderately W.B.

Narcissus – 5th Position

TRACK 59

Moderately W.B.

Sonatina in F Major – 5th Position

TRACK 60

Andante

The Commentator (Fifth Position)

TRACK 61

Guitar Solo

Carcassi – Bay

Allegretto

The Mixed Minor Scales

The **mixed** minor scale ascends in the **melodic mode** but descends in the **harmonic mode**.

Fifth-Position Etude #3

TRACK 62

Stallion at Daybreak – 5th Position

TRACK 63

Lively Tempo

W.B.

Riley McGurk – 5th Position

TRACK 64

Lively Tempo

W.B.

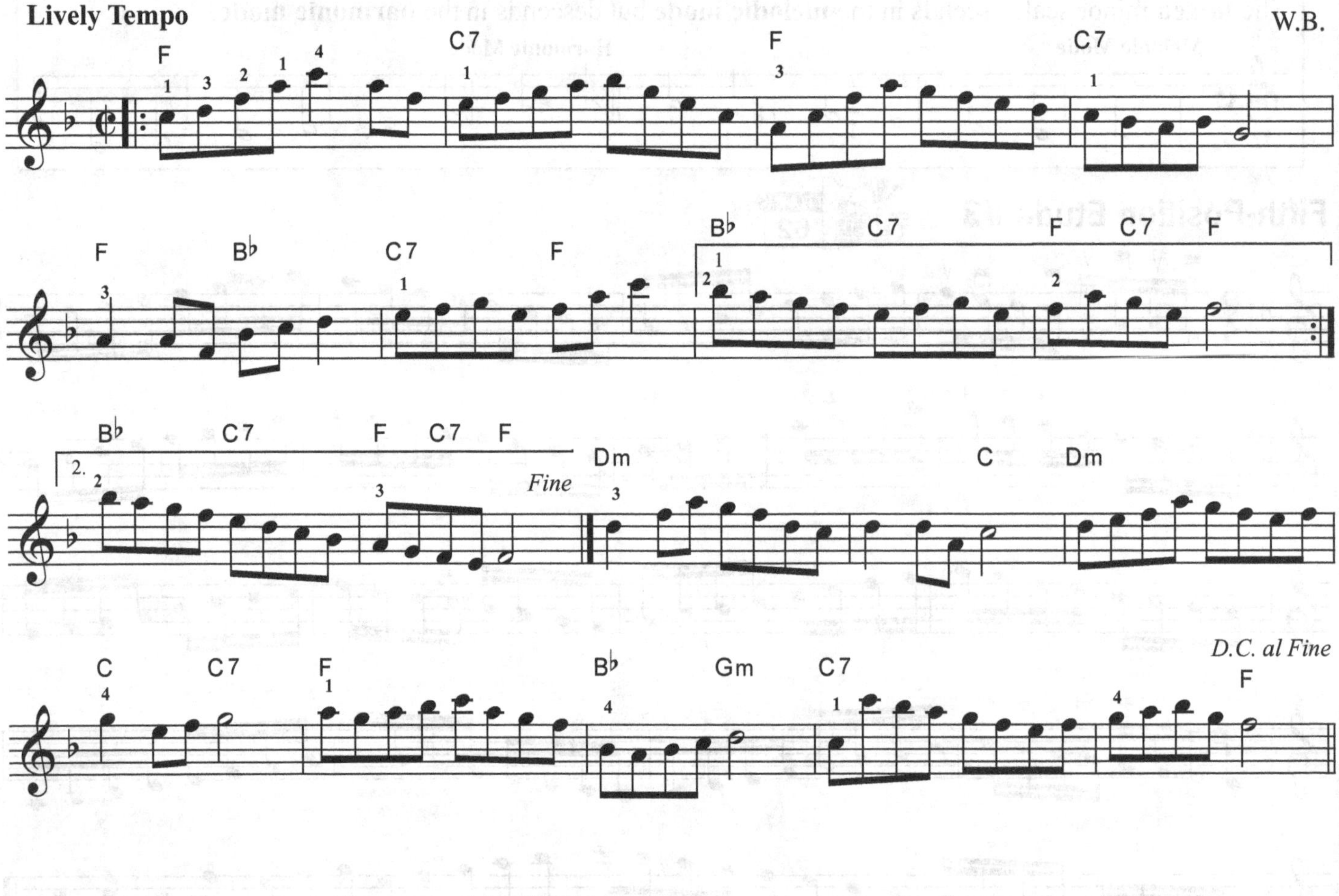

Dm Fifth Position

D Minor Scale / Harmonic Mode Scale – 5th Position

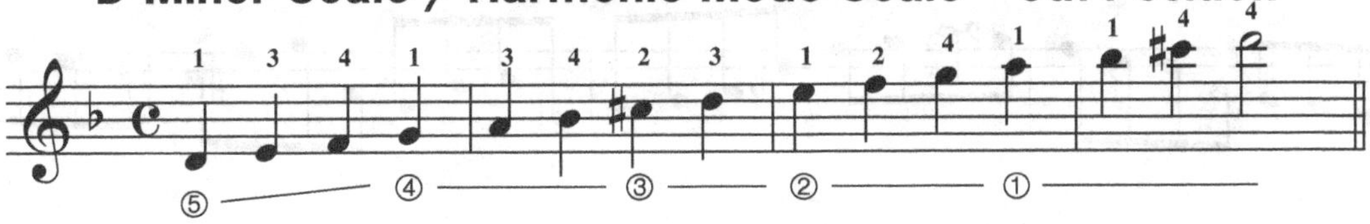

D Minor Arpeggio – 5th Position

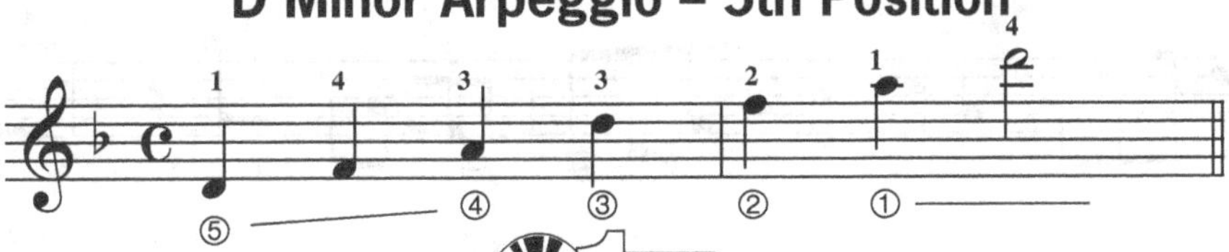

Levelland by Night – 5th Position

TRACK 65

Jonquil – 5th Position

TRACK 66

W.B.

Slowly

Sundance – 5th Position

TRACK 67

Slow Swing

W.B.

Clare Waltz – 5th Position

TRACK 68

W.B.

Slowly

High Five – 5th Position

TRACK 69

Swing Feeling

W.B.

Traverse Bay – 5th Position

TRACK 70

Medium Tempo

W.B.

Shadows

TRACK 71

Allegretto

Mazas – Bay

I
II
B♭
Dm
F dim
A7
A

Ballad – 5th Position

TRACK 72

Slowly

Divisee – Bay

River Glen – 5th Position

TRACK 73

Slowly

W.B.

Sailors Hornpipe – 5th Position

TRACK 74

Arr. by Mel Bay

Guitar Duet

Major Chord Etude #2

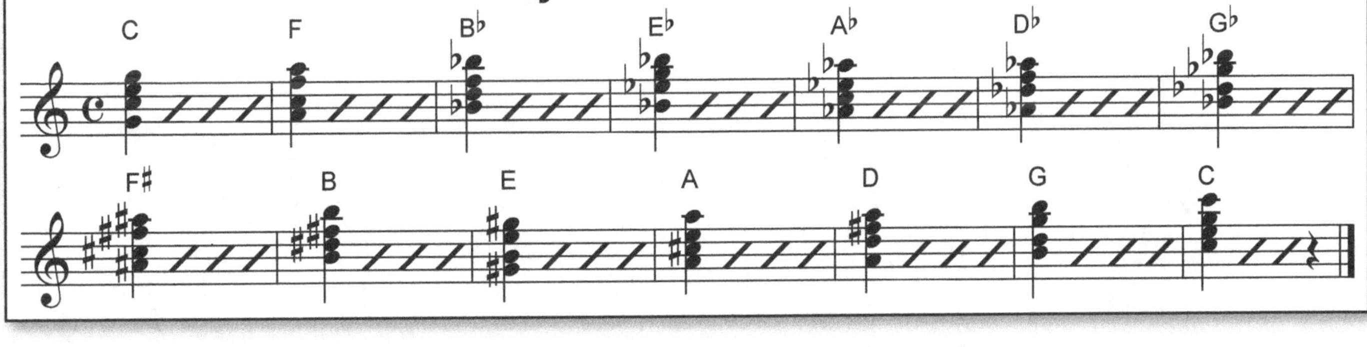

Key of C – 5th Position

C Scale – 5th Position

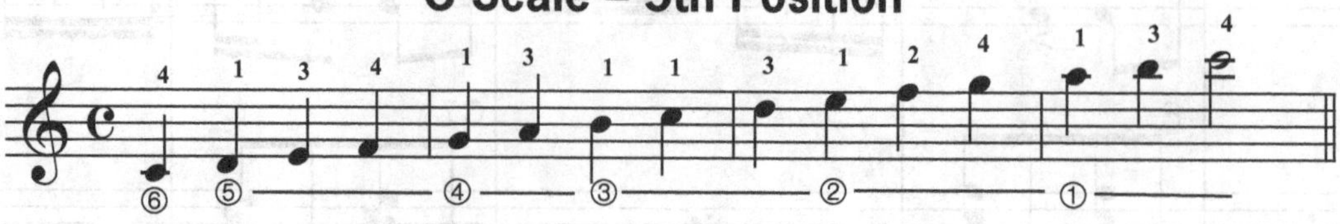

C Arpeggio – 5th Position

Meramec Echoes – 5th Position

TRACK 75

W.B.

Buena Vista – 5th Position

TRACK 76

Moderately

W.B.

Suffolk – 5th Position

TRACK 77

Moderately

W.B.

Shamrock – 5th Position

Allegro

W.B.

Ruby – 5th Position

Andante

W.B.

Key of Am – Fifth Position

A Minor Scale / Harmonic Mode Scale – 5th Position

A Minor Arpeggio – 5th Position

① TRACK 1

② TRACK 2

③ TRACK 3

Leipzig – 5th Position

Andante

W.B.

J.S. – 5th Position

Andante

W.B.

Dance – 5th Position

TRACK 6

Moderately

W.B.

Silouette – 5th Position

TRACK 7

W.B.

Starling – 5th Position

Andante

W.B.

Mirage – 5th Position

Allegro

W.B.

Key of B♭ – 5th Position

B Flat Scale – 5th Position

B Flat Arpeggio – 5th Position

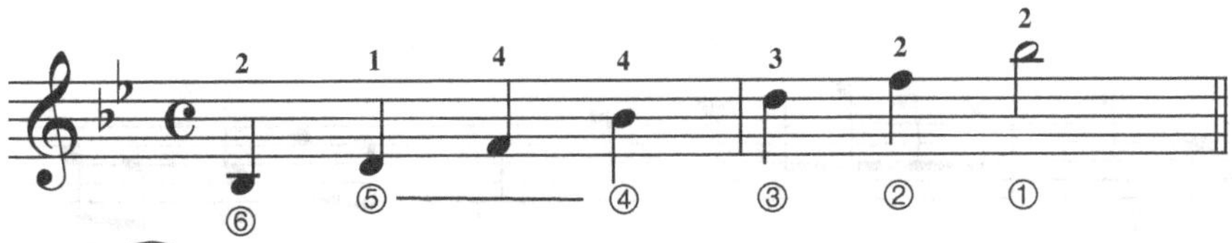

B♭ Scale Etude

TRACK 10

B♭ Studies – 5th Position

TRACK 11

①

Song – 5th Position

Allegro

W.B.

Exploration – 5th Position

Slowly

W.B.

Etude – 5th Position

Track 14

Minuetto

TRACK 15

Guitar Duet

(Both parts in V Pos.)

I. Pleyel, Opus 48

Arr. by Mel Bay

Two Triplet Etudes in the Fifth Position

TRACK 16

(Observe stroking.)

TRACK 17

DeSoto – 5th Position

TRACK 18

Allegro W.B.

Dora's Waltz – 5th Position

TRACK 19

Moderately W.B.

Key of E♭ – 5th Position

E Flat Scale – 5th Position

E Flat Arpeggio – 5th Position

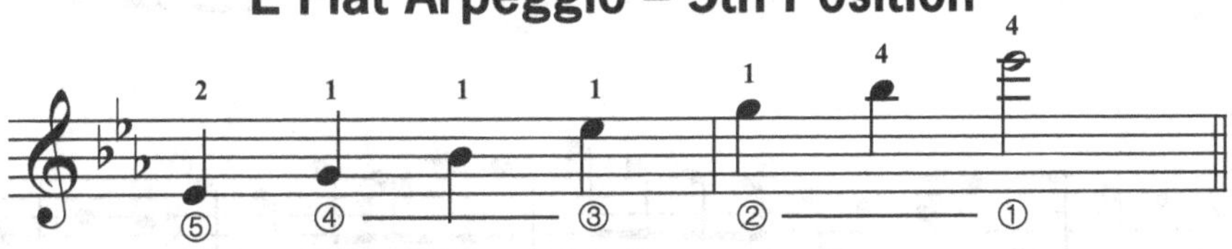

Erin's Waltz – 5th Position

W.B.

Cross Country – 5th Position

Allegro

W.B.

Snapshop – 5th Position

Moderately

W.B.

Major Chord Etude #3

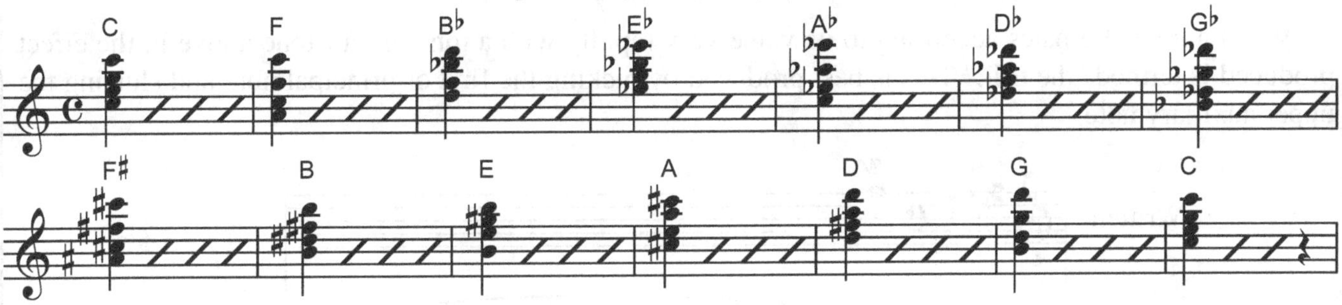

The Notation of the Major Chords

Poem

TRACK 23

Lento

Fibich
Arr. by Mel Bay

The Trill

When a note alternates according to its value very rapidly with a tone or half tone above it, the effect produced is termed "the trill." This is best produced by picking the first or principal note and slurring the upper auxiliary note.

The Major Chord Inversions

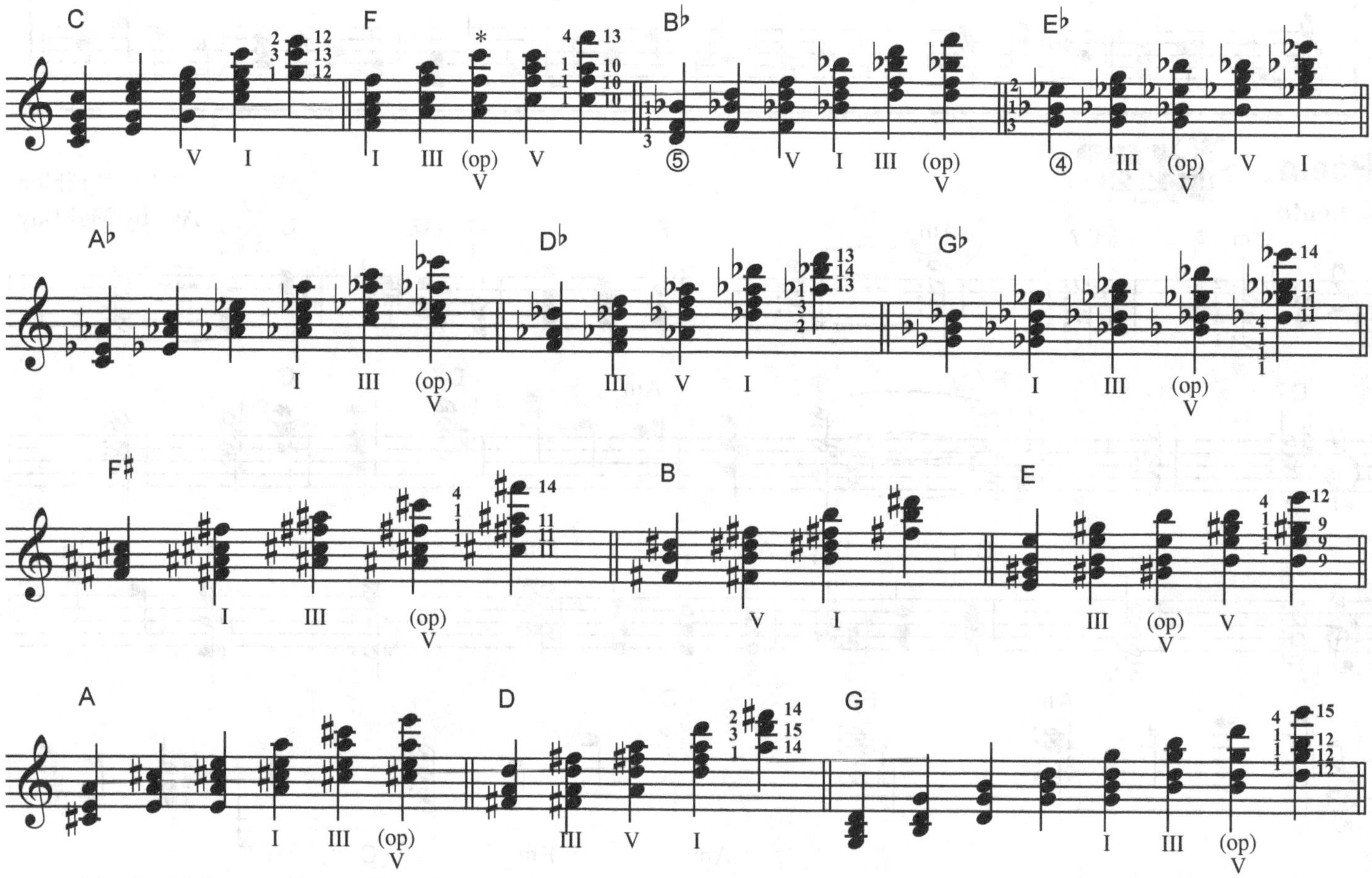

* In the higher positions where form V becomes difficult to finger, use the optional form V (op. V) as shown.

The Mordente

The mordente is a fragment of a trill. It is indicated by the sign 𝆗 .

The Minor Chords

The major and minor chords have the same note-spelling, but the third of the minor chord is a half step lower. Example: C (C-E-G), Cm (C-E♭-G). The intervals of the minor chord are root, min. 3rd, perfect 5th.

The Minor Chord Forms

The minor chord forms are designated as I_m, III_m, and V_m (m = minor).

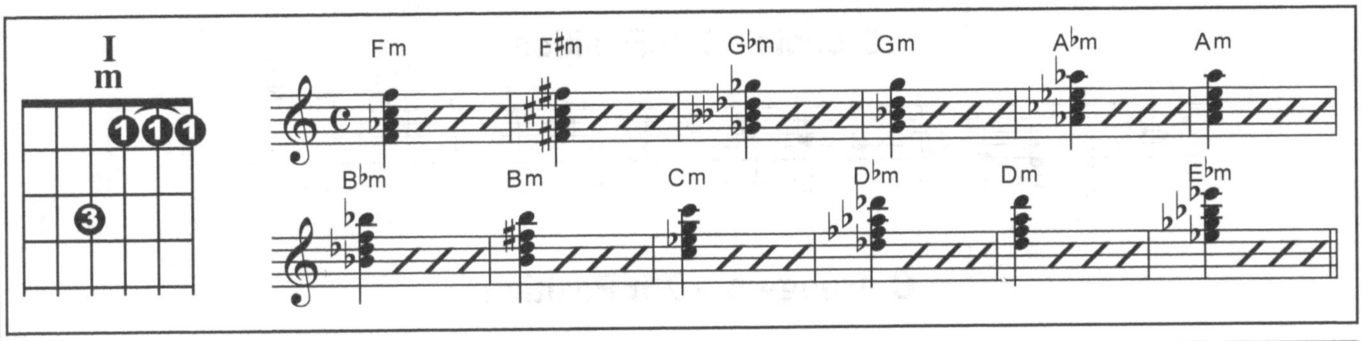

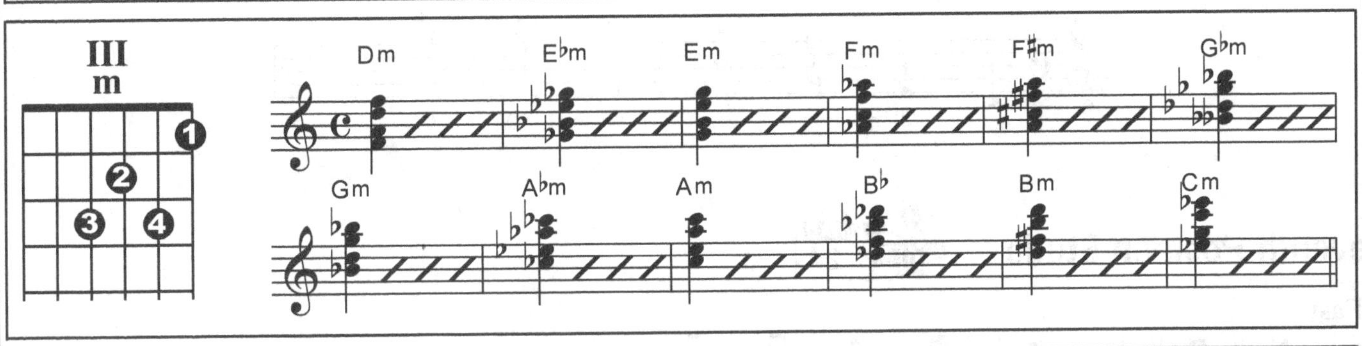

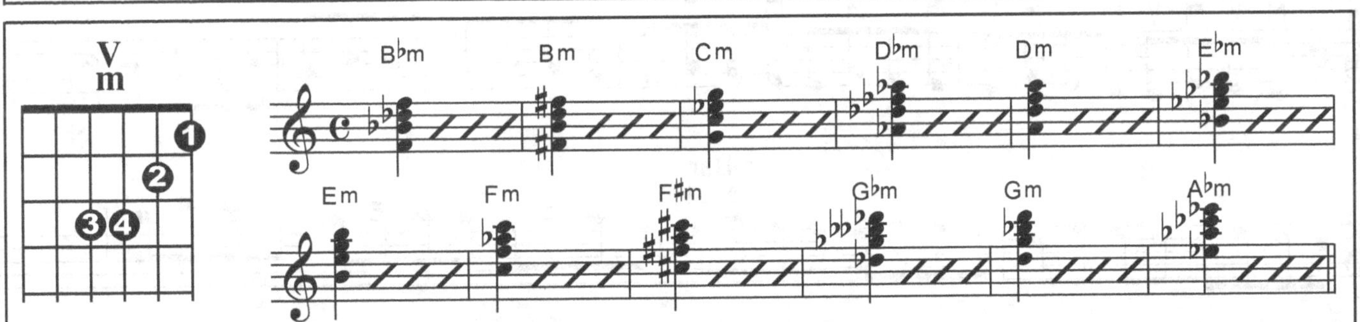

Minor Chord Etude #1

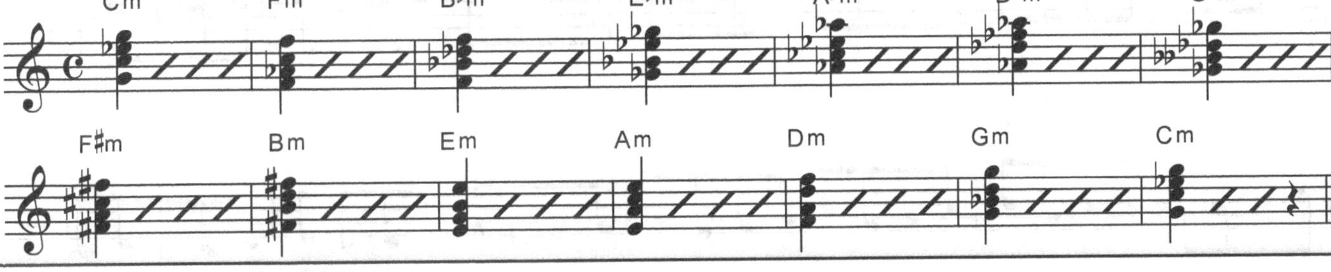

The Note-Spelling of the Major Chords

Cm (C-E♭-G)
D♭m (D♭-F-A♭)
Fm (F-A♭-C)
G♭m (G♭-B♭♭-D♭)
Am (A-C-E)
B♭m (B♭-D♭-F)
F♯m (F♯-A-C♯)
Dm (D-F-A)
E♭m (E♭-G♭-B♭)
Bm (B-D-F♯)
Gm (G-B♭-D)
A♭m (A♭-C♭-E♭)
Em (E-G-B)

The Seventh Position

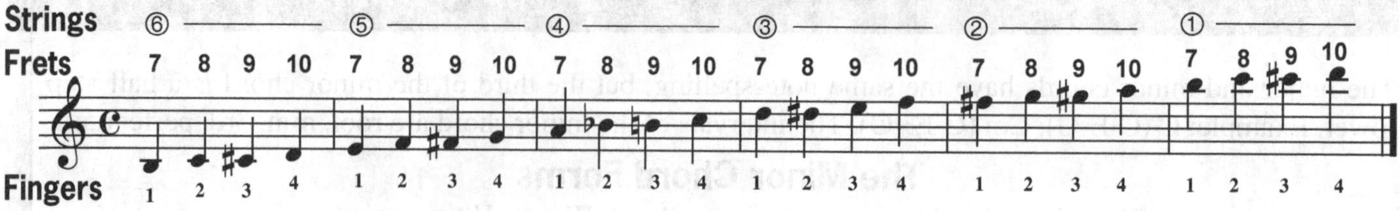

C Scale – 7th Position

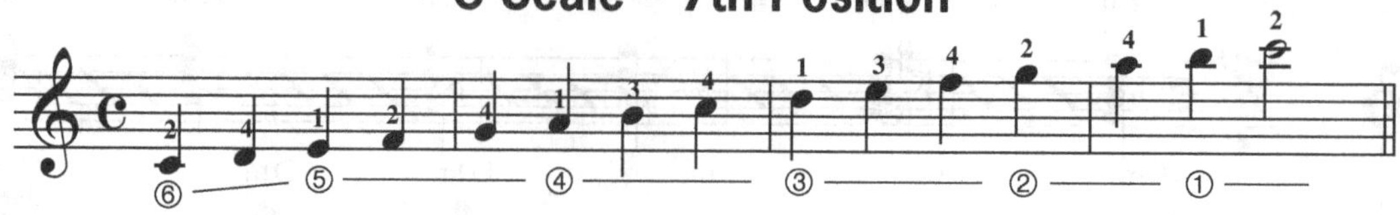

C Arpeggio – 7th Position

Seventh-Position Etude

TRACK 24

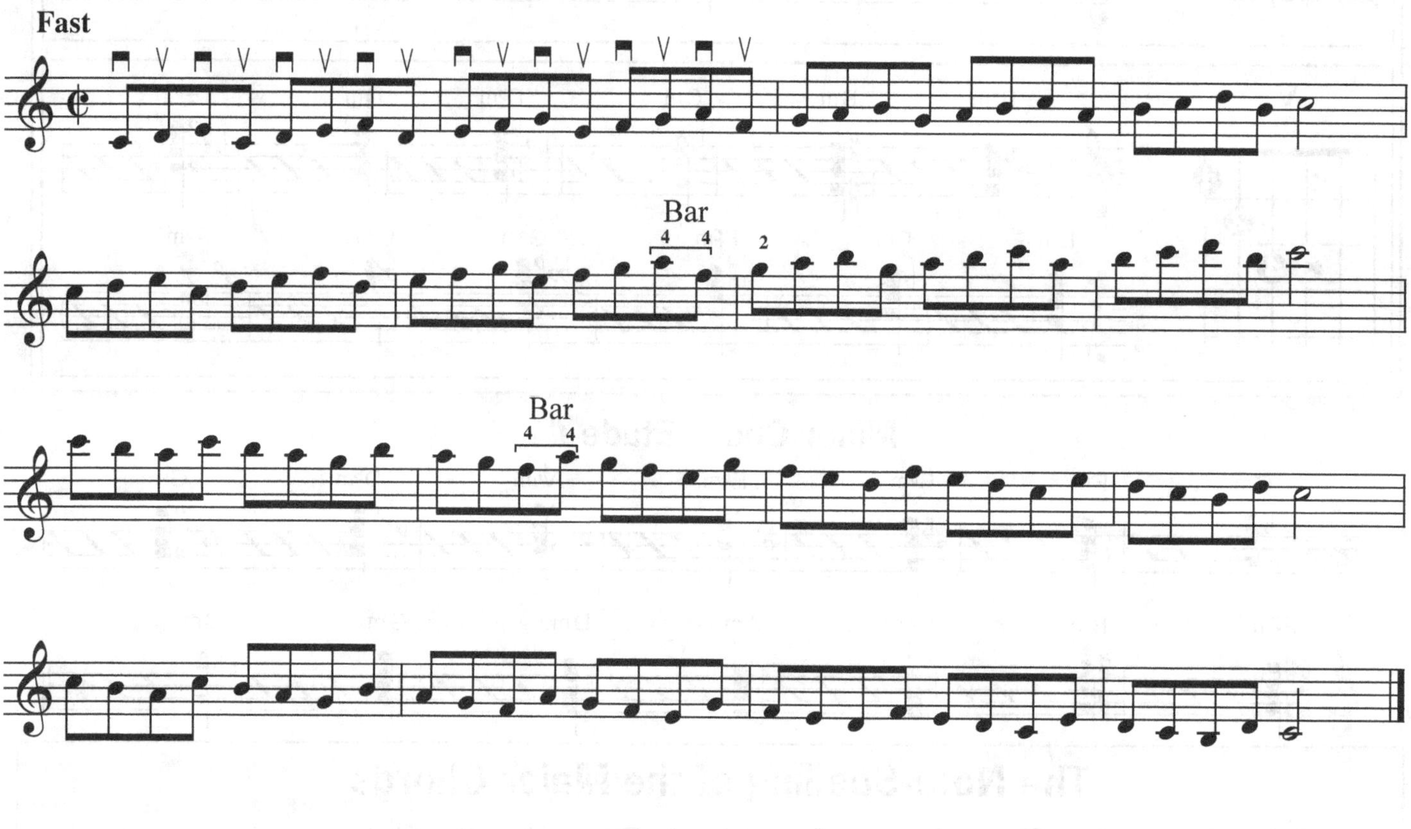

Waterfall – 7th Position

Allegro

W.B.

Joplin – 7th Position

Moderately

W.B.

Kreutzer's Etude – 7th Position

TRACK 27

Allegro moderato

Rudolphe Kreutzer

Key of G – 7th Position

G Scale – 7th Position

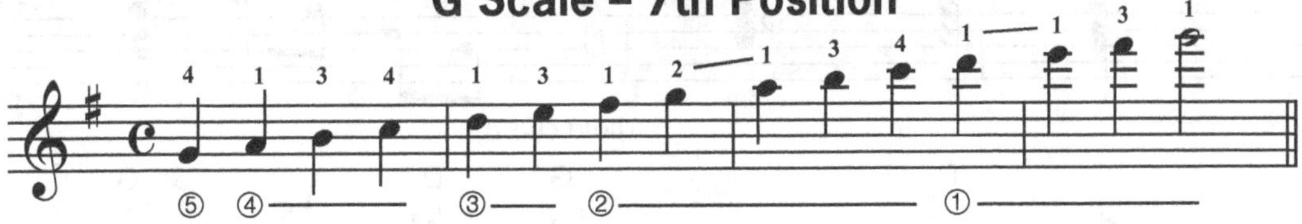

G Arpeggio – 7th Position

Seventh-Position Etude in G

TRACK 28

Sor's Song – 7th Position

TRACK 29

Lively

Breathe on Me, Breath of God

Slowly

Hymn
W.B.

Lucky Seven – 7th Position

Guitar Solo

Minor Chord Etude #2

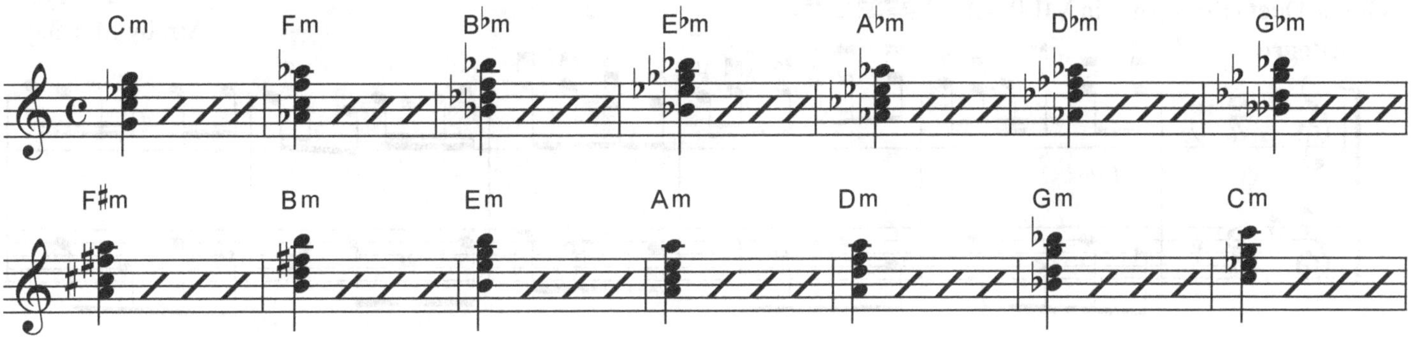

Minor Chord Etude #3

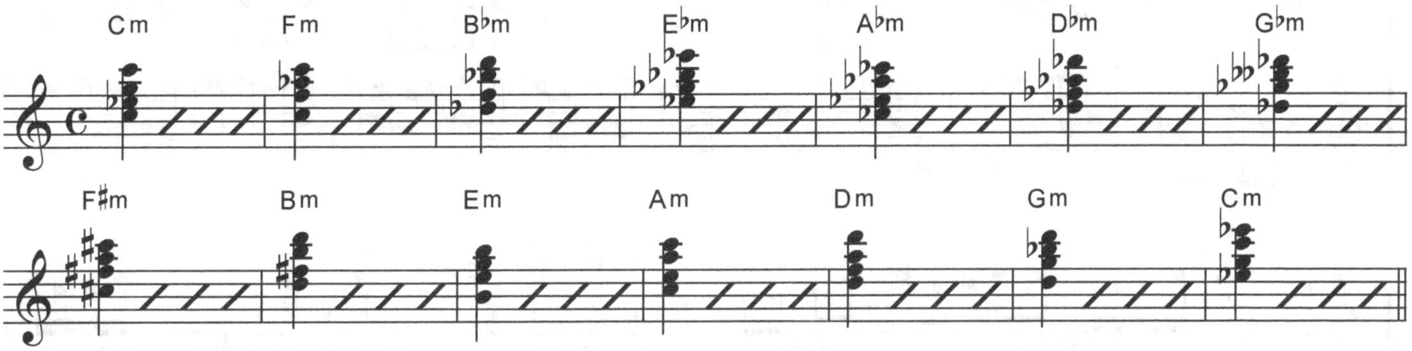

The Minor Chord Inversions

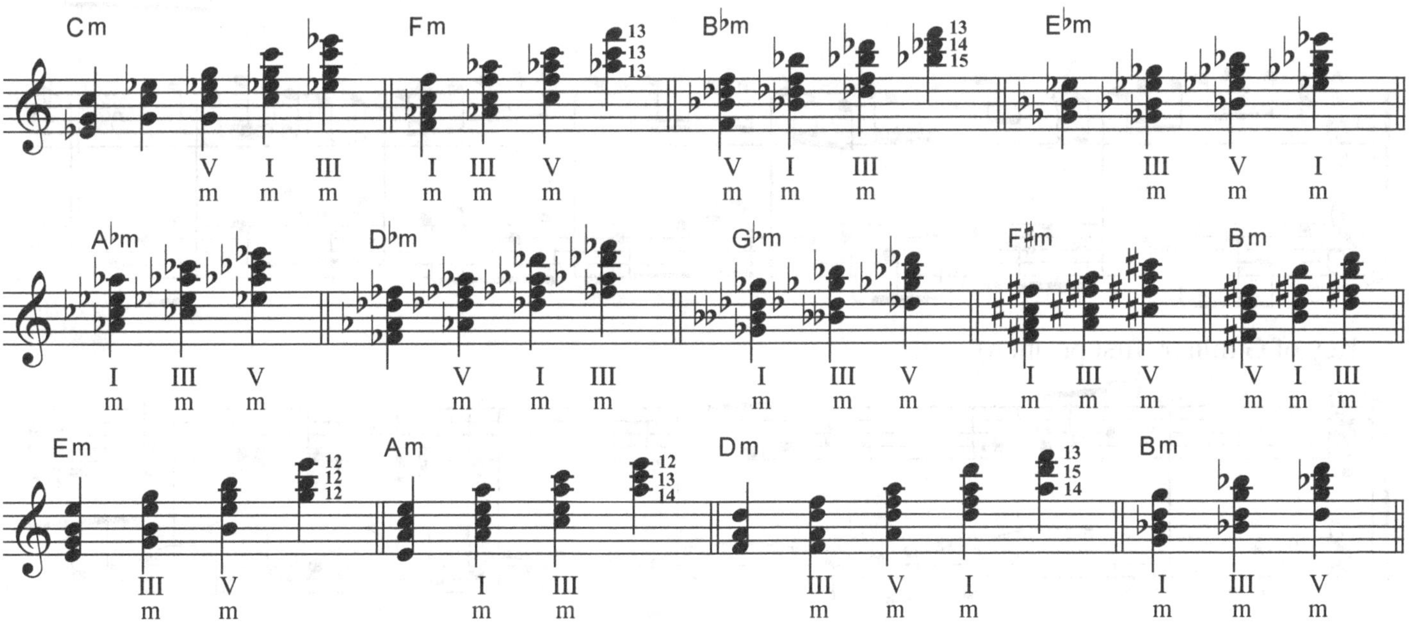

Rondo

Guitar Duet (Both parts in VII Pos.)

I. Pleyel
Arr. by Mel Bay

Allegro

Key of G minor (first position)

*By playing open, the student will be in the first position for minor portion.

G Major

Scale Study – 7th Position

TRACK 33

Gardenia – 7th Position

TRACK 34

Moderately

W.B.

The Dominant Seventh Chord

The intervals of the dominant seventh chord are root, major 3rd, perfect 5th, and minor 7th. The dominant seventh in the fundamental or root position consists of a major 3rd, minor 3rd, and a minor 3rd (see construction below).

The dominant seventh chord is named after the dominant (V) degree of the scale. The three principal chords in any major or minor key are the tonic, sub-dominant, and dominant seventh chords.

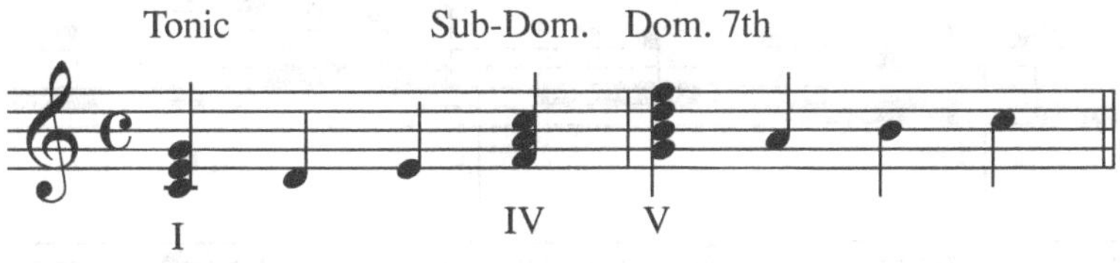

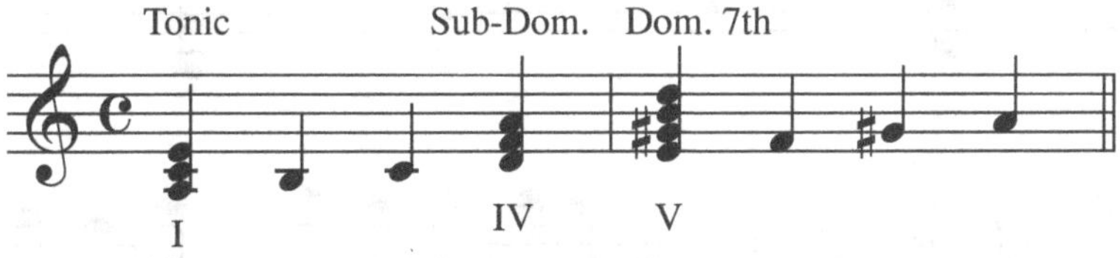

In this method, the student will be shown how the above chords are applied in the harmonizing and accompaniment of melodies with ear-training exercises.

The construction of a dominant seventh chord is best accomplished by taking the 1st, 3rd, 5th, and **lowered 7th** of any **major scale.**

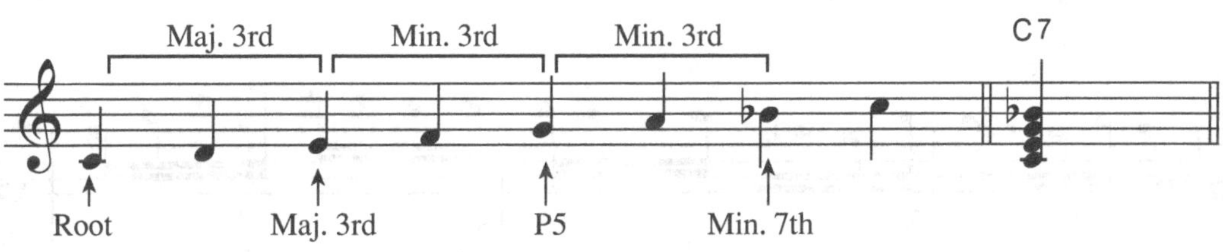

The student should write out all major scales, construct the dominant seventh chords by the above method and memorize the note-spelling of the chords.

The Notation of the Dominant Seventh Chord

Gypsy Rondo – 7th Pos.

TRACK 35

Joseph Haydn
Arr. by Mel Bay

Presto

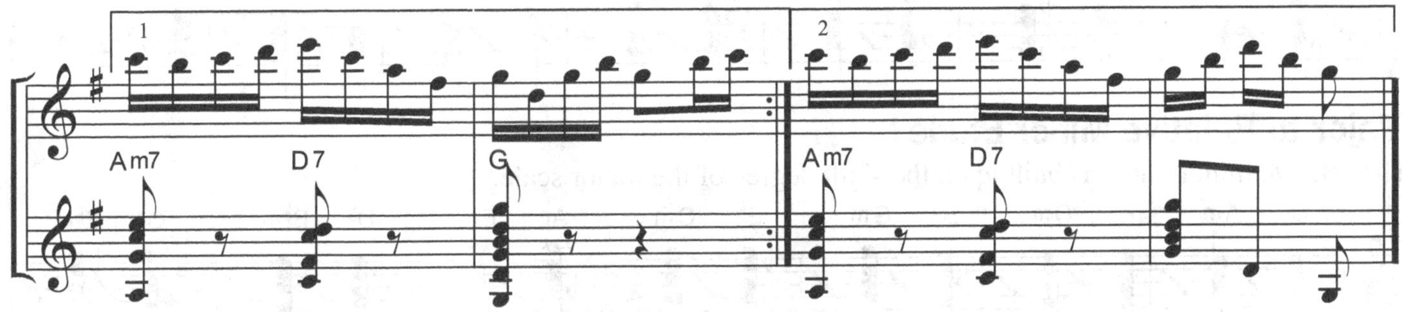

The following studies should be played by placing the first finger over the 1st, 2nd, and 3rd strings at the seventh fret. Hold the bar while playing the following passages.

Repeat 12 times.

The above passage can be found in the 1st, 2nd, 9th, 10th, 27th, and 28th measures of "Gypsy Rondo."

The following passages can be found in the 21st, 22nd, 23rd, and 24th measures of "Gypsy Rondo." Bar the seventh fret as shown above.

Repeat 12 times.

The following passages can be found in the 26th and 27th measures of the same selection and should be played by barring the seventh fret on the first three strings.

Repeat 12 times.

After carefully mastering the above passages, play "Gypsy Rondo," keeping the seventh fret barred throughout and lifting the bar only where necessary.

The Notation of the Major and Minor Chords

Memorize but do not play.

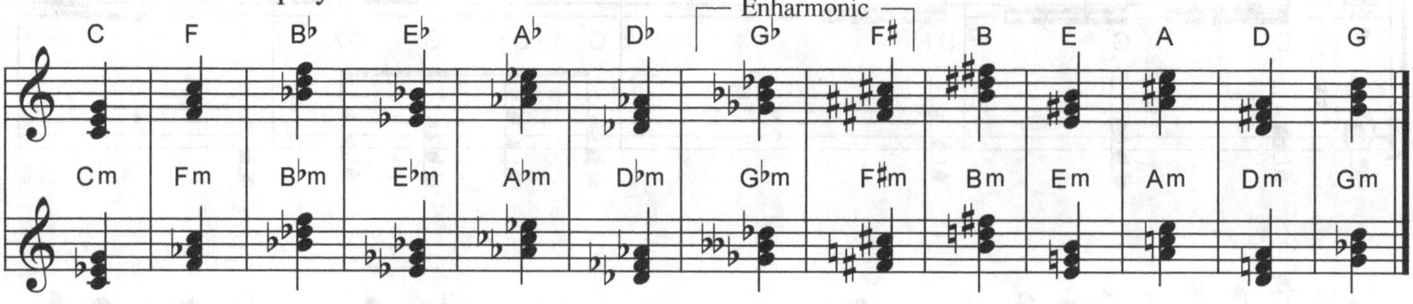

Major to Tonic Minor Etude

Major to Relative Minor Etude

The relative minor chord is built upon the sixth degree of the major scale.

Major to Tonic Minor Etude

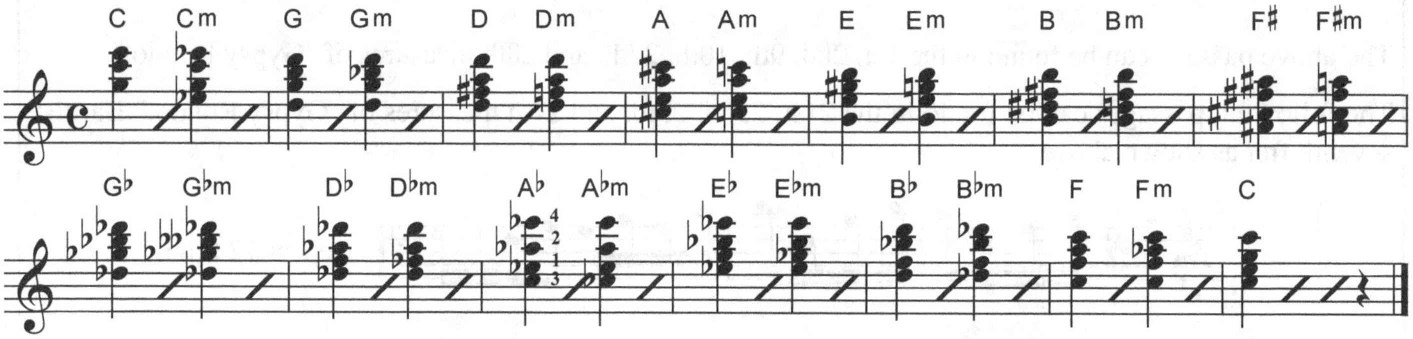

Major to Relative Minor Etude

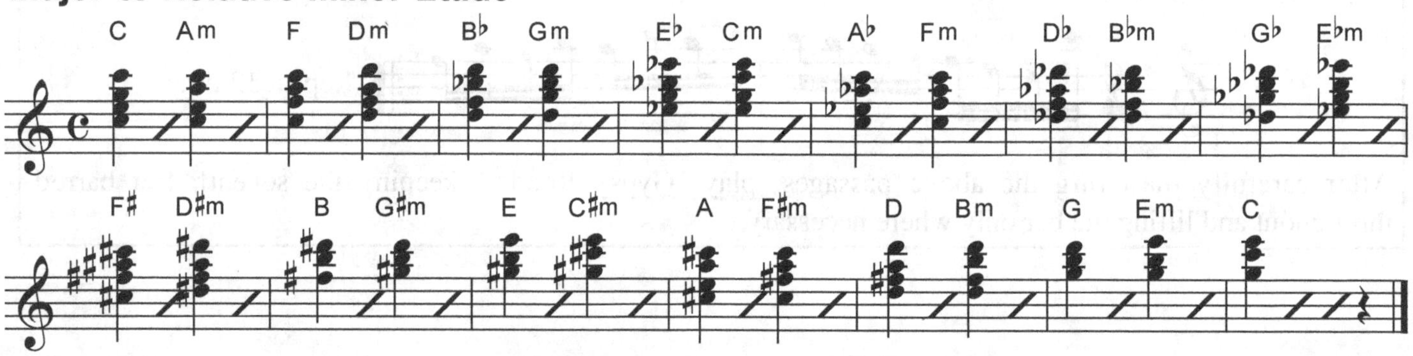

The Seventh Chords

The seventh chord forms will be numbered I7, III7, V7, AND VII7, corresponding to the chord intervals found on the first string. The note played on the first string is often referred to as the "top note" of the chord.

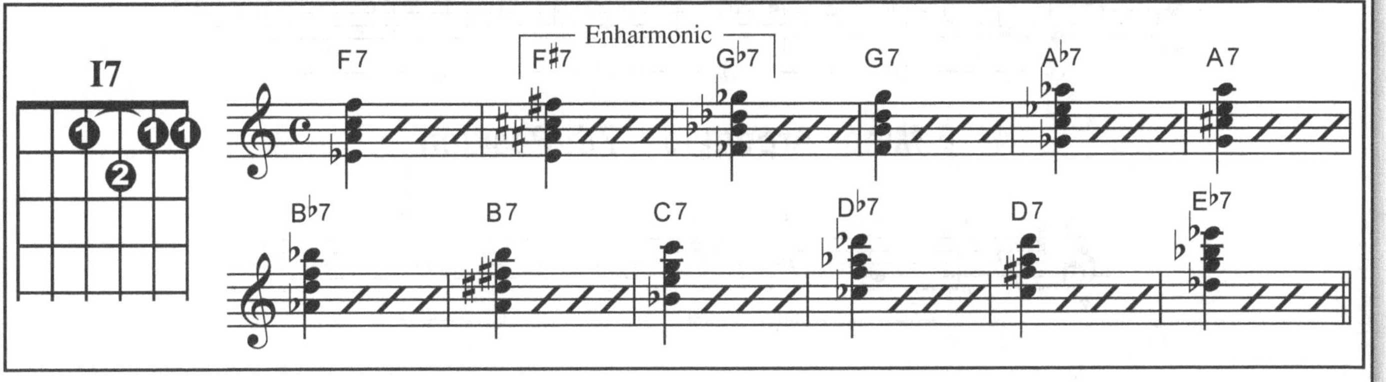

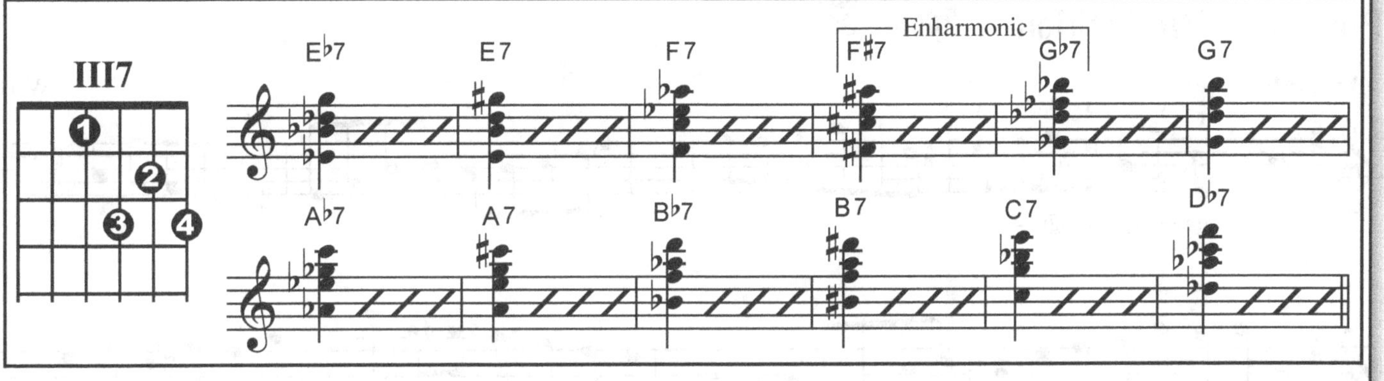

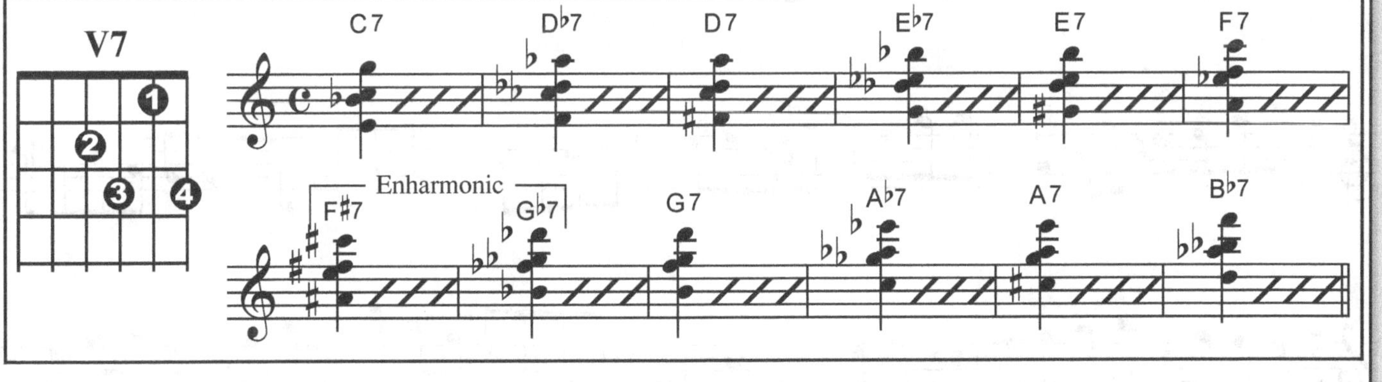

Key of Em – 7th Position

E Minor Scale / Harmonic Mode – 7th Position

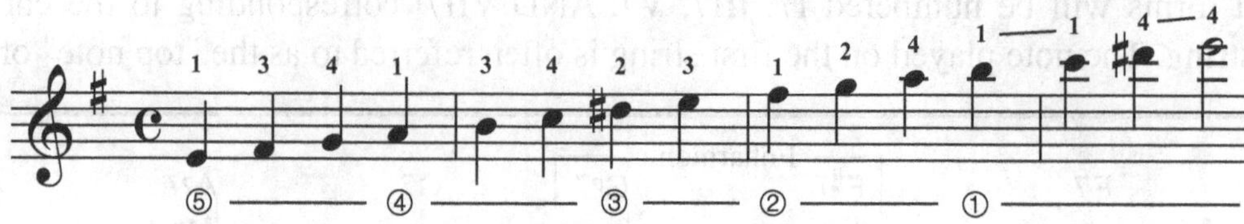

E Minor Arpeggio – 7th Position

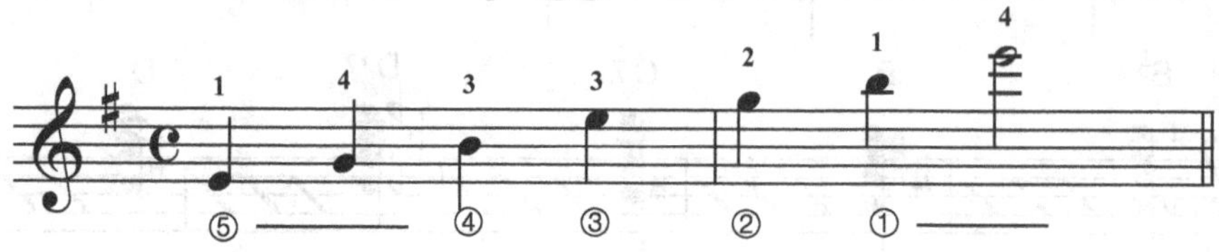

Portrait – 7th Position

TRACK 36

Andante

W.B.

Discovery – 7th Position

Andante

W.B.

Dawn– 7th Position

Moderately

W.B.

Key of Bm – 7th Position

B Minor Scale / Harmonic Mode – 7th Position

B Minor Arpeggio – 7th Position

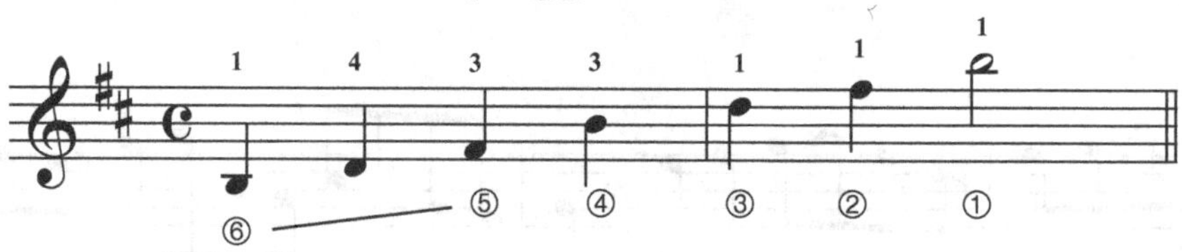

Passage – 7th Position

Andante W.B.

Misty Night – 7th Position

TRACK 40

Moderato

W.B.

Sierra – 7th Position

TRACK 41

Andante

W.B.

Key of F – 7th Position

F Scale – 7th Position

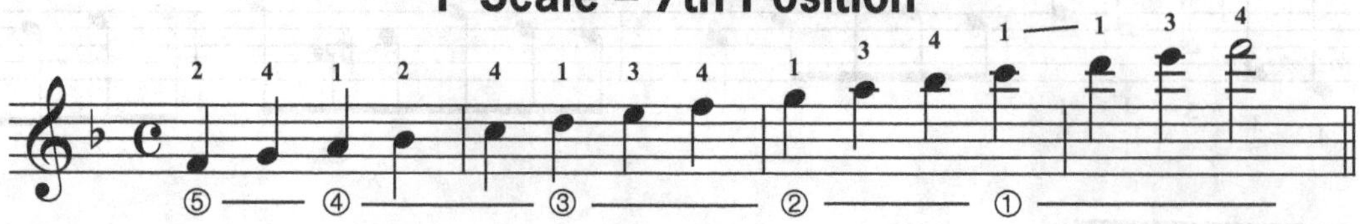

F Arpeggio – 7th Position

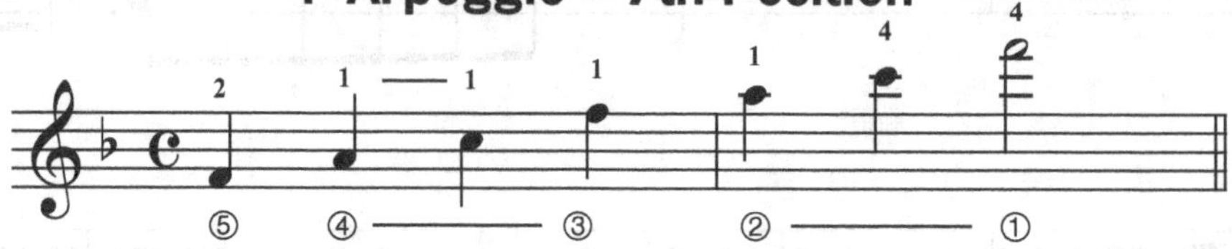

Vista – 7th Position

Andante

W.B.

Workout– 7th Position

Moderately

W.B.

Glasgow– 7th Position

Moderately

W.B.

Key of Dm – 7th Position

D Minor Scale / Harmonic Mode – 7th Position

D Minor Arpeggio – 7th Position

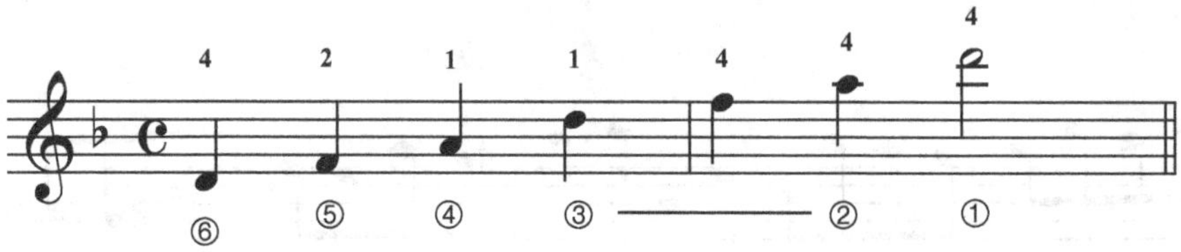

Sunset – 7th Position

Slowly

W.B.

Autumn – 7th Position

Andante

W.B.

Nightfall– 7th Position

W.B.

Key of D – 7th Position

D Scale – 7th Position

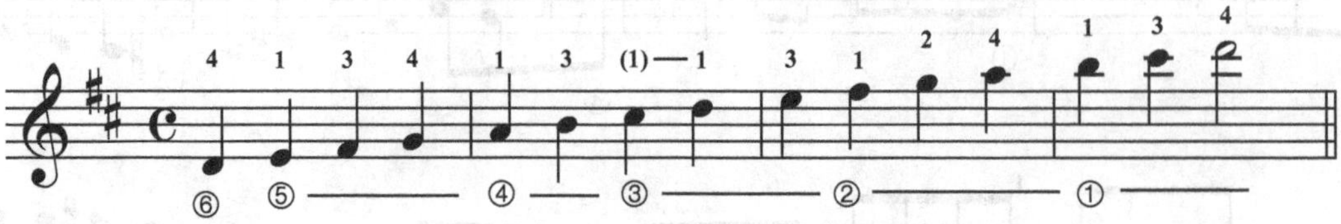

D Arpeggio – 7th Position

Cruising – 7th Position

TRACK 48

Moderately

W.B.

Muse – 7th Position

Allegro

W.B.

Snowfall – 7th Position

Moderately

W.B.

Key of Gm – 7th Position

G Minor Scale / Harmonic Mode – 7th Position

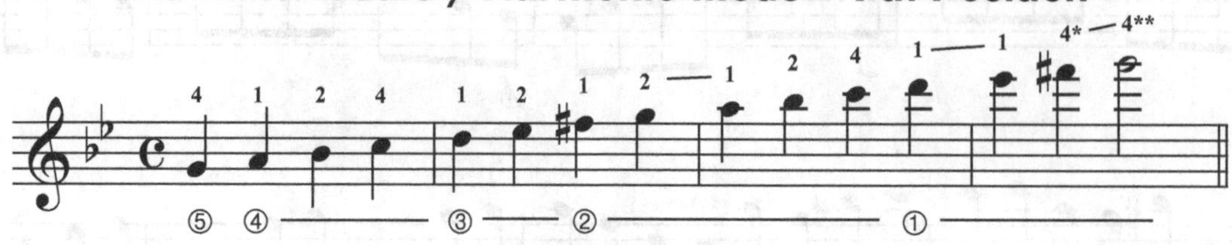

* 14th fret
** 15th fret

G Minor Arpeggio – 7th Position

Panorama – 7th Position

TRACK 51

Moderately

W.B.

Natasha – 7th Position

Slowly W.B.

Farewell – 7th Position

Allegro W.B.

The Ninth Position

Key of A – 9th Position

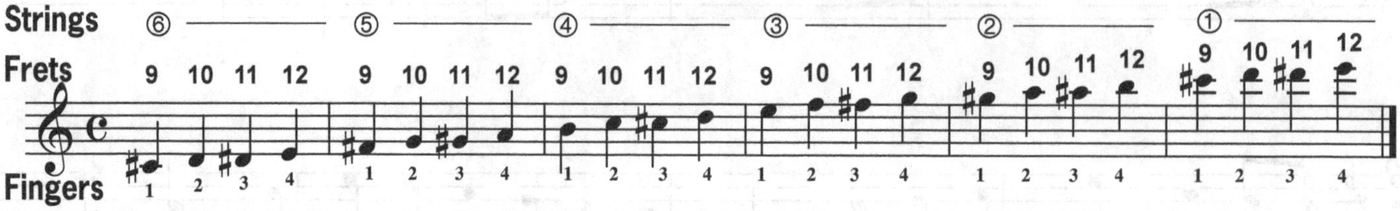

A Scale – 9th Position

A Arpeggio – 9th Position

Ninth-Position Etude #1

TRACK 54

Ninth-Position Etude #2

The Ninth Inning – 9th Position

Guitar Solo

Carcassi-Bay

Allegro

Maze – 9th Position

TRACK 57

Slowly

Seventh-Chord Etude #1

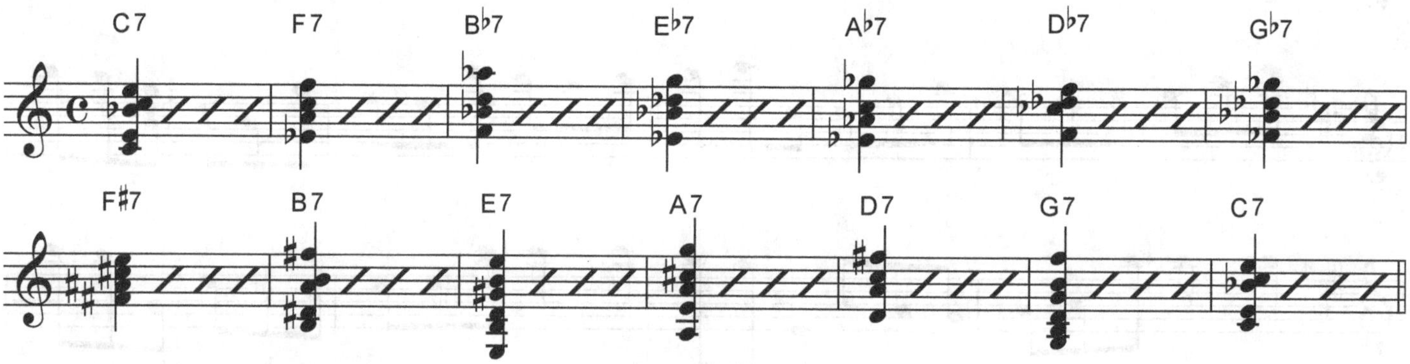

Seventh-Chord Etude #2

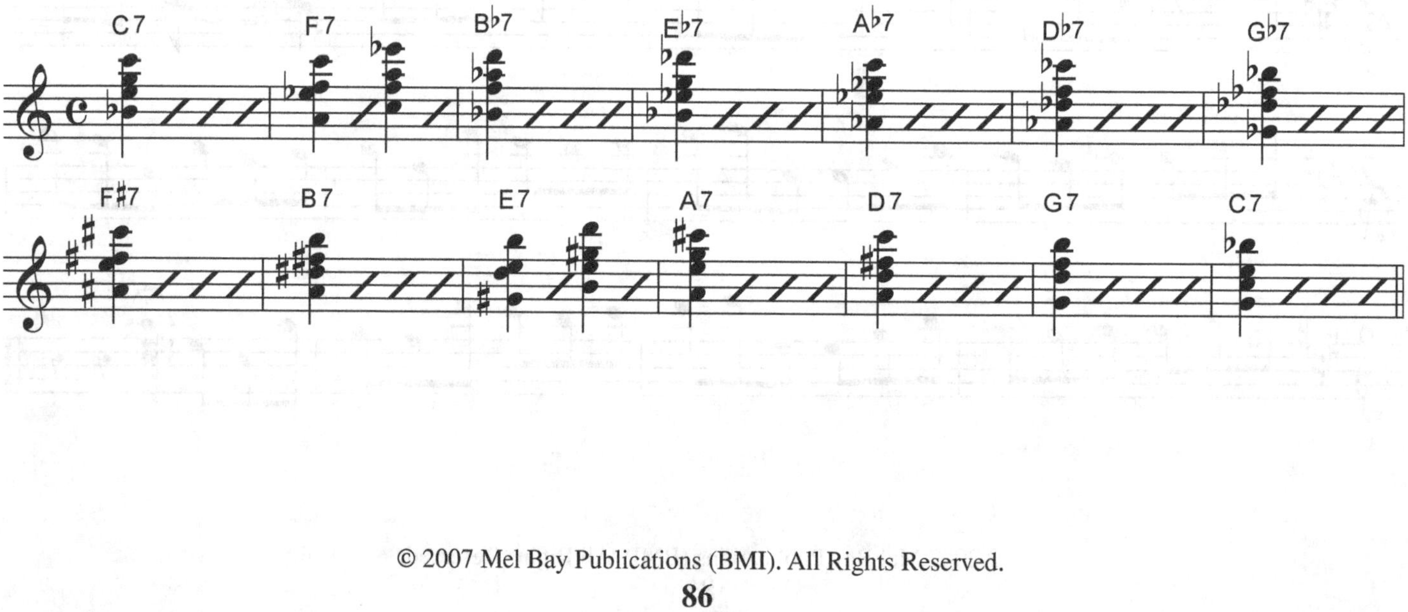

Seventh-Chord Etude #3

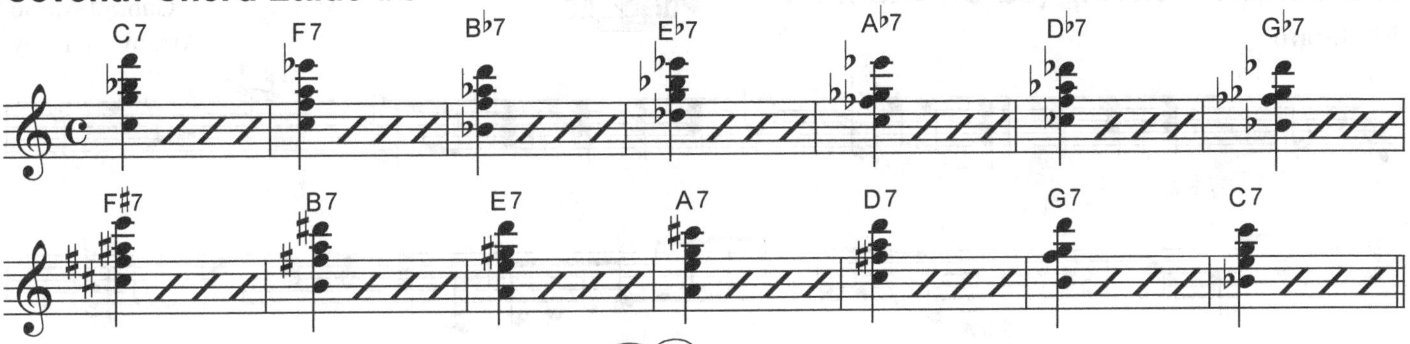

Susan Lynn – Multiple Positions

Guitar Solo

Allegretto

Carcassi-Bay

The Golden Wedding (La Cinquantaine)

Gabriel-Marie
Arr. by Mel Bay

Moderato

Inversions

Carcassi's Etude (A Major)

Guitar Solo

Carcassi

Norwegian Dance

Guitar Duet

Grieg, Opus 35
Arr. by Mel Bay

Key of A Minor

Allegretto

Excursion **(A Position Review)**

TRACK 62

Guitar Solo (Roman numeral = position)

Carcassi-Bay

VII
VII
VII
V
a tempo
rallentando
IV
V
II
IX
VII
V
IV
IX

VII
V
IV
cresc.
V
VII
V
cresc.
III
III
VII

Modulation One

Mel Bay

Modulation Two

Mel Bay

You are now ready to proceed with Grade 5!